LATINA AGENCY THROUGH NARRATION IN EDUCATION

Drawing on critical and sociocultural frameworks, this volume presents narrative studies by or about Latinas in which they speak up about issues of identity and education. Using narratives, self-identification stories, and testimonios as theory, methodology, and advocacy, this volume brings together a wide range of Latinx perspectives on education, identity, bilingualism, and belonging. The narratives illustrate the various ways erasure and human agency shape the lives and identities of Latinas in the United States, from primary school to higher education and beyond, in their schools and communities. Contributors explore how schools and educational institutions can support student agency by adopting a transformative activist stance through curricula, learning contexts, and policies. Chapters contain implications for teaching and come together to showcase the importance of explicit activist efforts to combat erasure and engage in transformative and emancipatory education.

Carmen M. Martínez-Roldán is Associate Professor of Bilingual/Bicultural Education, Teachers College, Columbia University, USA.

Language, Culture, and Teaching Series
Sonia Nieto, Series Editor

Dialoguing across Cultures, Identities, and Learning
Crosscurrents and Complexities in Literacy Classrooms
Bob Fecho, Jennifer Clifton

Language, Culture, and Teaching
Critical Perspectives, 3rd Edition
Sonia Nieto

Teaching Culturally Sustaining and Inclusive Young Adult Literature
Critical Perspectives and Conversations
R. Joseph Rodríguez

Teacher Evaluation as Cultural Practice
A Framework for Equity and Excellence
Maria del Carmen Salazar, Jessica Lerner

Teaching and Researching ELLs' Disciplinary Literacies
Systemic Functional Linguistics in Action in the Context of U.S. School Reform
Meg Gebhard

Culturally Sustaining Systemic Functional Linguistics Praxis
Embodied Inquiry with Multilingual Youth
Ruth Harman, Kevin Burke

Latina Agency through Narration in Education
Speaking Up on Erasure, Identity, and Schooling
Edited by Carmen M. Martínez-Roldán

For more information about this series, please visit: https://www.routledge.com/
Language-Culture-and-Teaching-Series/book-series/LEALCTS

LATINA AGENCY THROUGH NARRATION IN EDUCATION

Speaking Up on Erasure, Identity, and Schooling

Edited by Carmen M. Martínez-Roldán

Routledge
Taylor & Francis Group

NEW YORK AND LONDON

First published 2021
by Routledge
52 Vanderbilt Avenue, New York, NY 10017

and by Routledge
2 Park Square, Milton Park, Abingdon, Oxon, OX14 4RN

Routledge is an imprint of the Taylor & Francis Group, an informa business

© 2021 Taylor & Francis

Library of Congress Cataloging-in-Publication Data
Names: Martínez-Roldán, Carmen, editor.
Title: Latina agency through narration in education : speaking up on
erasure, identity, and schooling / edited by Carmen M.
Martínez-Roldán.
Description: New York, NY : Routledge, 2021. | Series: Language, culture,
and teaching series | Includes bibliographical references and index.
Identifiers: LCCN 2020039438 (print) | LCCN 2020039439 (ebook) | ISBN
9780367151010 (hardback) | ISBN 9780367151089 (paperback) | ISBN
9780429055065 (ebook) | ISBN 9780429621857 (adobe pdf) | ISBN
9780429617553 (mobi) | ISBN 9780429619700 (epub)
Subjects: LCSH: Hispanic American girls--Education. | Hispanic American
women--Education. | Hispanic Americans--Ethnic identity. | Culturally
relevant pedagogy--United States. | Agent (Philosophy)
Classification: LCC LC2669 .L335 2021 (print) | LCC LC2669 (ebook) | DDC
371.829/68073--dc23
LC record available at https://lccn.loc.gov/2020039438
LC ebook record available at https://lccn.loc.gov/2020039439

ISBN: 978-0-367-15101-0 (hbk)
ISBN: 978-0-367-15108-9 (pbk)
ISBN: 978-0-429-05506-5 (ebk)

Typeset in Bembo
by SPi Global, India

To all Latina women who have fought erasure, whether through small or big agentive and activist efforts; for those who have created networks of solidarity to lift up others and create more equitable learning contexts for our children. De un modo especial se lo dedico a la activista y guerrera incansable de la familia, my fearless sister María I. Reinat-Pumarejo. To my mother, Laura Martínez-Roldán, whose actions of love spoke louder than her voice, y para todas las mujeres en mi familia. Lastly, to my late colleague María Torres Guzmán, whose social imagination had no limits.

CONTENTS

BOXES

FIGURES

TABLES

FOREWORD

During much of the history of public education, both in the United States and in other societies, conventional wisdom held that students whose cultures and languages differed from the majority were functioning with a deficiency rooted in their very identities. As a result, long-held destructive notions of cultural, racial, and linguistic inferiority have often found their way into teacher education texts. In essence, the thinking has been that the sooner marginalized students assimilated to become more like the majority in culture, language, appearance, experience, and values, the easier would be their transition to the so-called "mainstream." By the latter part of the 20th century, these ideas finally began to be repudiated, largely but not exclusively by people from the very backgrounds whose identities were being disparaged. It is no accident that educational movements in favor of ethnic studies, bilingual and multicultural education, gender studies, and critical pedagogy all emerged at around the same time. These movements represented a denouncement of the ideologies that had heretofore excluded large segments of the population from achieving educational success.

In addition, traditional views of education have often conceived of education as little more than filling students' heads with knowledge, an idea that is still prevalent in many schools today. The books in the *Language, Culture, and Teaching* series challenge the view of education as the passive transmission of knowledge, instead viewing teachers and their students as active participants; that is, as agents in their own teaching and learning. The books also directly confront taken-for-granted assumptions about the identities of marginalized students as mired in deficiency. By focusing on the intersections of language, culture, and teaching—specifically on how language and culture inform classroom practice—the books ask readers to reflect, question, and respond to what they read by thinking more critically about their practice. Since the first book in the *Language, Culture, and Teaching* series was published in 2001, the goal has been to challenge conventional wisdom about the abilities and talents of students whose identities differ from the majority, and to help teachers reflect critically on their roles in promoting a liberatory pedagogy for their students. This is also certainly the case in *Latina Agency through Narration in Education*.

It is rare to come across a book that not only focuses on Latinas but that also seriously considers their personal stories and their commitments and trajectories as teachers, researchers, and activists. This is such a book, and it is indeed an honor to have it as the latest addition to the *Language, Culture, and Teaching* series. Knowing of her many years of extraordinary work with teachers whose approach to teaching children's literature included a critical understanding of literacy, several years ago I approached Carmen M. Martínez-Roldán about working on a book for this series. Because she had been teaching a course on Latina narratives for several years, she proposed the idea of a book about Latina teachers' *testimonios* and narratives. I found it to be an innovative idea that would fit in beautifully with the series, and I believed it could benefit both teachers and their students for a number of reasons. In the courses she taught, she was able to carve out a space for reflection, collaboration, and solidarity for and with the many graduate students, both Latinas and non-Latinas. The concept of *erasure*, so prominent in the daily lives and work of Latinas, became one of the foundational frames for the book. But because Carmen understands that Latina teachers' identities cannot be defined simply through the lens of oppression and erasure, she also insists that the concept of *agency* is central to this work. That is why the deeply agentive Latina practice of *testimonio*—that is, using the authors' experiences and autobiographies to understand both their lives and the political nature of education—is also central to the book's purpose, because it could add to teachers' understanding of the lives of their students. And, finally, *identity*—both the authors' and their students'—is equally significant in these chapters because it helps teachers understand what it means to teach Latinx students in this day and age. In the process of using their testimonios, the authors' writing also alludes to the necessity of multicultural, culturally sustaining, and nurturing curriculum and pedagogy. It is for these reasons that Professor Martínez-Roldán chose to frame the book with these four foundational concepts. The result is a book that is at once innovative, illuminating, and wise.

I was particularly taken with the idea that teachers' narratives are, in essence, models of activism. The result can be seen in chapters that are rich in theorizing and storytelling, and with insights that help elucidate what it means to critically use narratives to understand, advance, and critique their work, especially the education of Latinx students in U.S. schools. But the women who are the authors of these chapters do not speak with one voice: Although most are Latinas, they represent various ethnic, racial, social class, linguistic, gender identity, and immigrant/non-immigrant backgrounds, highlighting the tremendous diversity and intersectionality in our communities. This diversity is also evident in their teaching and life circumstances, whether in organizing Hispanic Heritage Month activities with their students, sitting at the dining room table in dialogue with their mothers, reclaiming the home language they had lost years ago, or challenging rigid definitions of what it means to be a Latina. In all these cases and more, the authors reflect critically on how their lived experiences can be placed in the service of their students' education.

It is my hope that as a result of reading these narratives, readers will get to know something about Latinx students and teachers. At the same time, I believe they will understand the tremendous power of story in their own lives and teaching. I hope too that they will revel in these teachers' stories and use the lessons in the narratives to appreciate that the young people with whom they work, like all of us, have their own stories to tell, and that part of our work as teachers and researchers is to help make these stories visible.

— Sonia Nieto, Amherst, MA

CONTRIBUTORS

Minosca Alcántara is the Chief of Scheduling at Metropolitan Transportation Authority Capital Construction. She is an experienced civil engineer with expertise in construction management in a variety of architectural, infrastructure, and wastewater management projects. Dr. Alcantara's children are following her example: Her oldest son and daughters are pursuing Ph.D.'s in Civil Engineering and Materials Engineering at MIT and Stanford, respectively. Her youngest daughter is at MIT majoring in Biological Engineering.

Marisol Cantú, a Mexican-American educator, has worked within higher education since 2014. Her expertise is in adult literacy, bilingual education, and culturally responsive curriculum. Marisol received her M.A. in Applied Linguistics with a concentration in Bilingual/Bicultural Education from Teachers College, Columbia University. In 2016, she was the recipient of the Televisa Graduate Research Fellowship on Latino Education. She serves as a board member of Things That Creep, a nonprofit science-education program in the Bay. In 2019, she returned home to teach English as a Second Language at her alma mater, Contra Costa College, in Richmond, California.

Eliza Clark first became interested in the mingling of language with identity during her high school years in Cambridge, Massachusetts. After spending several years traveling and teaching around Latin America, Eliza returned to the U.S. to receive an M.A. in Bilingual/Bicultural Education from Teachers College, Columbia University. She lives in Brooklyn with her small, bilingual family.

Daniela Conde is a community educator, scholar-activist, and doctoral student in Higher Education and Organizational Change at the University of California, Los Angeles. Daniela was born and raised in Puebla, México, but also considers San Diego, California (Kumeyaay land), home. They enjoy *cafecitos* with critical dialogue and creating art.

Diana Cordova-Cobo is a Ph.D. candidate in Sociology and Education at Teachers College, Columbia University, and a research associate for The Public Good and the Center for Understanding Race and Education (CURE). Her work focuses on the relationship between housing and school demographic change—particularly as it relates to racial/ethnic stratification and the experiences of Communities of Color. Prior to starting in the Sociology and Education program, Diana was a middle school teacher in the Washington Heights neighborhood of New York City.

Victoria Hernandez is a Program Manager at Masa, an organization that supports the Mexican and Latin American immigrant community in the South Bronx through education, civic engagement, and community organizing. Her research interests center on the transnational experiences of migrants from Honduras, Guatemala, and El Salvador. Victoria is committed to fighting for liberation alongside working-class immigrant communities in the United States.

Elise Holzbauer Cocozzo teaches first grade at Avenues: The World School in Manhattan. Her expertise is in early childhood education, and biliteracy and bilingual acquisition. She received her M.A. in Bilingual/Bicultural Education from Teachers College, Columbia University.

Martha Iris Rosas is a doctoral student in the International and Transcultural Studies Department at Teachers College, Columbia University. She has worked as a first-grade Spanish-English dual-language teacher in the New York City Public School System, as SEEK Counselor in Baruch College, and as the Director of Academic Support Services for the School of Education at Long Island University's Brooklyn Campus. Her research interests revolve around the knowledge-construction processes of students from ethnically, culturally, and linguistically diverse backgrounds in higher-education contexts; the intersections between writing and knowledge construction; and the use of culturally relevant knowledge and alternate knowledges in academic writing and mainstream platforms of knowledge dissemination.

Carmen M. Martínez-Roldán is an Associate Professor in Bilingual Bicultural Education at Teachers College, Columbia University. Her research seeks to advance both theory and practice related to young Latino bilingual children's literacy development. Her work contributes to understanding the ways in which this group's linguistic repertoire serves as a resource for meaning-making of texts and for supporting their academic identities. Her research also documents the ways teachers understand and address the particular literacy strengths and needs of bilingual students. Her work has been disseminated nationally and internationally through top-tier journals and through practitioner-oriented journals.

Maried Rivera Nieves is a project manager at the Center on Culture, Race, and Equity at Bank Street College of Education in New York City. Born in Puerto Rico and raised primarily in the suburbs of the Twin Cities, Maried is passionate about helping educators cultivate an anti-racist praxis and school environment, as well as writing and thinking individually and in the community about the intersections of race, culture, migration, colonization, and politics. Maried holds an M.A. in International Educational Development, with a focus on Latin American and Latino Education, from Teachers College, Columbia University. Her parents and sisters live in Minnesota. Since moving to the mainland 20 years ago, more family has done the same. Many of her family's elders remain in Yabucoa, Puerto Rico.

ACKNOWLEDGEMENTS

The journey leading to this book has been full of surprises and solidarities. I want to acknowledge the book contributors, those who opened their hearts, sharing their testimonios, and those who listened to and helped bring other women's testimonios forward. Thanks for your dedication to this project. Thanks to all the graduate students in my Latina Narratives course throughout the last eight years who listened to each other's stories with solidarity and awe. Thanks for your urgency towards fighting the inequities that surround the schooling of Latinx children, and for engaging in co-creating tools for advocacy and activism.

Thanks to the many friends, relatives, and colleagues in academia who have supported my thinking about narratives and transformation over the years, even before I knew I would be writing about narratives. My deep gratitude to those who responded to earlier drafts of these chapters, and especially to Sonia Nieto and Karen Adler, for believing in the project. I want to acknowledge graduate assistants and elementary bilingual teachers, Rene Minnocci and Inez Koberg, for your professionalism and careful attention to detail. Your students will be lucky to have such critical caring teachers committed to social justice and activism.

Lastly, thanks to my husband, Guillermo Malavé, who supported this work across the years with his encouragement and critical thinking.

1

NARRATING ERASURE, NARRATING AGENCY

Towards a Transformative Activist

Carmen M. Martínez-Roldán

This edited volume joins a line of research that uses narratives, self-identification stories, and *testimonios* as theory, methodology, and advocacy focusing on the lives of Latinas. Nine authors engaged in an inquiry into life experiences that have been relevant to the narrators' processes of *becoming*—becoming Latinas, students, anti-racist teachers, and advocates. Their narratives highlight experiences involving what can be described as *practices of erasure*, but more importantly, they feature a range of agentive actions and discourses with implications for the schooling of students from minoritized[1] communities, especially the schooling of Latinxs, who represent one-fourth of U.S. elementary, middle, and high-school students (IES National Center for Education Statistics, 2019).

My discussion of the narratives in this chapter is framed by an age-old question pursued by many scholars, and most recently raised by Anna Stetsenko (2017): "How can people be understood fundamentally as agentive persons choosing and making 'their way' and, at the same time, as constituted at the very core of their being and existence by the social forces and structures seemingly beyond themselves?" (p. 4). This question has shaped not only my own biography but also my inquiry on the interaction between educational contexts that constrain agency and those that open up spaces for teaching, learning, and agency. As Hall (1985) put it, echoing a Marxian principle: We make history and we can change history "but on the basis of anterior conditions which are not of our making" (p. 85). Working within this premise and challenging the individual/society dichotomy prevalent during his time, Vygotsky (1978, 2004) showed how individuals create, appropriate, and transform cultural tools and artifacts available to them for their own purposes. His proposal was profoundly agentive and his ideas about cultural mediation "as the main pathway for development were combined with, and embedded within, his social activism and a passionate quest for equality and justice" (Stetsenko, 2017, p. 89).

In her book, *The Transformative Mind: Expanding Vygotsky's Approach to Development and Education*, Stetsenko (2017) elaborates on these proposals and puts forth a dialectical view of agency called a Transformative Activist Stance in education. Her response to the question above on individuals' agency as enacted within social forces and structures beyond themselves resonates with my reading of the narratives presented in this volume, which center issues of identity, erasure, agency, and schooling. The central theme of Stetsenko's critical sociocultural proposal is that human development is a collaborative project of people changing and co-creating the world together, contributing change efforts oriented by social justice and equity goals. Within this premise, every person matters because the world is evoked and created "by each and every one of us, in each and every event of our being-knowing-doing-by us as social actors" (p. 7). We are "agents of communal practices and collective history, who only come about [as humans] within the matrices of these practices through realizing and co-authoring them in joint struggles and strivings" (p. 7).

Paraphrasing the premise of her proposal, it can be said that in fighting erasure and the structures that promote it, there are no insignificant contributions. Acknowledging that we live within contexts and structures that facilitate or stifle our agentive potential with real material consequences, every effort and story of each teacher, student, and parent counts and matters. These efforts, local and little as they may be, contribute to co-creating history; each one can help change the world; through each one we realize our humanity. Narratives, then, are approached in this book as a type of activism. Storytelling has been a core strategy of Latinx[2] communities' organized and ongoing struggle for a liberatory education. Teachers have often been central to those stories or their narrators as accomplices to the struggle for change. This volume recognizes that teachers' roles as activists are of critical importance in this struggle. Convinced of the power of stories and the power of teachers to generate change, we offer this edited volume.

As a Latina researcher and teacher educator working at a predominantly white institution of higher education that is committed to social justice through its mission and policies but that is still wrestling with how to better serve its students of color, I have been fortunate to teach a graduate methods class on 'Latina Women Narratives' every other year. The course has become a space where students not only engage with narrative methodologies but one in which Latinas' experiences are brought forth and centered into the curriculum, a rare occurrence at predominantly white institutions of higher education. It has been humbling to learn about my students' stories of struggle, survival, and self-identification processes. Their narratives raised many critical issues about the educational systems serving Latinx students, and I soon realized that these stories needed to be shared with Latinx communities and those interested in the education of students of color. The book then comes out of a collaborative process that spanned over eight years, in which a group of Latina and non-Latina students from different sections of the course who wanted to share their studies with a larger audience came together to think further about their narratives. As part of a mentoring process, the drafts of the chapters were read and discussed by a new group of students taking the same course in Fall 2019. Some of the authors participated in these discussions in which we engaged more deeply with the complexities of writing about Latinas' identities, about white privilege, including white Latino privilege, and about the role of schools and teachers in supporting students of color. These discussions led to further chapter revisions. The book features nine narrative studies: six testimonios, or autobiographical accounts by Latinas who chose to write about their life experiences or their families', and three narrative studies based on interviews with Latinas. Most of the contributors are or have been teachers and all are concerned with improving the educational experiences of students of color, especially of Latinx students.

In the chapters to follow, each contributing author pursues her own questions, resulting in entries that can stand on their own. While we hope these stories resonate with readers in various ways, in this introduction, I offer my perspective about the potential of the narratives as instantiations of transformative activism, acknowledging the value of narratives in shaping the narrators' subjectivities but also highlighting the political value of their stories. Through these narratives, the authors are doing something beyond just remembering past events (Bruner, 2004). I propose that although most of these are identification stories that reflect the narrators' processes of coming to know themselves and others through narrative, their stories contribute to collaborative transformative practices with clear implications for the development of a transformative activist educational project. The four concepts discussed next—erasure, agency, testimonios, and identity—frame my argument about the transformative, agentive nature of the narratives within this volume.

1.1 Narrating Erasure: A Sense of Urgency

Erasure is conceptualized in this volume as: practices and ideological discourses that dehumanize, silence, and render invisible Latinxs and other marginalized groups; practices and discourses that violate Latinxs' rights to preserve and cultivate our cultural, linguistic, and various social identities; and subtractive and at times violent schooling practices that stifle students' potential as learners and professionals, and their well-being (Allahar, 2005; Marquez Kiyama, Harris, & Dache-Gerbino, 2016; Valenzuela, 1999). *Subtractive schooling* takes place when educators do not recognize and build on students' and families' social and cultural resources (Valenzuela, 1999) and when schools engage in coercive assimilation practices (Stanton-Salazar, 2001). These systematic attempts at erasure of minoritized, colonized, and subjugated voices and histories have been effectively employed as strategies of social and cultural domination, especially, though not exclusively, through education (Spring, 2019).

Nowadays, such efforts at erasure are poignantly transparent in anti-immigrant and white supremacist ideological discourses (Hall, 1985; van Dijk, 1987) circulating with renewed energy in the United States and around the world. For instance, in his comparative study on ethnic prejudice, van Dijk (1987) found that despite the historical and socioeconomic differences between different countries of Western Europe and North America, white people's prejudices, and the structures and strategic uses of those prejudices, were very similar. For example, white people said sometimes identical things about Mexican immigrants in the United States and about Turkish guest workers in the Netherlands or Western Germany (p. 392). Their discourses were summarized in the following propositions: "THEY are different from US"; "THEY are deviant"; and "THEY are a threat to US" (van Dijk, 1996, pp. 17–18, emphasis in the original). van Dijk (1987) interpreted such ethnic prejudices "as functional in the maintenance of power and privileges of the dominant White majorities in these countries" (p. 392).

These discourses have devastating consequences, especially when openly endorsed and institutionalized by government authorities, such as in the United States under the Trump presidency. The 2018–2019 dehumanizing images of Latinx immigrant children in cages, deprived of their families and of schooling, along with ideological discourses criminalizing immigrants and people of color, are recurrent tragic enactments of white and state domination over immigrant groups and communities of color. Unsurprisingly, critical educational scholars have not shied away from naming the deeply embedded racism in U.S. systems and institutions, which casts white dominant culture as the norm in which the country's legal, political, and education systems, among others, have been steeped. The practices and policies that support white privilege hurt students of color in particular, as well as children from working-class families, which the U.S. educational system in general has historically failed (Delgado Bernal, 2002; Salinas, Fránquiz, & Nasseem Rodríguez, 2016; Shi, Jiménez-Arista, Cruz, McTier Jr., & Koro-Ljungberg, 2018[3]; Urrieta & Villenas, 2013). This sociopolitical climate, exacerbated by the death of innocent people at the hands of police officers, poses a sense of urgency that propelled the inquiry pursued in this book: How is erasure manifested and resisted in the lives of Latinas as expressed through their narratives on erasure, identity, and education? What are the implications of these narratives for education?

These narratives join the existing and extensive scholarship on narrative in not merely sharing experiences of erasure, but in demonstrating the agentive moves and resources activated by Latinas to challenge that erasure. Each narrative is grounded in a stance of resistance and agency that led to these more specific questions: What resources did these Latinas engage to resist or push down erasure? In what sense can these actions of resistance be considered transformative, agentic efforts with potential for a transformative activist educational project? After all, notwithstanding the role of educational institutions in contributing to erasure, schools can also create opportunities for student agency.

1.2 Narrating Agency: A Critical Sociocultural Perspective

In their critical sociocultural approach to learning, Moje and Lewis (2007) explicitly connect agency to the concepts of identity, power, and learning. They define agency as "the strategic making and remaking of selves, identities, activities, relationships, cultural tools and resources, and histories, as embedded within relations of power" (p. 18). Their definition contemplates both the subjective and contextual factors that encourage and stifle agency, including structures of power and collective histories (Enciso, 2007). In her transformative activist theory, Stetsenko (2017) also highlights as inherent aspects of agency "the situated dimensions of culture, politics, and power along with the ever-shifting interactivities and subjectivities" (p. 83), but she also contributes an ontological dimension, aligning with her interest in considering "the dialectics between the social and the individual, the external and the internal, the person and the world, the mind and the shared communal practices" (p. 2).

Stetsenko (2017) characterizes *commitment to change* as the formative co-constituent of human development and society when she states that "collaborative, purposeful transformation of the world is the core of human nature and the principled grounding for learning and development" (p. 474). As agents of change, individuals co-create reality in the present, striving for a better world, rather than merely hoping for the future's somehow predestined arrival, and they do so through struggle and contestation within their unique sociohistorical conditions (p. 32). Stetsenko's definition of agency highlights the future-oriented nature of these efforts, and thus agency is conceptualized as "a situated and collectively formed ability of human beings… to project into the future, challenge the existing status quo, and commit to alternatives in thus realizing the world and human development" (p. 84). Thus, human development, from a Transformative Activist Stance perspective, is a sociohistorical project, a continuously evolving process, and a collaborative achievement.

In her conceptualization of agency, Stetsenko (2008) pays explicit attention to cognitive processes, proposing a theory of the mind and agency that is grounded in ideals of social justice. Her theory of the mind addresses the relationship between memory, identity development, meaning-making, and the processes of individuals becoming agents of change. For Stetsenko, human subjectivity (mind and knowledge, self and agency) "is understood to emerge out of, within, and through collaborative transformative practices" (p. 484). Through these practices, individuals simultaneously come to know and transform themselves; through this, they come to be human (p. 484). Given the role of memory in this process, I will focus briefly on the relationship between memory and agency.

1.2.1 Memory and Agency

Eventually, the culturally shaped cognitive and linguistic processes that guide the self-telling of life narratives achieve the power to structure perceptual experience, to organize memory, to segment and purpose-build the very 'events' of a life. In the end, we become the autobiographical narratives by which we 'tell about' our lives.

(Bruner, 2004, p. 694)

From a sociocultural perspective, focusing on memory offers insights into the larger relationship between the individual and society. Of interest here is addressing the question: What does memory have to do with agency? The idea of memory as a mental storage of past events, where memories remain unchanged until we retrieve them, has been extensively challenged (Stetsenko, 2017). Scholars working from different traditions have proposed that telling stories and listening to others' stories shape memories in significant ways. Autobiographical narratives have the power to structure perceptual experience and organize memory (Bruner, 1986, 2004); likewise, the texts and narratives we read and listen to mediate both individual and collective memory (Wertsch, 2002). However, narratives also project into the future:

The ways of telling and the ways of conceptualizing that go with them become so habitual that they finally become recipes for structuring experience itself, for laying down routes into memory, for not only guiding the life narrative up to the present but directing it into the future.

(Bruner, 2004, p. 708)

To this existing work on memory, Stetsenko (2017) contributes a theory of the mind that further highlights its orientation to the future and its agentive, transformative nature. Paraphrasing Vygotsky, Stetsenko describes the higher mental functions, such as memory, as "a process of *authorially taking up* social practices, in contributing to changing them, by actors of society and history in always creative, novel, agentive, and transformative—that is, *activist*—ways" (p. 321, emphasis in the original). In line with the work previously presented, Stetsenko starts with the premise that all acts of remembering the past are actually never just about the past; they serve goal-directed thought and action and commitments to change the present. From this perspective, human memory is a form of action. Remembering is the work of keeping things, persons, and experiences alive because they are relevant to us on some level; it is the work of continuously recreating the past and recruiting its resources in the service of one's becoming, a becoming that occurs through changing the world within community practices (p. 305). For Stetsenko, memory then is a tool of creating novelty and inventing the future, "reimagining what is possible and who one wants to be within the overall work of identity development and becoming" (p. 305).

An agentive view of memory and narrative has also been developed by Black feminist scholars in their work around Endarkened Feminist epistemologies. In her study of an African American young female and future teacher engaging with Africa and African knowledges, Dillard (2016) offers the concept of (re) membering as radical activism and spiritual and sacred activism, especially for diasporic Black women. These (re)membering processes have implications for healing, humanizing, and ultimately transforming teaching, learning, and teachers' lives (p. 406). These epistemologies and (re)membering methodologies are becoming increasingly relevant for scholars, teachers, students of color, and their communities (González, 2001; Medina, in press). One type of narrative that most strongly illustrates this authorial and activist nature of remembering and narratives is the genre of testimonios.

1.3 Testimonios: An Agentive Practice

In the first 1981 edition, reprinted in 2015, of *This Bridge Called My Back: Writings by Radical Women of Color*, Anzaldúa writes a letter to women of color in which she contemplates writing as a tool for self-preservation, personal and collective transformation, and combating erasure:

> I write to record what others erase when I speak, to rewrite the stories others have miswritten about me, about you. To become more intimate with myself and you. To discover myself, to preserve myself, to make myself, to achieve self-autonomy.
>
> (2015, p. 167)

Such an invitation demonstrates a view of women of color's autobiographical writing as an agentive, transformative act that impacts the personal and the collective; it is an agentive power that Anzaldúa encourages Latinas to assume in her foreword to the second edition in 1983 of that same volume:

> With This Bridge…hemos comenzado a salir de las sombras; hemos comenzado a reventar rutina y costumbres opresivas y a aventar los tabúes; hemos comenzado a acarrear con orgullo la tarea de deshelar corazones y cambiar conciencias (*we have begun to come out of the shadows; we have begun to break with routines and oppressive customs and to discard taboos; we have commenced to carry with pride the task of thawing hearts and changing consciousness*).
>
> (1983, p. v, emphasis in original)

And she was heard.

Nowadays, as part of an increasing body of educational scholarship on the topic, life narratives are seen as an agentive practice. Testimonios, in particular, document scholars of color's and their communities' commitment to change, resistance, and activism. Testimonios play an important role in developing collective memory that combats erasure and master narratives. Entire volumes and journal issues have been dedicated to the genre of testimonios as they relate to experiences of discrimination but more importantly, of agency (Delgado Bernal, Burciaga, & Carmona, 2016; Espinoza, Cotera, & Blackwell, 2018; The Latina Feminist Group, 2001; Solinger, Fox, & Irani, 2008; see the 2012 issue of *Equity and Excellence in Education*, Vol. 45, and the 2017 issue of the *Journal of Literacy Research*, Vol. 49).

Freire (1970) advances the notion of "testimonio" (p. 228) as an essential element in the struggle for the liberation of the oppressed people. According to Freire, the leaders pursuing unity and organization should bring forth authentic testimonios (to bear "witness") before the people to demonstrate "that the struggle for liberation is a common task" (1993, p. 157). Popularized in Latin America during times of political struggle and change, testimonio is a narrative genre that centers narrators remembering silenced or untold experiences. In the United States, testimonios often address how Latinas experience education as racialized, gendered, and linguistically minoritized individuals, inscribing into history those lived realities "that would otherwise succumb to the alchemy of erasure" (The Latina Feminist Group, 2001, p. 2). The process of sharing their testimonios is healing (Pérez Huber, 2017), liberating, and empowering for marginalized individuals and communities. Testimonios have been described as a genre in which tellers recast their memory to accentuate certain experiences that then serve as a reconstructive epistemology (Blackmer Reyes & Curry Rodríguez, 2012, p. 527). However, testimonios convey not only personal, but, more importantly, political and social realities that are then used to respond to and resist dominant practices, laws, and policies that perpetuate inequity and, more broadly, to elicit social change (Delgado Bernal, Burciaga, & Carmona, 2012, p. 364; see also, Espinoza et al., 2018).

Schools have not only functioned as sites of erasure but also as sites that support testimonios, as Cervantes-Soon's (2012) study illustrates. In her study, the personal narrative became a means of agency for a group of Chicana students from Ciudad Juárez and for the author, who identified as a member of the community she was studying. The school supported narratives of *autogestión* and agency through a social justice curriculum that used Chicana students' counternarratives as pedagogical tools, incorporating their epistemologies into their schooling. In the very act of sharing their narratives or documenting others' testimonios, scholars of color have become agentive and engaged in resistant moves as ways of combating erasure. They have used testimonios to break the silence and challenge deficit perspectives about students, families, communities of color, and teachers. Testimonios have allowed narrators to negotiate contradictions and ambiguities and to affirm and agentively reclaim their various identities, promoting solidarity and producing transformative research (Castillo-Montoya & Torres-Guzmán, 2012; Castillo-Speed, 1995; Delgado Bernal et al., 2016; Delgado Bernal, Elenes, Godinez, & Villenas, 2006; Flores, 2018; Gibbs Grey & Williams-Farrier, 2017; Martínez-Roldán & Quiñones, 2016; Moraga & Anzaldúa, 1981; Quiñones, 2015, 2018; Ramirez & De La Cruz, 2016; Sosa-Provencio, Sheahan, Fuentes, Muñiz, & Prada Vivas, 2019).

More recent autobiographical work provides narratives and autobiographical accounts that also offer insights into educational scholars' lives, educational commitments, and the sociocultural contexts of teaching and learning (Medina, 2003; Mercado, 2019; Nieto & López, 2019). These autobiographical narratives demonstrate the creative and agentive ways used by Latinas to overcome discrimination in their communities as they become bi- or multilingual teachers, teacher educators, and educational scholars. Their narratives show what is possible within the constraints and possibilities of educational systems that should operate equitably for all students.

1.4 Identity: Sociocultural Perspectives

In line with the critical sociocultural and historical perspectives described in this chapter, identity is defined as a process of becoming that is situated, mediated by sociocultural and historical forces and by language (that is, discursively constructed). At the same time, this definition takes into account the different positions individuals agentively enact or perform in various contexts and relations (Lewis, Enciso, & Moje, 2007, p. 4; see also Holland, Lachicotte, Skinner, & Cain, 1998).

1.4.1 Identity as a Storytelling Activity

Concerned about conceptualizations of identity that aim to capture 'who one is,' Sfard and Prusak (2005) instead propose the idea of identity-making as a communicational practice, a storytelling activity, a collection of identifying stories. They assert that it is our vision of our own or other people's experiences (expressed in narratives), and not the experiences as such, that constitutes our identities. As stories, identities are human-made, "collectively shaped even if individually told, and they can change according to the authors' and recipients' perceptions and needs" (p. 17). How we identify ourselves (our first-person, self-told identities) and how others identify us (designated identities) have potentially significant impacts on our actions. Designated identities/narratives, especially institutional narratives (e.g., a school grade report or school-based diagnoses related to one's abilities), can impact our actions. These have a particular capacity to supplant stories that are already part of our designated identities (p. 18). This conceptualization leads Sfard and Prusak to propose that the focus of inquiries on identity should address the complex dialectic between identity-building and other human activities. Human agency and the dynamic nature of identity come to the forefront in this definition of identity as a narrative.

For most narrators in the next chapters, their self-identifying narratives center on the processes, challenges, and/or contradictions involved in becoming or storying themselves as Latinas and on responding to designated identities that include or exclude them from this social identity. The concept of Latina used in these narratives challenges a single, unified experience for Latinas in the United States, in the same way the term 'Black,' as used in different countries, conveys differences and specificities within different, even if related, histories (Hall, 1985, p. 108). Collectively, however, designated identities, like the broad categories of 'women of color' or 'Latina,' have been embraced by individuals who otherwise self-identify in more local terms. Behind these choices, there are often political and social justice purposes, such as developing solidarity and fighting for political representation without ignoring the intragroup differences within the various Latinx ethnic groups and local communities (Zentella, 2005). In the narratives presented in this book, individuals move between (and in and out of) self-identification narratives and collective narratives/identities while being transformed through a dialectic process in which they mobilize funds of knowledge (González, Moll, & Amanti, 2005) and funds of identity (Esteban-Guitart & Moll, 2014).

1.4.2 Funds of Identity

An agentive view of identity as a mobilization of resources is offered by Esteban-Guitart and Moll (2014). They submit a perspective on identity that enables an inquiry into identity-building and other human activities, yet still addresses subjective aspects of the self through the concept of individuals' 'emotional experiences' or 'lived experiences,' a concept borrowed from Vygotsky (1994), which seeks to break the dichotomy between individual and environment. The concept of lived experiences recognizes how each situation affects each individual differently depending on how the person understands, feels, and lives it, that is to say, by an individual's consciousness, which involves psychological phenomena such as motivation, perception, memory, and self-concept. Through these subjective processes, people respond to cultural factors and "generate culturally appropriate behavior and particular identities to meet the requirements of the situation" (p. 34). At the same time, identities are mediated by signs, symbols, and interactions. Esteban-Guitart and Moll (2014) note that "people define themselves through other people and through the artifacts and resources—visible and invisible—of their social and cultural worlds" (p. 36). Situated in the Vygotskian theoretical sociocultural approach to learning and in the empirical context of the funds of knowledge approach, Esteban-Guitart and Moll contribute the concept of 'funds of identity' and define these as "historically accumulated, culturally developed, and socially distributed resources that are essential for people's self-definition, self-expression, and self-understanding" (p. 37).

This perspective on identity highlights people's agency in the way they orchestrate, use, and transform artifacts (cultural and psychological signs and tools) to create, express, and develop their identities. Social institutions, practices, social relationships, geographies, and less-visible artifacts such as ideologies, beliefs, values, and cultural models (especially as they are expressed in narratives and discourses), are also part of these systems and materials from which we generate our self-understanding and develop self-definitions (Esteban-Guitart & Moll, 2014; González, 2001). Learning about the funds of identity of a particular group of students in their processes of identification may support teachers in their efforts to develop culturally relevant and sustaining curricula (Ladson-Billings, 1995; Paris & Alim, 2017) that affirm students' linguistic and cultural identities without assuming an "unidirectional correspondence between race, ethnicity, language, and cultural ways of being" (Paris, 2012, p. 94). Such efforts would require: to keep in mind the dynamic and mediated processes of becoming for both students and teachers; to recognize the fluidity with which individuals choose to respond, whether it is appropriating, creating, or rejecting the artifacts, discourses, and identity stories that surround them; and to acknowledge the collective histories, power, and ideological struggles of different social groups.

1.5 Enacting a Transformative Activist Stance

In this section, I bring together the concepts of erasure, agency, testimonios, and identity as they intersect in the narratives presented in the following chapters around the argument that, collectively, the narratives are instantiations of a transformative activist educational project in that they reflect a stance that resists, pushes down erasure, and, through struggle and contestation, contributes to futures in the making.

While some of the authors have worked as community organizers or in more overt collaborative activist efforts, their narratives generally speak to more personal experiences in their process of becoming Latinas, women, students, or advocates. From a Transformative Activist Stance perspective, transformative agency is recognized not only when overt challenges and disruptions of oppressive structures occur or when material conditions are changed as the result of agentive actions. Transformative agency is also recognized when more subtle changes occur at the personal and/or collective levels (acknowledging that from a Vygotskian perspective, the personal is always social, and that from a more contemporary critical perspective, the personal is also always political). These subtle changes and contributions can be characterized, borrowing the metaphors by sociologist Silvia Rivera Cusicanqui (Cacopardo, 2018) and Walsh (2013, 2017), as fissures, *resquebraduras*, that open up possibilities, and as narratives that widen the cracks of a transformative and decolonial educational project (Mignolo, 2000).

Going back to the questions posed earlier, I propose that Latinas in these narrative studies engaged in agentive moves, discourses, and actions that contribute to a transformative activist educational agenda in several ways discussed next: a) the narrators author themselves as they mobilized funds of knowledge and funds of identity that challenged erasure and supported their agency; b) they situate their narratives on erasure and agency within larger historical practices of marginalization and advocacy that bring to the forefront the relationship between collective histories and individual stories; c) the authors use writing as activism to develop networks of solidarity; and d) lastly, the chapters contribute to a transformative activist educational project by addressing the implications of their narratives for the development of more equitable, humanizing, and decolonizing education for Latinx students and all students of color, a contribution that will be the focus of the last chapter.

1.5.1 Mobilizing Funds of Knowledge and Funds of Identity

As discussed in the section on memory, remembering is the work "of continuously recreating the past and recruiting its resources in the service of one's becoming," (Stetsenko, 2017, p. 305) with a healing and activist potential to transform who we are and the work we do as educators (Dillard, 2016). Esteban-Guitart and Moll (2014) characterize those resources we mobilize through remembering as funds of identity. In the very act of narrating their experiences, the narrators featured in the upcoming chapters mobilized and orchestrated funds of identity that enabled them to authorially take up social practices, artifacts, activities, and discourses to author themselves and to resist and push down erasure. The range of funds of identity the authors made salient in their narratives speaks to the intersectionality of Latina identities.

While the book title highlights two social identities in the word 'Latinas,' namely ethnicity and gender, identity is constructed in the chapters through experiences and processes related to their ethnicities (often more than one ethnicity), race, language, gender, class, immigration status, and educational experiences, among others. In the end, embracing a situated Latina identity in its inherent intersectionality, even with the ideological struggles the category 'Latina/o/x,' may prompt, for some, opened-up opportunities for solidarity, for feeling part of a collective, for advocating for Latinx students, women, and other marginalized groups.

In my reading of the chapters, salient funds of identity organizing the narratives involve the authors' mobilization of their ethnicities and nationalities. Latinas in this volume *story* themselves (and dis-identify) using one or more of these social identities: Black Latina, Chicana, Mexicana, Mexican American, Poblana, Cuban, Dominican, Honduran, Indigenous, Panamanian, Puerto Rican, Salvadoran, gringa, immigrant, and undocumented. A clear tension emerges in the narratives from the desire to belong (mostly as Latinas, but for some, also as Americans), while at the same time rejecting designated identities that serve to dismiss intersectionality. The chapters contribute a view of identity as situated and fluid, as the narrators move in and out of the category of 'Latina' in relational and contested ways. While biculturalism and interculturalism are embraced by some, the narrators' unique voices and perspectives offer nuances about, expand upon, and complicate what it means to live and identify as a Latina in the United States, contending with erasure while at the same time contributing to co-creating history. Oftentimes, the narrators' sense of ethnicity and nationality appears strongly connected to their sense of place (Brukitt, 2005; Harnett, 2010). Several chapters highlight how moving across geographical contexts became a critical source for identity formation, whether such places affirmed or constrained their process of becoming.

Another salient source of identity formation recruited by the narrators in their remembering processes are the social relationships developed with significant people in their lives, particularly family, including their ancestors. The narrators also orchestrated what Esteban-Guitart and Moll (2014) refer to as institutional funds of identity. That is, in their remembering, the tellers mobilized institutions as spaces that mediated identities, constraining or opening up spaces for self-authoring. For eight of the nine narratives, those institutions were educational, and most of them were associated with experiences of erasure or subtractive schooling practices (Valenzuela, 1999). However, institutions also became a source for identifying stories of affirmation, which speaks to the critical role teachers can play in affirming students' identities and embracing critical pedagogies that promote student agency (Antrop-González & De Jesús, 2006; Darder, 1995; Nieto & Bode, 2018; Rolón, 2000; Stetsenko, 2017).

The authors in this volume also mobilized their academic funds of knowledge and identity as they developed their academic voice, even if it was employed to challenge the very structures that sustain academia. The authors appropriated theoretical concepts that placed their narratives within scholarly traditions and discussions concerned with educational issues and the topics of erasure, agency, and identity. That is to say that, in my reading of their narratives, using theory was more than an academic exercise: the various conceptual frameworks used became artifacts or funds of identity as the authors storied or created identity narratives about themselves or interpreted those of others. This theoretical move also inserted the authors within the historical efforts for liberation made by our communities, our ancestors, and the scholars that have preceded us. In the end, orchestrating these theoretical constructs and using the language of academia could have potentially silenced the voices of these Latina young women, as others have experienced. On the contrary, theory was used in agentive ways for combating erasure, gaining new self-understandings, developing an academic identity, and building solidarity, with the potential for decolonizing academia from within.

Mignolo proposes that each one of us is responsible for our own decolonial liberation (in Mignolo & Walsh, 2018, p. 105) and that the fundamental task of decolonialism is to decolonize knowledge and ourselves (p. 136). I propose that the mobilization of funds of knowledge and identity by the narrators, including the use of epistemologies from different traditions, such as those coming from communities of color, sociocultural theories, decolonial frameworks, and even some concepts from postructuralism, to think about their experiences and their participants' experiences, inserts their narratives agentively within a larger decolonial project.

1.5.2 Contributing to Collective Histories of Erasure and Agency

As with all autobiographical accounts, the narratives included in this volume are not just individual accounts but are social at their core, mediating and mediated by individual and collective memory. From their unique perspectives, the contributors join the voices of other narrators aimed at transforming oppressive practices and discourses while being themselves transformed in the process. These are stories of solidarity. One way in which this collective perspective is reflected is through the contextualization of the narratives within larger minoritized groups' cultural, ideological, and historical struggles (Denzin, 1989, p. 73), especially within practices of marginalization and advocacy. The authors join the voices of others who have come before them and use the 'texts' of their lived experiences to call for interrogating systems, educational institutions, and ideologies that privilege some individuals and exclude others on the basis of race, gender, language, and/or social class, among others.

The narrators recall experiences of exclusion in interactions that questioned their belonging and/or in the process of navigating white-dominant spaces that felt like expressions of white supremacy. Some narratives join collective histories of 'forced' migration and survival experienced by Latinxs due to socioeconomic reasons (e.g., Puerto Ricans in the Midwest and Indigenous, Mexicans, and Latin Americans in the Southwest, California, and New York City); they also speak about the consequences of colonialism and transnationalism. Some narratives are inserted within traditional migration patterns of families from rural areas moving to the city and/or from the city to the United States in search of better socioeconomic opportunities for their children, especially for women moving from small communities where established gender roles stifled their possibilities. Drawing from their parents' or communities' experiences, some of the narratives denounce low-wage labor practices imposed on immigrants, especially on undocumented immigrants who labor sunrise to sunset in order to provide for their families in the United States and Latin America.

Their narratives are located within the struggles of working-class neighborhoods across the United States, whose schools are underfunded, affecting the school quality for many Latinx students and in schools impacted by English-only/monolingual and monocultural ideologies and policies, a lack of bilingual education, and a whitewashed curricula, which contribute to the deculturalization of Latinx. Their narratives offer insights into how these macro-level issues manifest in communities and families at the micro-level, how they impact individual Latinas, and how Latinas speak back to these practices in the process of transforming themselves and their communities.

1.5.3 Writing as Activism

Not only through their content but in the very act of writing their testimonios, analyzing, and/or sharing their narratives, the authors and narrators enact a Transformative Activist Stance that is about inventing the future rather than expecting passively for a more just future to arrive (Stetsenko, 2017). The process of writing about their experiences or their participants' experiences, and their decision to share their narratives, as Anzaldúa (1983) proposed, constitute an agentive act, an example of writing as activism. The writing process was described by the authors creating their testimonios as a spiritual and healing journey (Victoria, Chapter 5), but also became an opportunity for them to author themselves as bicultural Latinas or Indigenous and activists on their own terms (Daniela, Chapter 10). Writing their stories led some to become "an active agent of social change moving past her own moments of oppression to empowerment" (Diana, Chapter 2). For some, using Spanish in the writing of their testimonio journals, even when aware that Spanish was once imposed, felt like resistance, agency, and recovery of a part of themselves (Maried, Chapter 3; Marisol, Chapter 6). Writing was also used to build solidarity. By writing these narratives, the authors and participants demonstrate their orientation to the future and commitment to change, as well as their commitment to transform contexts and ideologies that dehumanize Latinxs and erase their contributions to society from the official curriculum and larger dominant narratives.

1.5.4 Advocating for Latinx Students

Lastly, I propose that all the authors engage in transformative agency through considering the implications of their stories for students, teachers, and schooling. They call for educators to rethink curricula and pedagogical practices—to become culturally responsive and sustaining educators and provide multicultural, anti-racist, and bi/multilingual teaching while holding high expectations of their students (Minosca, Chapter 8; Eliza, Chapter 9). However, the authors recognize, being teachers and educators themselves, that teachers do not work in a vacuum but within structures that support or stifle their professionalism. Thus, the authors call for supporting teachers, especially white teachers and school staff with the time and resources to learn how to reflect on and understand the impact of race, culture, and gender (among other identity markers) on their practice, and to become teacher-researchers (Elise, Chapter 7). The authors address the need to include more culturally responsive family engagement opportunities, recognize and affirm families' and communities' funds of knowledge (Martha, Chapter 4), and increase the number of teachers, administrators, and staff members of color, especially those who are bi/multilingual.

1.6 Overview of the Book

The book is organized in three sections, emphasizing different, although overlapping, ways that the authors engage in transformative, agentive efforts and activism.

Part I, *Mobilizing Funds of Knowledge and Funds of Identities: Negotiating Bicultural Identities*, includes four chapters in which transformative activism is enacted through testimonios that illustrate how the authors mobilize funds of knowledge and funds of identity to resist invisibility, take an agentive stance, and affirm their bicultural or intercultural identities. This section opens with Chapter 2, *Soy Un Amasamiento: A Critical Self-Narrative on Latina Identity Development*, Diana Cordova-Cobo's testimonio as a daughter of Salvadoran parents, mestiza, teacher, and mother affirming her place within the Latinx community following a period of self-exclusion. While she co-founded a Central-American student organization in college and co-organized the Hispanic Heritage Month at her school, for her, resistance has come to signify small, individual actions she takes on a daily basis, such as the conversations she has with her students to combat the narrow understandings of what it means to be Latina in the United States. Diana highlights how understanding the varied experiences of Latinas and their identity development has implications for the choices educators make about curriculum and pedagogy, from preschool to graduate school, and calls for schools to create equitable power structures where all students feel included.

In Chapter 3, *Growing Old/Growing Up Gringa: Negotiating Puertorriqueñidad and Americanism in the Midwest*, Maried Rivera Nieves writes an autobiographical narrative about her mother's and her own national, ethnic, and linguistic identities as Puerto Rican Latinx Spanish-English bilinguals living most of their lives in the midwestern United States. She shares her process of making sense of their different responses to migration and how differently a mother and daughter can negotiate their American and Puerto Rican selves. Her mother intentionally recruits different funds of identity depending on the immediate context and describes her biculturalism through the metaphor of the *va y ven*. Maried's awareness of Puerto Rico's neocolonial status leads her to strive for more political and social awareness, accompanied by the desire to act. She states how her narratives have implications for education, particularly teacher and school preparation, curriculum design, and the development of more culturally sustaining family/community engagement strategies, something that was denied to her.

Likewise, in Chapter 4, *Armonía con Una Palita de Conflicto: A Latino Relationship as Intercultural*, Martha Iris Rosas analyzes how her parents negotiated differences between their Cuban and Puerto Rican backgrounds and the insights she gained from this process. Her narrative addresses how her parents resisted unfavorable designated identities and acted agentively by undoing normative categories of what it means to be Cuban or Puerto Rican. They did that by mobilizing language as a resource, relationships, and the intimate knowledge they have of each other. She describes her parents' relationship as intercultural, even if they come from two Latinx communities, and argues that teachers of bicultural and intercultural students can benefit from integrating the knowledge of intercultural families as they address diversity in classrooms. Teachers can also develop pedagogies in which each child's household languages and cultures are affirmed, ensuring that all students gain more concrete knowledge about their classmates' cultures.

In Chapter 5, *Unearthing el Árbol de Mis Raíces as a First-Generation Graduate Student*, Victoria Hernandez offers her testimonio as a Latina first-generation graduate student in a predominantly white institution where she feels both marginalized and empowered. Her agency was enacted as she found/created counterspaces in academia, where she was able to establish her sense of self and affirm her Honduran and Mexican Indigenous and working-class roots. Mobilizing her pedagogies of the home and a connection to her ancestors are presented as critical for the development of her academic identity, but also in her journey to become an anti-racist educator. Victoria became a student organizer and advocated for the needs of other first-generation students of color, working at supporting academic identities anchored in their cultural identities while simultaneously decentering whiteness and demystifying graduate school for other first-generation students.

Part II, *Mobilizing Places and Voice: Authoring Linguistic and Academic Identities*, includes three chapters in which Latinas' agency is enacted through the reclaiming of their linguistic and/or academic identities, and/or through advocating for students. In Chapter 6, *Reclaiming La Lengua: A Self-Narrative on Language Loss, Learning, and Identity*, Marisol Cantú, a fifth-generation Mexican American, narrates her struggles associated with the intergenerational language loss in her family as a consequence of subtractive language education policies and punitive practices in schools. For her, language and identity were strongly interwoven. She offers a counterstory of her agency in her decision to immerse herself in a Latin American context as an opportunity to recover Spanish as a young adult. Marisol's experience involved the negotiation of identities as she saw how she was excluded from an American identity in the United States and was assigned a gringa identity in Latin America, all while trying to affirm her Mexican American identity. Her story highlights the need to address educational policies that promote not only English as a second language and heritage language programs, but especially bilingual education and bicultural identities in adult and K-12 classrooms.

Elise Holzbauer Cocozzo's narrative study in Chapter 7, *It Takes a Village: Advocating for Bilingual Student with Dis/Abilities*, highlights the weight of educational policy decisions and their consequences for a bilingual child with dis/abilities, which seriously limited spaces for agency for the three Latinas she interviewed: a paraeducator, a mother, and a teacher. The narratives make salient the effects of policies that normalize assimilatory practices. The Latinas' agency and advocacy, more quietly than overtly exercised, is noticeable in the nuanced ways they were able to narrate what happens when cultural funds of knowledge, including students' languages, are not mobilized to support a Latinx child with dis/abilities. Elise calls on those involved in policy-making, teaching, and services for bilingual students with dis/abilities to consider the role of language and culture in students' academic success. She also advocates for supporting teachers to become researchers themselves in their classrooms by way of time, resources, and professional development to engage in the development of more culturally responsive teaching.

In Chapter 8, *Teachers' Mentoring Role, or Lack Thereof, in Latinas' Erasure of a STEM Identity*, Minosca Alcántara, a Latina civil engineer working in a field dominated by men, addresses some of the factors associated with the lack of representation of Latinas in STEM fields. She focuses on the narratives of Graciela, a Dominican high school student who graduated at the top of her class, but whose interest in math and science was erased through her academic journey. Poor-quality schools, tracking systems in math, and inconsistent teacher efficacy, caring, and expectations seemed to play a role in Graciela's disengagement from math and influenced the quality of her relationships with teachers. These relationships mediated her negative self-perception as a math learner and her positive self-image as an English learner. To reverse the trend of Latinas' under-representation in STEM careers, Minosca calls for supporting schools that serve low-income communities by providing them with the resources needed to hire and maintain high-quality math and science teachers.

Part III: *Mobilizing Networks of Solidarity: Creating Spaces for Agency*, includes three chapters in which the development of networks of solidarity and activism are more overt.

In Chapter 9, *Fill a Void to Create New Space: The Narrative and Counternarratives of Zoraida López*, Eliza Clark, a former bilingual teacher, features the counter-narratives of Zoraida, a self-identified Afro-Latina artist, activist, and student of Panamanian background. Eliza wanted to learn how much agency Zoraida felt over her positioning in demographic 'stories,' and what is lost/gained and resisted/accepted in this positioning. The chapter includes three narratives: a story about Zoraida's mother's reaction to a speech pathologist who advised her to stop speaking in Spanish to her daughter; a narrative about Zoraida's agentive positioning on issues of race; and a narrative of Zoraida's professional commitments as an artist teaching photography to incarcerated women in Colombia. Zoraida shares a counternarrative that highlights the women's humanity and their agentive moves in using photography to portray themselves in particular ways. Eliza considers the implications of the narratives for her work as a teacher and on her role as a white researcher listening to Zoraida's and her own students' stories.

Lastly, in Chapter 10, *Transgressing Pedagogical Borders of Oppression: A Poblana/Mexicana Indígena-Migrante Praxis,* Daniela Conde centers the intergenerational experiences of erasure and agency of Poblana Mexicana Indigenous migrant women. She also centers Indigenous epistemologies by focusing on her self-narratives and her aunt's counternarratives. Her chapter discusses Dolores' narratives as an undocumented migrant who found her voice and mobilized other women in ESL classes to advocate for their children's educational rights. Her narratives serve as a testament to the liberatory potential of educational spaces that live out a vision of social justice. Daniela and Dolores propose a Poblana Mexicana Indígena-Migrante Praxis enacted through a cyclical process that involves survival, healing, resistance, and empowerment as a framework to understand their experiences. Their narratives have implications for the development of culturally sustaining pedagogies.

The book ends with Chapter 11, *Narratives as Tools for Agency: Teachers and Students as Activists*, in which I elaborate on the implications of the narratives for the development of a transformative activist educational project in preK-higher education for Latinx and all students of color through pedagogies of critical caring and daring. Such a project would imply shifting the goal of education from adaptation and participation to contribution. The proposed shift calls for creating the conditions for transformative and decolonizing education by developing together—teachers, students, parents, and teacher-educators—tools for agency and activism in schools. Examples of pedagogical practices and 12 tools with potential to support children's and teachers' activism in classrooms are presented. The chapter includes eight tables listing literature for children and adolescents that could support critical conversations.

Through the process of preparing this volume, I have read the narratives featured here countless times, and with each reading, the narratives move me deeply. The narrators' fight, resistance, and agentive decisions are inspiring. By sharing their stories, the tellers faced emotions and contradictions and made themselves vulnerable, aware that these are unfinished stories and identities still in the making. Because it has been a long time since they wrote their testimonios and counterstories, some of the narrators have wondered how they might reinterpret their narratives in different ways now that their experiences have provided them with new insights, especially regarding issues of race in relationship with Latinidad and new understandings of identity politics. The same is true for me, as I have also been transformed during this journey. The perspectives on narrative and identity put forth in this volume rest on the premise that we are all in a process of becoming. It is with this spirit that we offer these narratives and invite you to bring your own as the field of education comes together to generate new equitable and transformative activist educational contexts for teachers and students, especially for Latinxs, immigrants, and all students of color.

Notes

1 The concept of 'minoritized' rather than 'minority,' proposed by McCarty (2002) when referring to Navajo communities and largely used in the United States to include other groups, "conveys the power relations and processes by which certain

groups are socially, economically, and politically marginalized within the larger society. This term also implies human agency" (p. xv).

2 The term 'Latinx' aims to be inclusive of people in the United States with roots in Spanish-speaking nations or Latin America who do not identify within the gender binary of masculinity or femininity, and represents the various intersections of gender (Salinas & Lozano, 2017, p. 10). The term, though, has not been uniformly used throughout this volume. Some authors decided to use it only if participants self-identified as Latinx as recommended by Salina and Lozano, whereas others applied the term to refer to communities but not to individuals, unless they knew how the individual self-identified. In this chapter, I apply the latter use.

3 In solidarity with other scholars of color, we will list up to five authors the first time of an in-text citation throughout the volume.

References

Allahar, A. (2005). Identity and erasure: Finding the elusive Caribbean. *Revista Europea de Estudios Latinoamericanos y del Caribe* [European Review of Latin American and Caribbean Studies], *79*, 125–134.

Antrop-González, R., & De Jesús, A. (2006). Toward a theory of *critical care* in urban small school reform: Examining structures and pedagogies of caring in two Latino community-based schools. *International Journal of Qualitative Studies in Education, 19*(4), 409–433.

Anzaldúa, G. (1983). Foreword to the second edition. In C. Moraga & G. Anzaldúa (Eds.), *This bridge called my back: Writings by radical women of color* (2nd ed.) (pp. iv–v). Kitchen Table: Women of Color Press.

Anzaldúa, G. (2015). Speaking in tongues: A letter to third world women writers. In C. Moraga & G. Anzaldúa (Eds.), *This bridge called my back: Writings by radical women of color* (4th ed., pp. 163–172). State University of New York Press.

Blackmer Reyes, K., & Curry Rodríguez, J. E. (2012). Testimonio: Origins, terms, and resources. *Equity & Excellence in Education, 45*(3), 525–538.

Brukitt, I. (2005). Situating auto/biography: Biography and narrative in the times and places of everyday life. *Auto/Biography, 13*, 93–110. https://doi.org/10.1191/096755 0705ab025oa

Bruner, J. S. (1986). *Actual minds, possible worlds.* Harvard University Press.

Bruner, J. S. (2004). Life as narrative. *Social Research, 71*(3), 691–710.

Cacopardo, A. (2018, April 18). *Historias debidas VIII. Entrevista a Silvia Rivera Cusicanqui* [Video]. Youtube. https://www.youtube.com/watch?v=1q6HfhZUGhc&feature=yo utu.be

Castillo-Montoya, M., & Torres-Guzmán, M. (2012). Thriving in our identity and in the academy: Latina epistemology as a core resource. *Harvard Educational Review, 82*, 540–558. https://doi.org/10.17763/haer.82.4.k483005r768821n5

Castillo-Speed, L. (1995). *Latina: Women's voices from the borderlands.* Simon & Schuster.

Cervantes-Soon, C. G. (2012). Testimonios of life and learning in the borderlands: Subaltern Juárez girls speak. *Equity & Excellence in Education, 45*(3), 373–391. https://doi.org/10.1080/10665684.2012.698182

Darder, A. (1995). *Buscando America:* The contributions of critical Latino educators to the academic development and empowerment of Latino students in the U.S. In. C. Sleeter & P. McLaren (Eds.), *Multicultural education, critical pedagogy, and the politics of difference* (pp. 319–347). State University of New York.

Delgado Bernal, D. (2002). Critical race theory, Latino critical theory, and critical race-gendered epistemologies: Recognizing students of color as holders and creators of knowledge. *Qualitative Inquiry, 8*(1), 105–126.

Delgado Bernal, D., Burciaga, R., & Carmona, J. F. (2016). *Chicana/Latina testimonios as pedagogical, methodological, and activist approaches to social justice*. Routledge.

Delgado Bernal, D., Burciaga, R., Flores Carmona, J. (2012). Chicana/Latina testimonios: Mapping the methodological, pedagogical, and political. *Equity & Excellence in Education, 45*(3), 363–372. https://doi.org/10.1080/10665684.2012.698149

Delgado Bernal, D., Elenes, C., Godinez, F., & Villenas, S. (Eds.). (2006). *Chicana/Latina education in everyday life: Feminista perspectives on pedagogy and epistemology*. State University of New York Press.

Denzin, N. K. (1989). *Interpretative biography*. SAGE Publications.

Dillard, C. B. (2016). Turning the ships around: A case study of (re)membering as Transnational Endarkened Feminist inquiry and praxis for Black teachers. *Educational Studies, 52*(5), 406–423.

Enciso, P. (2007). Reframing history in sociocultural theories: Toward and expansive vision. In C. Lewis, P. Enciso, & E. B. Moje (Eds.), *Reframing sociocultural research on literacy: Identity, agency, and power* (pp. 49–74). Lawrence Erlbaum.

Espinoza, D., Cotera, M. E., & Blackwell, M. (2018). *Chicana movidas: New narratives of activism and feminism in the movement era*. University of Texas Press.

Esteban-Guitart, M., & Moll, L. C. (2014). Funds of Identity: A new concept based on the Funds of Knowledge approach. *Culture & Psychology, 20*(1), 31–48. https://doi-org.tc.idm.oclc.org/10.1177/1354067X13515934

Flores, T. T. (2018). Chicas fuertes: Counterstories of Latinx parents raising strong girls. *Bilingual Research Journal, 41*(3), 329–348. https://doi.org/10.1080/15235882.2018.1496955

Freire, P. (1970). *Pedagogía del oprimido*. Siglo XXI.

Freire, P. (1993). *Pedagogy of the oppressed* [New rev. 20th-anniversary ed., 1993]. (Trans. M. Bergman Ramos). Continuum. (Original work published 1970)

González, N. (2001). *I am my language: Discourses of women and children in the borderlands*. The University of Arizona Press.

González, N., Moll, L. C., & Amanti, C. (Eds.). (2005). *Funds of knowledge: Theorizing practices in households, communities, and classrooms*. Lawrence Erlbaum.

Grey, T. G., & Williams-Farrier, B. (2017). #Sippingtea: Two black female literacy scholars sharing counter-stories to redefine our roles in the academy. *Journal of Literacy Research, 49*(4), 503–525.

Hall, S. (1985). Signification, representations, ideology: Althusser and the post-structuralist debates. *Critical Studies in Mass Communication, 2*(2), 91–114.

Harnett, P. (2010). Life history and narrative research revisited. In A. Bathmaker & P. Harnett (Eds.), *Exploring learning, identity, and power through life history and narrative research* (pp. 159–170). Routledge.

Holland, D., Lachicotte, J. W., Skinner, D., & Cain, C. (1998). *Identity and agency in cultural worlds*. Harvard University Press.

IES National Center for Education Statistics. (2019). *Status and trends in the education of racial and ethnic groups*. https://nces.ed.gov/programs/raceindicators/indicator_rbb.asp

Kiyama, J. M., Harris, D. M., & Dache-Gerbino, A. (2016). Fighting for *respeto*: Latinas' stories of violence and resistance shaping educational opportunities. *Teachers College Record, 118*(12), 1–50.

Ladson-Billings, G. (1995). Toward a theory of culturally relevant pedagogy. *American Educational Research Journal, 32,* 465–491.

Latina Feminist Group. (2001). *Telling to live: Latina feminist testimonios.* Duke University Press.

Lewis, C., Enciso, P., & Moje, E. B. (2007). *Reframing sociocultural research on literacy: Identity, agency, and power.* Lawrence Erlbaum.

Martínez-Roldán, C. M., & Quiñones, S. (2016). Resisting erasure and developing networks of solidarity: Testimonios of two Puerto Rican scholars in the academy. *Journal of Language, Identity, and Education, 15*(3), 151–164. https://doi.org/10.1080/1534845 8.2016.1166059

McCarty, T. L. (2002). *A place to be Navajo: Rough Rock and the struggle for self-determination in Indigenous schooling.* Lawrence Erlbaum.

Medina, C. (2003). Puerto Rican subjective locations: Definitions and perceptions of literacy. *Journal of Hispanic Higher Education, 2*(4), 392–405.

Medina, C. L. (in press). Barruntos: Youth improvisational work as decolonial literacy actionings in Puerto Rico. *Research in the Teaching of English.*

Mercado, C. I. (2019). *Navigating teacher education in complex and uncertain times: Connecting communities of practices in a borderless world.* Bloomsbury Academic.

Mignolo, W. D. (2000). *Local histories/global designs: Coloniality, subaltern knowledges, and border thinking.* Princeton University Press.

Mignolo, W. E., & Walsh, C. (2018). *On decoloniality: Concepts, analytics, praxis.* Duke University Press.

Moje, E. B., & Lewis, C. (2007). Examining opportunities to learn literacy: The role of critical sociocultural literacy research. In C. Lewis, P. Enciso, & E. B. Moje (Eds.), *Reframing sociocultural research on literacy: Identity, agency, and power* (pp. 15–48). Lawrence Erlbaum.

Moraga, C., & Anzaldúa, G. (1981). *This bridge called my back: Writings by radical women of color.* Persephone Press.

Nieto, S., & Bode, P. (2018). *Affirming diversity. The sociopolitical context of multicultural education* (7th ed.). Pearson.

Nieto, S., & López, A. (2019). *Teaching, a life's work: A mother–daughter dialogue.* Teachers College Press.

Paris, D. (2012). Culturally sustaining pedagogy. *Educational Researcher, 41*(3), 93–97.

Paris, D., & Alim, H. S. (2017). *Culturally sustaining pedagogies: Teaching and learning for justice in a changing world.* Teachers College Press.

Pérez Huber, L. (2017). Healing images and narratives: Undocumented Chicana/Latina pedagogies of resistance. *Journal of Latinos and Education 16*(4), 374–389. https://doi.org/10.1080/15348431.2016.1268963

Quiñones, S. (2015). Negotiating entangled contradictions: Nudos (knots) in the lives of bilingual latina teachers. *NABE Journal of Research and Practice, 6,* 1–39.

Quiñones, S. (2018). "I get to give back to the community that put me where I am": Examining the experiences and perspectives of Puerto Rican teachers in Western New York. *Urban Education, 53*(5), 621–639.

Ramirez, P. C., & De La Cruz, Y. (2016). The journey of two Latino educators: Our collective resilience. *Journal of Latinos and Education, 15*(1), 58–65. https://doi.org/10.108 0/15348431.2015.1045142

Rolón, C. A. (2000). Puerto Rican female narratives about self, school, and success. In S. Nieto (Ed.), *Puerto Rican students in U.S. schools* (pp. 141–165). Lawrence Erlbaum.

Salinas, C., & Lozano, A. (2017). Mapping and recontextualizing the evolution of the term Latinx: An environmental scanning in higher education. *Journal of Latinos and Education, 18*(4), 1–14. https://doi.org/10.1080/15348431.2017.1390464

Salinas, C. S., Fránquiz, M. E., & Nasseem Rodríguez, N. (2016). Writing Latina/o historical narratives: Narratives at the intersection of critical historical inquiry and LatCrit. *Urban Review, 48*(2), 264–284.

Sfard, A., & Prusak, A. (2005). Telling identities: In search of an analytic tool for investigating learning as a culturally shaped activity. *Educational Researcher, 34*(4), 14–22. https://doi.org/10.3102/0013189X034004014

Shi, Y., Jiménez-Arista, L.E., Cruz, J., McTier Jr., T.S., & Koro-Ljungberg, M. (2018). Multilayered analyses of the experiences of undocumented Latinx college students. *The Qualitative Report, 23*(11), 2603–2621.

Solinger, R., Fox, M., & Irani, K. (Eds.). (2008). *Telling stories to change the world: Global voices on the power of narrative to build community and make social justice claims.* Routledge.

Sosa-Provencio, M. A., Sheahan, A., Fuentes, R., Muñiz, S., & Prada Vivas, R. E. (2019). Reclaiming ourselves through *Testimonio* pedagogy: Reflections on a curriculum design lab in teacher education. *Race Ethnicity and Education, 22*(2), 211–230. https://doi.org/10.1080/13613324.2017.1376637

Spring, J. (2019). *The American school: From the Puritans to the Trump era* (10th ed.). Routledge.

Stanton-Salazar, R. D. (2001). *Manufacturing hope and despair: The school and kin support networks of U.S.-Mexican youth.* Teachers College.

Stetsenko, A. (2008). From relational ontology to transformative activist stance on development and learning: Expanding Vygotsky's (CHAT) project. *Cultural Studies of Science Education, 3,* 471–491.

Stetsenko, A. (2017). *The transformative mind: Expanding Vygotsky's approach to development and education.* Cambridge University.

Urrieta Jr., L., & Villenas, S. (2013). The legacy of Derrick Bell and Latino/a education: A critical race testimonio. *Race Ethnicity and Education, 16*(4), 514–535.

Valenzuela, A. (1999). *Subtractive schooling: U.S.-Mexican youth and the politics of caring.* State University of New York Press.

van Dijk, T. A. (1987). *Communicating racism: Ethnic prejudice in thought and talk.* SAGE Publications.

van Dijk, T. A. (1996). *Discourse, racism and ideology.* RCEI Ediciones La Laguna.

Vygotsky, L. S. (1978). *Mind in society.* Harvard University Press.

Vygotsky, L. S. (2004). Thinking and speech. In R. Rieber & D. Robinson (Eds.), *Essential Vygotsky* (pp. 33–148). Kluwer Academic/Plenum.

Vygotsky, L. V. (1994). The problem of the environment. In R. van der Veer & J. Valsiner (Eds.), *The Vygotsky reader* (pp. 338–354). Blackwell.

Walsh, C. (2013). Introducción. Lo pedagógico y lo decolonial: Entretejiendo caminos. [Introduction: The pedagogical and decolonial: Interweaving roads.] In C. Walsh (Ed.), *Pedagogías decoloniales. Prácticas insurgentes de resistir, (re)existir y (re)vivir, Tomo I.* [Decolonial Pedagogies. Insurgent Practices of Resisting, (Re)existing and (Re)living, Volume I] (pp. 23–68). Abya-Yala.

Walsh, C. (2017). (Ed.). *Pedagogías decoloniales: Prácticas insurgentes de resistir, (re)existir y (re)vivir. Tomo II.* [Decolonial Pedagogies. Insurgent Practices of Resisting, (Re)existing and (Re)living. Volume II]. Abya-Yala.

Wertsch, J. V. (2002). *Voices of collective remembering.* Cambridge University Press.

Zentella, A. C. (2005). Premises, promises, and pitfalls of language socialization research in Latino families and communities. In A. D. Zentella (Ed.), *Building on strength: Language and literacy in Latino families and communities* (pp. 13–30). Teachers College Press.

PART I

Mobilizing Funds of Knowledge and Funds of Identities

Negotiating Bicultural Identities

2

SOY UN AMASAMIENTO

A Critical Self-Narrative on Latina Identity Development

Diana Cordova-Cobo

In 2004, I read *The House on Mango Street* for the first time as a high school student. Esperanza, the protagonist who struggles to belong and wishes to "jump out of her skin," became my literary mirror. Esperanza writes:

> I want to be
> like the waves on the sea,
> like the clouds in the wind,
> but I'm me.
> One day I'll jump
> out of my skin.
> I'll shake the sky
> like a hundred violins.

(Cisneros, 1984, pp. 60–61)

Like Esperanza, as a teenager I wished to be anyone but me. I watched my friends and classmates proudly proclaim their cultural identities and I could not identify my own. I struggled to grasp my place in between the American identity imposed on me by my birthplace and the Salvadoran identity imposed on me by my ancestry. While others found a way to fluidly navigate in between, I stumbled through both of these worlds–never quite sure if I belonged in either.

Five years later, I read *Borderlands/The New Mestiza* as an undergraduate student. Just as Esperanza had once echoed my thoughts, it felt as if Anzaldúa (1987) reflected my most intimate deliberations. By this time, I had affirmed my place within the Latinx[1] community—a standing that has been further solidified with each subsequent stage of my life. I related most to how Anzaldúa questioned the labels and expectations imposed on her by others as a result of her cultural identity. While I am no longer struggling to "find" my cultural identity, I found myself with no understanding of how that transition happened at the inception of this study. I know *who* I am without an understanding of *how* I became this person.

Recently, as I engaged in conversations with friends, I realized that many of them also struggled to navigate multiple worlds as adolescents, only to reject complete immersion in any of them as adults. Given the rapid growth of the Latinx population, understanding how individuals come to see themselves as part of this larger community becomes an essential step in strengthening the influence of the Latinx community in the United States. Additionally, the growth in the Latinx population overall is currently fueled by the growth in Latinx births instead of from an influx of immigration from Latin America (Krogstad & Fry, 2014). In fact, in 2018, more than a quarter of the nation's newborns were Latinx (Krogstad, 2019). Teachers and administrators at all grade levels stand to benefit from understanding how the choices they make about pedagogy and curriculum can support their students as they navigate multiple identities. The same is true for policymakers, who hold the power of direct funding and resources towards different education initiatives that can empower or further marginalize Latinx students.

This self-narrative study is therefore centered on the following questions: How do my past experiences mediate my current understandings about my identity as a Latina and my perceived positionality in various contexts? What were the major turning points in my identity development and why were these moments particularly impactful? Essentially, I aim to understand my own identity development as a Latina in the United States with the intent of furthering the research on Latina identity past the *who* to the *how*. Within the scope of this study, my identity development is generally defined as the process by which I came to understand my positionality and subjectivity as a Latina in the current context of the United States. While I consider many characteristics central to my identity, throughout my analysis it became clear that—within the scope of my study—'Latina' and 'mother' were the most salient.

2.1 Theoretical Perspectives and Literature Review

In reviewing the existing narrative research that focuses on the experiences of Latinas in the United States, most narrative studies are grounded in Critical Race Theory (CRT) and, more specifically, Latino Critical Theory (LatCrit). Considering the lack of Latina voices in academia and research overall, CRT and LatCrit provide a theoretical framework for those who employ narrative strategies with a critical/radical lens as a means of resisting erasure and combating oppression within educational institutions.

At its inception, CRT was the result of internal critiques of the existing critical theory movement that urged researchers within the field to improve their work by including the experiences of People of Color[2] who experienced racism in their daily experiences (Delgado & Stefancic, 2001). The third and fourth tenets of CRT are particularly relevant to a self-narrative. They outline a commitment to social justice and transformative research in response to racial oppression and emphasize the centrality of the experiential knowledge of people of color (Solórzano & Yosso, 2001). CRT is also based on the belief that racism exists for most people of color as "ordinary... the usual way society does business" (Delgado & Stefancic, 2001, pp. 6–7).

LatCrit, as an extension of CRT, brings attention to the "way in which conventional, and even critical, approaches to race and civil rights ignore the problems and special situations of Latino people—including bilingualism, immigration reform, the binary black/white structure of existing race remedies law, and much more" (Stefancic, 1997, p. 1510). Latinx individuals do not always fit neatly into the larger narratives around race in the United States. Extending the CRT framework to include LatCrit for this particular self-narrative is integral to understanding the nuances of my experiences and identity development.

The reality of intersectionality in the experiences of many of the Latinas whose narratives are included in the existing body of research also speaks to the importance of also drawing on Latina/Chicana feminism (Alarcón, 1990; Anzaldúa, 1987; Moraga & Anzaldúa, 2002). CRT advocates using other critical frameworks like feminist theory to provide a full analysis of racialized individuals or groups (Delgado & Stefancic, 2001). There are three concepts within Latina/Chicana feminism that are particularly useful in understanding my identity development thus far: theory in the flesh, living in the borderlands, and *conocimiento*. Theory in the flesh is "where the physical realities of our lives—our skin color, the land or concrete we grew up on, our sexual longings—all fuse to create a politic born out of necessity" (Moraga & Anzaldúa, 2002, p. 21). Related to this concept, living in the borderlands refers to "living on borders and in margins... keeping intact one's shifting and multiple identity and integrity" (Anzaldúa, 1987).

Finally, conocimiento (Anzaldúa, 2002) speaks to the impact of engaging in this type of research. Within this conocimiento process, the researcher becomes an active agent of social change, moving past moments of oppression to empowerment. The existing body of literature on Latina narratives points to the ability of Latinas to turn their experiences with oppression and marginalization into moments of resistance and empowerment. This is true within the multiple ways Latinas self-identify, such as 'mother' (Villenas, 2001), 'student' (Carrillo & Rodriguez, 2016; Espino, Muñoz, & Kiyama, 2010; Gómez, 2010; Pérez Huber & Cueva, 2012), and 'academic' (Prieto & Villenas, 2012; Rodriguez, 2006), among others.

2.2 Research Design and Methodology

In line with CRT, this self-narrative is used as a form of counterstory to the homogenized understanding of Latina identity that is often put forth by non-Latinxs in academia and popular culture (Solórzano, 1998; Solórzano & Yosso, 2001). *Testimonios* are used as a form of counternarrative (a transformative narrative) that is based in Latina/Chicana feminism and brings the experiences of Latinas to the center (Anzaldúa, 1990; Delgado Bernal et al., 2009; Flores Carmona, 2010; Latina Feminist Group, 2001; Pérez Huber, 2009). Testimonios "engage the personal and collective aspects of identity formation while translating choices, silences, and ultimately identities" (Delgado Bernal, Burciaga, & Flores Carmona, 2012, p. 2).

For this self-narrative, I engaged in four separate testimonios that were audio-recorded and transcribed. After years in graduate school, I find myself writing much more formally than I speak. Given that this is an exploration of my personal experiences, which are not always located within academia, it was more appropriate to record my testimonios and transcribe them afterwards. Audio-recording instead of journaling allowed me to switch in and out of speech patterns that may not be as evident in writing.

Each of these testimonios were between 30 and 45 minutes of audio recordings that were then transcribed; these transcriptions totaled 67 pages of written text for analysis. The testimonios progressively narrowed in scope. The first explored how and why I divided up my life into four chronological sections: high school, undergraduate, move to New York City, and motherhood. Each of the subsequent testimonios focused on specific aspects of each section that most related to my research questions. These later testimonios were characterized by elaborate descriptions of specific experiences, whereas the first focused on the broad themes and understandings I have of my life thus far. The testimonios took place once a week in my home—again, emphasizing the personal nature of this study.

With respect to data analysis, software for qualitative data analysis and open-coding was used. The analysis began with a holistic-content analysis and moved to a holistic-form analysis as the second stage of data review (Lieblich, Tuval-Mashiach, & Zilber, 1998). Holistic-content analysis in narrative research aims to uncover textual themes across data and requires multiple reviews of the text until patterns emerge. However, in general, the analysis was an iterative process, with themes constantly revisited as I listened to audio recordings multiple times and reread the transcripts during coding. The sequencing of analyzing and concluding did not fit a neat linear progression, as I often attempted to employ Jackson and Mazzei's (2011) ideas about looking for the complexities instead of the coherence within the data. The use of holistic-form analysis was an addition to the original data review as I became interested in the language I used during my testimonios. An analysis based on form requires a careful examination of aspects like the use of repetitive words/phrases throughout a narrative. In my case, a careful holistic-form analysis across testimonios led to the otherness and exclusion-finding I discuss below that transcended the specific setting of the stories being recounted in each audio recording.

2.3 Findings

Upon completion of my data analysis, I was left with three thematic findings that spoke to my identity as a Latina in the United States. The first finding centers on the concepts of othering and exclusion as the process by which I defined my *Latinidad*—or lack thereof. An overall understanding of the trajectory of my identity as nonlinear and continuous follows. Finally, the third finding highlights how I engage in and define resistance as a function of the development of my identity. Within each finding, I attempt to connect my experiences to previous research in both CRT and Latina/Chicana feminism as well as discuss the broader implications of my understandings about my own identity development for the Latinx community.

2.3.1 Otherness and Exclusion

> …we're afraid the other will think we're agringadas because we don't speak Chicano Spanish. We oppress each other trying to out-Chicano each other….There is no one Chicano language just as there is no one Chicano experience.
>
> (Anzaldúa, 2012, p. 80)

In the United States—like many other countries—the structures of power and privilege hinge on the ability to stratify groups of people. At the same time that we define the group that is allotted power and place them at the top of the social hierarchy, we define the groups that are excluded from a privileged status. The privileged group becomes our normative reference and, in comparison to the normative group, we define the "other" (Spivak, 1985). "Othering" is a multidimensional process based on various levels of social differentiation and can be seen as the consequences of racism, sexism, classism, and any combination thereof. In this country, the stratification system that determines the "other" is primarily built on race, where your position is determined by your proximity to whiteness. The patterns of "othering" against the Latinx community are self-evident in the United States. A cursory reading of history will provide you with multiple examples, including the lynching of Latinxs in the Southwest (Delgado, 2009), the school segregation of Latinx students based on skin color (Valencia, 2005), and the SB 1070 immigration law that essentially allowed for the racial profiling of Latinx individuals in Arizona (Cohn, 2012).

Less evident and discussed in empirical research is the process of secondary marginalization that occurs within the Latinx community. Cohen (1999), in her work on AIDS and the politics of Black communities, describes secondary marginalization as the process by which more privileged members of marginalized communities police the boundaries of group identity and therefore maintain control over who or what determines a group's political and social interests.

More specifically, within the Black community, the process of secondary marginalization is built on differences in behavior, attitude, and socioeconomic status. Cohen describes this as a common reaction within marginalized communities that have been defined as "inferior" as they attempt to redefine the definitions of their group for both themselves and the larger public.

In Anzaldúa's (2012) excerpt at the beginning of this section, she is essentially describing this reality within the Latinx community and the insecurities it elicits within group members. How we define Latinidad within our own community is less clear and varies by context—sometimes it simply conforms to mainstream definitions of Spanish-speaking and brown-skinned. In my experience, the boundaries of Latinidad often vary by the dominant subgroup within a geographic context. At the same time that my identity has developed in response to the popular depiction of Latinas in the United States, it has also developed in response to the messages I received from within the Latinx community about what it meant to be Latina. More specifically, it developed in response to the messages I received about what I was not. What follows in this section are excerpts from my testimonios that speak to this reactionary development and discussions of these excerpts as they relate to the larger trends in the data.

In the excerpt below, I describe how my definition of Latinidad led to my self-exclusion from the Latina label in high school:

> I signed up for a Latin American history class during tenth grade…. Aside from one classmate who self-identified as Dominican and was born in New York, it felt as if the entire class was made up of recent immigrants… this was my first consistent interaction with these students who spoke Spanish at a speed I could not. If I think about the classroom, I see my Dominican classmate and myself in a corner while the rest of the students congregated. The class became a social hour and I found myself left out. I stumbled over my Spanish sometimes and I was embarrassed. That, on top of the negative comments I got from Latinxs about my boyfriend—who was not Latino—I think did something to my understanding of what it meant to be Latina at that time in my life. Like, I wasn't Latina enough to really be Latina. "My parents are from El Salvador," I would say… sometimes I would even add, "but I was born here."

In the above excerpt, exclusion shapes my understanding of where I stood within the Latinx community—that I did not stand within the community at all. I perceived the exclusion from my classmates and the comments from adults as a message that I did not belong within their community. I had somehow broken the rules of Latinidad as I perceived them at the time—I did not speak Spanish well enough and my boyfriend was not Latino. At various other points of my testimonios about high school, I describe individuals who had broken one of these "rules," and I still label them as Latina. Ultimately, my understanding at that time—that I did not meet the minimum requirements to be Latina, or that I was not "Latina enough"—shaped my self-exclusion from this group.

However, at the next stage of my life, and the subsequent stages that follow, my identity is largely developed by my inclusion within Latinx spaces and my exclusion from "white spaces." Upon entering college, I suddenly found myself in the extreme racial/ethnic minority. Thus, instead of identifying the difference between myself and other Latinx students on campus, I clung to our similarities as a response to the glaring differences between the white students I encountered and myself. The excerpt below is an example of many that pointed to the lines I redrew in college around my identity.

> I remember walking past sorority row to get to the bus stop from where I parked my car. It was called sorority row, but it wasn't all the sororities. These houses were for the white sororities. I heard about these houses throughout college but never stepped inside. Honestly, it was not for me. I was not one of them. I was not white. Hell, they had to pay over $1,000 a semester just to be in the sorority. So I guess not only was I not white, I couldn't afford that. Years later, my husband told me about an experience he had with a white fraternity where he blatantly felt discriminated against because he was Latino. I told him that is how I felt in a lot of spaces at UF.

These feelings of being the "other" in white spaces only continued as I moved to New York City. New York City has one of the most diverse populations in the world while also having persistent neighborhood segregation (Ellen, Yager, & Austensen, 2019; Logan & Stults, 2011) and one of the highest levels of school segregation in the country (Kucsera & Orfield, 2014). The exception to this in recent years has been rapidly gentrifying neighborhoods, where school racial segregation decreased even as the number of intensely segregated schools increased in non-gentrifying neighborhoods (Mordechay & Ayscue, 2019). That said, gentrification is more likely to end in resegregation instead of sustained diversity without adequate policy interventions—a process that is most harmful to low-income residents and Communities of Color. So really what you end up having is a scenario where you think you are coming to a liberal-heaven, but racism is waiting for you behind some thinly veiled message of "the melting pot." Below is an excerpt of one encounter on the Upper East Side of Manhattan that represents more of the norm whenever I am in that section of the city:

> I hate going to the Upper East Side… I always have a negative interaction. The most recent one was a woman at a bar… middle-aged, white, maybe wealthy… who looked at my husband and me and asked what neighborhood we were from. The assumption, of course, being that we were not from that one. It wasn't in an inquisitive way. It was in a condescending way like she was appalled we were allowed to be in there. I honestly have no idea

what we did to prompt it aside from being obviously Latinos in a mostly white bar. Maybe she didn't like us so close to her chair. But the bar was so tiny. We stuck out. We did not belong. That was the message she was giving us. We left eventually and complained to the bouncer. He empathized with us, but I don't think anything got done. I didn't expect it to. It never does. I guess I just needed someone else to verify I wasn't going crazy. In that neighborhood, they always win.

These two examples mark the persistence of how I define the "they" in the "they versus us" conversation post-undergraduate degree. As I have progressed in my education, I have increasingly been in white spaces—something I did not have to experience until after high school. As much as I look to others who I deem as part of the "us" for support, I realized through the content analysis that my language lingers on the negative associations instead of the positive. In other words, instead of focusing on which groups I am part of, I include many phrases centered on which groups I do not belong to. I constantly say, "I am not _____" or "I did not belong."

The fact that these speech patterns persist today, at a time when I affirm my Latina identity, marks an important divergence in how we understand identity development. Instead of focusing solely on unity as a source of empowerment, it brings into question why that empowerment is even necessary, because we continue to be excluded and "othered" within spaces that are predominantly white. This reality calls for systemic change at the same time that universities and cities work to affirm the cultural identities of students. It is not enough to encourage affinity groups on campus as a source of empowerment for Students of Color. We must also interrogate the systems and ideologies of people within those spaces that make it necessary to have those groups in the first place. As long as individuals continue to feel excluded in schools, an equitable power structure will largely evade us. This is also true within the Latinx community.

2.3.2 Latina Identity Development as Nonlinear and Continuous

The struggle is inner: Chicano, indio, American Indian, mojado, mexicano, immigrant Latino, Anglo in power, working class Anglo, Black, Asian—our psyches resemble the bordertowns and are populated by the same people. The struggle has always been inner, and is played out in outer terrains. Awareness of our situation must come before inner changes, which in turn come before changes in society. Nothing happens in the "real" world unless it first happens in the images in our heads.

(Anzaldúa, 2012, p. 109)

Analyzing the overall trend in my identity development began with a division of my life into the four timeframes mentioned earlier: high school, undergraduate, move to New York City, and motherhood. These categories highlight the importance of context and how a shift in place or an important life event either changed or cemented my understanding about my identity as a Latina in that specific context. The trajectory described below is essentially a way of understanding how Moraga and Anzaldúa's (2002) theory in the flesh is reflected in my narrative. With each stage of my life, the changes in the physical realities of my existence—mainly my geographic location and which racial/ethnic group was dominant in these spaces—resulted in a shift of the politics of my identity as a Latina. The particular salience of place in constituting self has been further echoed by Brukitt's (2005) and Martínez-Roldán and Quiñones's (2016) descriptions of how places helped shape aspects of their identities. For Martínez-Roldán and Quiñones (2016), the movement in between Puerto Rico and the United States and in between a Spanish-speaking household and school, respectively, played a role in cementing their identities as "bilingual learners."

Following a holistic-form analysis based on the salience of the label "Latina" to my self-identification, it was clear my comfort with the label has increased or decreased with each of the four stages. My first noticeable decrease happened in high school, where I felt as if I had no true connection to the "Latina" identity as a result of feelings of exclusion from Latinx social groups. It is important to note that prior to this time period, my family's traditions and summer trips to El Salvador played an integral role in my understanding that I was Central American—though not necessarily "Latina." This is followed by a rise in comfort with the label during college and a period of stability until I moved to New York City. My affinity to my Latina identity then surged again and was followed by another period of stability during my time as a middle school teacher. The second drop in my positive association or comfort with the "Latina" label occurred when I simultaneously entered motherhood and my doctorate program.

This nonlinear and continuous development in my self-identification as Latina serves as a counterstory to the myth in popular culture and in research that once an individual claims their Latina identity and uses it as a source of resistance, that identity does not waver. This is especially evident in my testimonio from the period of my life where I simultaneously became a mother and started my doctorate program. At these points, my identity as a Latina—and my understanding of what that means—wavers and succumbs to fears rooted in marginalization and oppression, even once I consider myself firmly rooted in my beliefs about Latinidad. Below is an excerpt that exemplifies this during my pregnancy:

> My coworker asked me what I thought she would look like. I had no clue at that moment, but her question haunted me for days. The joy I felt when I thought about having a little girl quickly transformed into fear. At its worst, I wanted her to look nothing like me. I wanted her to pass. To walk into a room and not be labeled as Latina or Brown. All my years of education and all the work I did to resist my insecurities evaporated into thin air. I wanted

her to look white and I wanted her to have straight hair. I'm embarrassed to say that out loud.

This above excerpt, and others like it, largely illuminate responses that are rooted in fear instead of self-hatred. Internal colonialism (Gutiérrez, 2004), the concept that we internalize the larger oppressive messages about People of Color, largely leads to self-hatred or secondary marginalization as outcomes. This concept often gets pointed to as the reason for an excerpt like the one above both within and outside of the Latina community. This is not that. This is fear. This is the fear that comes with knowing about and being able to identify oppressive forces that function to subvert my personal and professional success.

Constantly navigating microaggressions (Sue et al., 2007) and seeing People of Color marginalized by white people in white spaces that are supposed to be "liberal" and "accepting" can feel overwhelming. I succumb to these thoughts, rooted in fear, because I am fatigued. As a mother, like most mothers, my instinct is to protect my child. That includes a protection from oppression and exclusion. At that moment, I did not want her to pass for white because I believed she would be more beautiful or more intelligent if she were. I wanted her to present as white because I felt she would be more protected if she were. She would inevitably end up in a white space where she would be susceptible to experiencing exclusion and be forced to defend herself against the assumptions placed on her because of her perceived racial and ethnic group.

The very real emotional and psychological costs of being aware of oppression and racism as adults and academics need to be further explored if we are to combat the homogenized understanding of Latina identity. The rejection of Latina identity may at times be rooted in fear instead of inferiority. Similarly, it is important to emphasize to those struggling to navigate the many parts of their identity that even those who seem firmly grounded in their racial/ethnic identities may waver at times and succumb to their fears. That experience needs to be normalized and accepted if we are to truly create a unified Latinx community across the various contexts and experiences that exist in the United States.

2.3.3 Marginalization as a Site of Resistance

By creating a new mythos—that is, a change in the way we perceive reality, the way we see ourselves, and the ways we behave—la mestiza creates a new consciousness. The work of mestiza consciousness is to break down the subject–object duality that keeps her a prisoner and to show in the flesh and through the images in her work how duality is transcended.

(Anzaldúa, 2012, p. 102)

In the existing narrative research on Latinas, a theme often emerges about resisting marginalization through the use of counterspaces (Espino et al., 2010;

Pérez Huber & Cueva, 2012) and counterstories (Gómez, 2010; Reyes & Ríos, 2005; Rodriguez, 2006; Villenas, 2001) both inside and outside of a predominantly white academia. While my narrative finding on the theme of resistance largely aligns with this, it also builds on the theme to include the battle against the normative understandings within the Latina community that may get passed down to the next generation. The excerpt below is an example of the trends in the data that showed my use of my Latina identity as a means of subverting normative understandings within the Latinx community. This was especially true when it came to individuals that I felt personally invested in—like my students.

> It must have been my second year teaching when I had this conversation with one of my Latina students. One of my kids asked me why I talked like a 'white girl.' She was in my classroom after school and was watching as I explained a shortened version of a history lesson to a seventh grader… We spent thirty minutes talking through why she thought the way I spoke was reserved for white people and whether she felt like all Latinas could only speak one way. This wasn't the first time or the last time that happened. But I had the conversation every time, and I think it was largely because I didn't want my kids to place themselves or others in a box.

Being responsible for others and becoming a teacher is essentially what led me to start speaking out within the Latinx community, especially amongst family and friends. By making my classroom a space where students could share their stories and commentary freely, I became better attuned to how the actions of adults within and outside of the Latinx community could impact my students' perceptions of themselves—both negatively and positively. I place an exorbitant amount of emphasis on these individual conversations, which speak to my larger beliefs about how change can occur within a community.

Similarly, I see my resistance against the norms placed on me by non-Latinxs as grounded in the choices I make when I interact with public institutions or how I respond to microaggressions in the classroom. Again, the emphasis with non-Latinxs is also on smaller actions and conversations I engage in instead of the times I was part of organized activism. The excerpt below is an example of an individual action that I characterize as resistance, even though it is related to a simple form.

> Filling out forms in this country as a Latina requires either indifference or some type of active resistance. I am not Black, white, or Native in the United States context. I can check off white and Native American because of the colonial history of El Salvador—I'm Mestiza. But then I get prompted for a tribal number. Even 'mixed' doesn't mean me. Now, I just write in Latina. If they are going to force me to pick in a country that racializes Latinas in

every other place and space except a form… well, then I am Latina all the time, even if I have to draw my own box.

When I carefully considered what I chose to exclude or include in my recordings during analysis, it forced me to think critically about what I view as active resistance under the idea that marginalization can be used as a space for resistance. For example, in college I co-founded the Central American student organization as a way of providing a safe space for students, and yet I did not include that in the testimonio that focused on my time as an undergraduate. Similarly, I never spoke about my efforts to co-organize the Hispanic Heritage Month celebration as a teacher. These efforts were overshadowed by the smaller, individual actions and conversations I engage in on a daily basis. Therefore, in my identity development, resistance has come to signify the individual actions I take on a daily basis to combat the narrow understandings of what it means to be Latina in the United States.

Upon further analysis, it was also clear that these modes of resistance were how I attempted to keep the "shifting and multiple" parts of my identity intact. At the points in my life when I did not readily identify as Latina—particularly in high school—I was less likely to push back on the homogenized understandings of what it means to be Latina in the United States. As Anzaldúa (1987) notes in her conception of living in the borderlands, those who navigate in between multiple identities often learn "to swim in a new element, an 'alien' element" as a way of keeping their identities intact. For me, acts of resistance against a homogenous definition of Latinidad serve to further cement for myself—and for others—that I belong to the Latinx community despite the parts of me that others perceive as being outside of their conception of what it means to be Latina.

2.4 Conclusion

Soy un amasamiento, I am an act of kneading, of uniting, and joining that not only has produced both a creature of darkness and a creature of light, but also a creature that questions the definitions of light and dark and gives them new meanings.

(Anzaldúa, 2012, p. 103)

Ultimately, in trying to understand how my past experiences mediated my current understandings about my identity as a Latina, I came to the conclusion that my self-identification as Latina—and my confidence in identifying as such—was a reaction to feelings of otherness at various stages of my life, as well as the shifts that occurred in my physical location and social context. My perceived positionality within various contexts—both within and outside of the Latinx community—hinged on negative and positive social messages about what it means to be Latina. Furthermore, the four major turning points I highlighted in my testimonios were moments in my life that moved me from one social context to another. Even motherhood—though not tied to a physical location—represented a shift socially in how others perceived me and whom I chose to surround my family with, following several moments of fear like the one described above.

The three findings discussed in this chapter highlight the necessity to continue to provide counterstories to the homogenized understandings of Latina identity. Continued research needs to be done to understand the experiences of Latinas and Latina identity outside of a binary whereby individuals either reject their Latina identity or embrace it fully. Furthermore, what it means to be Latina in the expanding diaspora needs to be updated and complicated. Given that this self-narrative study focuses on identity development, it presents the possibility that Latina identity is a spectrum and is not fixed for individuals, as it is contextually bound. Narratives generally allow for a look at how an individual's identity might evolve over time given multiple events over their life course. Prioritizing research that aims to understand the experiences of individuals who have lived in between mainstream America and their parents' cultural expectations since they were children has significant implications for education policy, considering that the fastest growing group of public school students are Latinx children born in the United States.

Understanding the varied experiences of Latinas and their identity development also has implications for the choices educators make about curriculum and pedagogy from preschool to graduate school and the education initiatives administrators and policymakers choose to fund. Several of the excerpts from my narrative analysis took place in educational spaces or were related to my position within the educational world. I often thought about that Latin American history class from high school as a graduate student training to be a teacher. How could that teacher have better structured the class to facilitate discussions and understanding between the different Latinx subgroups? Would the class have turned out differently if the teacher himself were Latino? Would it have been different if my school or district had prioritized ethnic studies or culturally relevant education and trained my teacher in these pedagogies?

While I had many invested and effective teachers throughout my schooling, very few—if any—explicitly incorporated pedagogies or curriculum in their teaching that we would consider to be culturally relevant (Ladson-Billings, 1992, 1995; Nieto, 2004) or culturally sustaining (Paris, 2012). That said, this may also be due to a lack of training provided for teachers on these pedagogies and the increased pressures teachers face to "teach to the test" in K-12 education under waves of accountability reforms and high-stakes testing environments. It was not until college in a U.S. Women of Color class that I was exposed to many of the Scholars of Color that influence my work today. As a teacher, I saw firsthand that the lessons that often stuck with my students the most were the ones where they felt personally connected to the historical content or the literature. They were also more likely to participate and be invested in their work when I made my classroom a safe space and when they felt valued. Even as a graduate student, I find myself more engaged in classes where the professors make an intentional effort to bring in their students' perspectives and include Scholars of Color in their syllabi.

Finally, with respect to building networks of empowerment for Latinxs in the United States, as I read the narratives of other Latinas in preparation for this self-narrative, I saw many of my experiences and frustrations mirrored in their writing. Instead of further frustration, this realization brought me hope and a sense of empowerment. There is a lack of Latina representation in higher education as students (Krogstad, 2016) and professors (National Center for Education Statistics, 2019). Thus, most of my time in academia has been spent fighting off the "imposter syndrome" (Clance & Imes, 1978) that inevitably sets in time and time again when I am one of the few—if not the only—Latinas in a class or at a research meeting. Engaging in this self-narrative reaffirmed my identity and gave me additional perspective as both a researcher who is focused on the Latinx community and as a mother raising Latinas. As Anzaldúa (2002) describes in her concept of conocimiento, the process of this self-narrative and the sharing of this self-narrative allow me to become an active agent of social change moving past my own moments of oppression to empowerment. By sharing my narrative with others, I also hope to provide this same sense of relief and assurance to Latinas who feel marginalized and isolated within their own ivory towers.

Notes

1 Throughout the chapter, I use Latinx to describe the group as a whole, and Latina or Latino when the gender construct is identified by the author of the source I am discussing, or when I am talking about myself, because I identify as Latina.
2 I capitalize People of Color, Communities of Color, Students of Color, and Scholars of Color to position groups historically marginalized in the United States in a place of importance, where they do not exist merely in relation to the numerical white majority. As Yosso, Smith, Ceja, and Solórzano (2009) note, this capitalization under a CRT lens calls into question the "institutionalized practices that subtly minimize the role of race ... or repeat practices of marginalization" (p. 681).

References

Alarcón, N. (1990). Chicana feminism: In the tracks of 'the' native woman. *Cultural Studies*, 4(3), 248–256.
Anzaldúa, G. (2012). *Borderland/La frontera: The new mestiza* (4th ed.). Aunt Lute Books.
Anzaldúa, G. (1990). Introduction: Haciendo caras, una entrada. In G. Anzaldúa (Ed.), *Making face, making soul/Haciendo caras: Creative and critical perspectives by women of color* (pp. xv–xxvii). Aunt Lute Foundation.
Anzaldúa, G. (2002). Now let us shift…The path of conocimiento…Inner work, public acts. In G. Anzaldúa, & A. Keating (Eds.), *This bridge we call home: Radical visions for transformation* (pp. 540–578). Routledge.
Brukitt, I. (2005). Situating auto/biography: Biography and narrative in the times and places of everyday life. *Auto/Biography*, 13(2), 93–110.
Carrillo, J. F., & Rodriguez, E. (2016). She doesn't even act Mexican: Smartness trespassing in the new south. *Race, Ethnicity and Education*, 19(6), 1–11.

Cisneros, S. (1984). *The house on Mango street.* Arte Público Press.

Clance, P. R., & Imes, S. A. (1978). The imposter phenomenon in high achieving women: Dynamics and therapeutic intervention. *Psychotherapy Theory, Research & Practice, 15*(3), 241–247.

Cohen, C. J. (1999). *The boundaries of blackness: AIDS and the breakdown of black politics.* University of Chicago Press.

Cohn, M. (2012). Racial profiling legalized in Arizona. *Columbia Journal of Race and Law, 1*(2), 168–186.

Delgado Bernal, D., Burciaga, R., & Flores Carmona, J. (2012). Chicana/Latina testimonios: Mapping the methodological, pedagogical, and political. *Equity & Excellence in Education, 45*(3), 363–372.

Delgado Bernal, D., Flores Carmona, J., Alemán, S., Galas, L., & Garza, M. (Eds.). (2009). *Unidas we heal: Testimonios of the mind/body/soul.* University of Utah.

Delgado, R. (2009). The law of the noose: A history of Latina lynching. *Harvard Civil Rights-Civil Liberties Law Review (CR-CL), 44,* 297–312.

Delgado, R., & Stefancic, J. (2001). *Critical race theory: An introduction.* New York University Press.

Ellen, I. G., Yager, J., & Austensen, M. (2019). Housing: The paradox of inclusion and segregation in the nation's melting pot. In B. Bowser & C. Davedutt (Eds.), *Racial inequality in New York City since 1965* (pp. 25–46). SUNY Press.

Espino, M. M., Muñoz, S. M., & Kiyama, J. M. (2010). Transitioning from doctoral study to the academy: Theorizing trenzas of identity for Latina sister scholars. *Qualitative Inquiry, 16*(10), 804–818.

Flores Carmona, J. (2010). *Transgenerational educacion: Latina mothers' everyday pedagogies of cultural citizenship in Salt Lake City, Utah.* [Unpublished dissertation]. University of Utah, Salt Lake City.

Gómez, M. L. (2010). Talking about ourselves, talking about our mothers: Latina prospective teachers narrate their life experiences. *The Urban Review, 42*(2), 81–101.

Gutiérrez, R. A. (2004). Internal colonialism: An American theory of race. *Du Bois Review: Social Science Research on Race, 1*(2), 281–295.

Jackson, A. Y., & Mazzei, L. A. (2011). *Thinking with theory in qualitative research: Viewing data across multiple perspectives.* Routledge.

Krogstad, J., & Fry, R. (2014, August 18). *Dept. of Ed. projects public schools will be 'majority-minority' this fall.* Pew Research Center. http://pewrsr.ch/1t9N6OP

Krogstad, J. M. (2016). *5 facts about Latinos and education.* Pew Research Center. http://pewrsr.ch/2a76XJd

Krogstad, J. M. (2019, July 31). *A view of the nation's future through kindergarten demographics.* Pew Research Center. https://pewrsr.ch/2MuOI6D

Kucsera, J., & Orfield, G. (2014). *New York state's extreme school segregation: Inequality, inaction and a damaged future.* The Civil Rights Project/Proyecto Derechos Civiles. https://www.civilrightsproject.ucla.edu/research/k-12-education/integration-and-diversity/ny-norflet-report-placeholder/Kucsera-New-York-Extreme-Segregation-2014.pdf

Ladson-Billings, G. (1992). Reading between the lines and beyond the pages: A culturally relevant approach to literacy teaching. *Theory into practice, 31*(4), 312–320.

Ladson-Billings, G. (1995). But that's just good teaching! The case for culturally relevant pedagogy. *Theory into practice, 34*(3), 159–165.

Latina Feminist Group. (2001). *Telling to live: Latina feminist testimonios.* Duke University Press.

Lieblich, A., Tuval-Mashiach, R., & Zilber, T. (1998). *Narrative research: Reading, analysis, and interpretation* (Vol. 47). SAGE Publications.

Logan, J. R., & Stults, B. J. (2011). *The persistence of segregation in the metropolis: New findings from the 2010 census.* Census Brief prepared for Project US2010. http://www.s4.brown.edu/us2010/Data/Report/report2.pdf

Martínez-Roldán, C. M., & Quiñones, S. (2016). Resisting erasure and developing networks of solidarity: Testimonios of two Puerto Rican scholars in the academy. *Journal of Language, Identity & Education, 15*(3), 151–164.

Moraga, C., & Anzaldúa, G. (2002). Entering the lives of others: Theory in the flesh. In C. Moraga & G. Anzaldúa (Eds.), *This bridge called my back: Writing by radical women of color* (3rd ed., pp. 19–21). Third Woman Press.

Mordechay, K., & Ayscue, J. B. (2019). *School integration in gentrifying neighborhoods: Evidence from New York City.* The Civil Rights Project/Proyecto Derechos Civiles. https://www.civilrightsproject.ucla.edu/research/k-12-education/integration-and-diversity/school-integration-in-gentrifying-neighborhoods-evidence-from-new-york-city/NYC-031019.pdf

National Center for Education Statistics. (2019). *The condition of education 2019.* https://nces.ed.gov/programs/coe/indicator_csc.asp

Nieto, S. (2004). *Affirming diversity: The sociopolitical context of multicultural education* (4th ed.). Pearson.

Paris, D. (2012). Culturally sustaining pedagogy: A needed change in stance, terminology, and practice. *Educational researcher, 41*(3), 93–97.

Pérez Huber, L. (2009). Disrupting apartheid of knowledge: Testimonio as methodology in Latina/o critical race research in education. *International Journal of Qualitative Studies in Education, 22*(6), 639–654.

Pérez Huber, L., & Cueva, B. M. (2012). Chicana/Latina testimonios on effects and responses to microaggressions. *Equity & Excellence in Education, 45*(3), 392–410.

Prieto, L., & Villenas, S. (2012). Pedagogies from Nepantla: Testimonio, Chicana/Latina feminisms and teacher education classrooms. *Equity & Excellence in Education, 45*(3), 411–429.

Reyes, X. A., & Ríos, D. I. (2005). Dialoguing the Latina experience in higher education. *Journal of Hispanic Higher Education, 4*(4), 377–391.

Rodriguez, D. (2006). Un/masking identity healing our wounded souls. *Qualitative Inquiry, 12*(6), 1067–1090.

Solórzano, D. G. (1998). Critical race theory, race and gender microaggressions, and the experience of Chicana and Chicano scholars. *International Journal of Qualitative Studies in Education, 11*(1), 121–136.

Solórzano, D. G., & Yosso, T. J. (2001). Critical race and LatCrit theory and method: Counter-storytelling: Chicana and Chicano graduate school experiences. *Qualitative Studies in Education, 14*(4), 471–495.

Spivak G. C. (1985). The Rani of Sirmur: An essay in reading the archives. *History and Theory, 24*(3), 247–272.

Stefancic, J. (1997). Latino and Latina critical theory: An annotated bibliography. *California Law Review, 85*(5), 1509–1584.

Sue, D. W., Capodilupo, C. M., Torino, G. C., Bucceri, J. M., Holder, A. M., Nadal, K. L., & Esquilin, M. (2007). Racial microaggressions in everyday life: Implications for clinical practice. *American Psychologist, 62*(4), 271–286.

Valencia, R. R. (2005). The Mexican American struggle for equal educational opportunity in Mendez v. Westminster: Helping to pave the way for Brown v. Board of Education. *Teachers College Record, 107*(3), 389–423.

Villenas, S. (2001). Latina mothers and small-town racisms: Creating narratives of dignity and moral education in North Carolina. *Anthropology & Education Quarterly, 32*(1), 3–28.

Yosso, T., Smith, W., Ceja, M., & Solórzano, D. (2009). Critical race theory, racial microaggressions, and campus racial climate for Latina/o undergraduates. *Harvard Educational Review, 79*(4), 659–691.

3

GROWING OLD/GROWING UP GRINGA

Negotiating Puertorriqueñidad and Americanism in the Midwest

Maried Rivera Nieves

The purpose of this narrative-autobiographical study is to explore the ways a Latinx mother and daughter navigate and negotiate Puerto Rican and American culture and identity. It should be said that I neither conflate Puerto Rico with the continental United States nor "American" with "Puerto Rican"; the two remain distinct entities, tethered but in tireless tension, as they are in my mind. This study focuses on my mother's and my national, ethnic, and linguistic identities as Puerto Rican Latinx Spanish-English bilinguals living most of our lives in the United States.

Upon moving from Puerto Rico to the Midwest, I took my Puerto Rican ethnicity and Spanish fluency for granted, and, feeling pressured to assimilate into American culture, I subconsciously began to shed that part of myself. My schooling played a significant role in how I perceived my puertorriqueñidad. My mother, on the other hand, experienced a more conscientious assimilation, taking Adult English as a Second Language classes, urging her children to remember who we were and where we came from, and progressively taking on more American cultural practices. She and I share many personality traits, but we differ in how we integrated into U.S. society, and our relationship has shifted as a result. I have always been interested in this dynamic and about my mother's life story, as well as what connections or contrasts can be drawn with mine.

Gómez (2010) asserts that understanding Latinxs' relationships with their mothers, their stories, and consejos is crucial to understanding how Latinx women negotiate their identities. From an educational perspective, insight into students' relationships and critical reflection on their own life experiences is important for educators wishing to cultivate transformative classroom experiences that respect and validate students' identities.

I do not expect to answer any questions regarding the self and those I love; answering questions with questions is a more fulfilling reality. Scaffolding this work, however, are some curiosities: How do mother–daughter Puerto Rican migrants to the United States experience and negotiate identity? How have they experienced integration into U.S. culture? How do they negotiate their American and Puerto Rican selves?

As I collected data, analyzed, and wrote, I considered nuances that would impact how I understood and wrote about my mother. I considered generational differences between my mother, myself, and those of im/migrants in the United States more broadly. I wrestled with whether I am considered a first- or second-generation migrant, or neither, and did not come to a satisfactory conclusion. Am I any more a migrant than someone who moves across United States state lines? Puerto Ricans call la Isla un país—is it? Am I an American? Do I want to be? What is "American"? This is another way in which Puerto Rico's neocolonial status limits my ability to know myself, even if it is through technocratic terms my people did not generate for themselves.

3.1 A Complicated Affair: The Puerto Rico–United States Relationship

Puerto Rico, only 100 miles wide, boasts a strong national identity that transcends borders and language. Mired by legal, political, and economic uncertainty, we are a diasporic nation caught between two geographic entities—the mainland United States and the island. Puerto Ricans are tethered between full-scale and second-class citizenship, beneficiaries of legal status often made invisible and thwarted by oppressive policies that fail to understand the intricacies of the Puerto Rican experience.

After the Spanish-American War, Puerto Rico was recolonized by the United States. The island represented a new model of neoliberalism and capitalist development (Grosfoguel, Negrón-Muntaner, & Georas, 1997). Today, Puerto Rico's importance to the United States on these fronts is arguable, but the two maintain an active political and "institutionalized migratory" relationship (Martínez-San Miguel, 2014, p. 79). This relationship "has produced a long-standing debate on the limits of the decolonization process from metropolitan societies," with Puerto Rico embodying a struggle between assimilation and autonomy (p. 80). The same can be said of the Puerto Rican diaspora on the mainland. Puerto Ricans have suffered the tyranny of the continent and quarreled with the Stockholm Syndrome from perpetual colonization. After Hurricane María, the chasm is even more pronounced: more than 135,000 Puerto Ricans have since left the island (Center for Puerto Rican Studies, 2018).

While Puerto Rican migration was originally concentrated in the U.S. northeast, migration to the Midwest began in the mid-twentieth century (Vélez, 2017). Migrants were recruited by regional private and public agencies, a "solution" to the "problematic" concentration of Puerto Ricans in New York City (De Genova & Ramos-Zayas, 2003). Many became steel, factory, and domestic workers (Vélez, 2017, p. 128). Today, Puerto Rican migration feeds foundational hubs like Chicago and new destinations like Florida and Arizona (Duany, 2002; Vélez, 2017). Migrants in the rural Midwest in particular receive less attention; I explore this omission later.

This narrative runs parallel to my self-education about the political, economic, and sociocultural conditions in Puerto Rico—a frustrating and revealing journey. Namely, it has unveiled a reality I never knew existed: that of a resistant Puerto Rican people. While different from that of Puerto Ricans elsewhere, this story remains universal: my family's migration was facilitated by an imposed legal status and motivated by economic and educational privileges. It was bold, but safe; voluntary, yet necessary. The palm trees and the mountains, a motley of concrete and pasture, were replaced by neat sidewalks, flat fields, and white faces.

3.2 Theoretical Framework and Literature Review

In examining our narratives, I pull from Anzaldúa's borderlands, *nepantla*, and *entremundos* concepts as well as Antonia Darder's *critical biculturalism* as theoretical frameworks. I complement them with critical discourse on migration, nationalism, and assimilation. Nepantla, a Nahuatl word meaning "in-between space" (Keating, 2006, p. 8), "speaks to and informs the difficult and often overlapping spaces of cultural dissonance, conciencia con compromiso, and cariño" (Cortez, 2001, as cited in Prieto & Villenas, 2012, p. 424). While nepantla can represent a painful experience characterized by "turmoil and frustration" (Prieto & Villenas, 2012, p. 415), anxiety, and invisibility, it can also represent a rebirth. Nepantla is central to my identity formation and I explore how it interacts with my mother's understanding of living in between worlds. Entremundos speaks to the phenomenon that nepantla elucidates in the Chicano/a context:

> For Puerto Ricans, entremundos is part of an ongoing polemic on national identity that has permeated Puerto Rico's colonial history… the entremundos experience is part of a complex, dynamic process which is also influenced by other variables such as gender, social class, race, personal values, political forces, and generational status.
>
> (Zavala Martínez, 1994, p. 30)

Darder's (2012) critical biculturalism also plays a foundational role in this work; she defines it as a process wherein individuals navigate two contrasting sociocultural environments, one of which is dominant over the other (p. 45). Biculturalism allows us to live transnationally, to step in and out of various identities. Critical biculturalism is political, involving the "ongoing process of identity recovery construction, and re-construction" (Darder, 2011, p. 44). In this study, I consider my mother's and my understanding and enacting of biculturalism as we become 'American.'

I also draw from Fred Arroyo's (Interview with Moreno, 2015a, 2015b) commentary on the Puerto Rican experience in the Midwest. Arroyo sheds light on our long-silenced migratory history outside of urban centers, particularly that of seasonal agricultural workers and those with destinations in the rural Midwest (Moreno, 2015b). These days, research on non-urban Puerto Rican migration concerns the burgeoning Puerto Rican population in Orlando, Florida. But what is life like for Puerto Rican migrants living in the rural Midwest? While Arroyo focuses on expanding diasporic narratives, his argument also applies to social and educational research. After all, the experiences of rural migrants are not statistically negligible; in Minnesota, Puerto Ricans are the second-most populous group among Latinxs/Hispanics. Between 1990 and 2010, their population quadrupled and is expected to double by 2030 (Minnesota State Demographic Center [MSDC], 2015).

Importantly, Ariza (2010) invites us to consider the variability in the immigrant experience and transcend a uniform framework to understand how immigrants are incorporated into societies. She alludes to Aranda's work (2007a) on Puerto Ricans as migrants who cross "geopolitical, social, and cultural" borders, but not international ones (p. 21). For Duany (2010), the contrasts between Puerto Rico and the United States are sufficient enough to consider migrants transnational. Being a nepantlera, though, means interrogating 'the nation' and how we construct national identities (Berila, 2005). Anzaldúa, through Berila (2005), beckons us to see national identity as "multiple, relational, and contestatory" (p. 122), much like the discourse on Puerto Rico's status and future.

Puerto Ricans encounter the force of assimilation in the United States in myriad ways. For Portes and Zhou (1993), segmented assimilation accounts for variability in immigrant incorporation, depending on "human capital, context of reception, place of residence, and other variables" (Duany, 2010, p. 92). The transnationalism of Puerto Rican migration further influences how Puerto Ricans fare on the mainland, and may result in 'dislocations,' Parreñas's (2001) concept from which Aranda's (2007b) work on middle-class Puerto Ricans' incorporation departs. Aranda (2007b) argues that while middle-class, non-Black Puerto Ricans—like my family—have the resources to bridge dislocations, most notably from kinship networks, these attachments can affect their assimilation, and ultimately, their settlement decisions. For those who remain, selective acculturation describes how "second-generation youths combine aspects of their parents' home society culture with elements of the host society culture into bicultural, hybrid identities" (Portes & Rumbaut, 1996, 2001, as cited in Aranda, 2007b, p. 200), of which there are indications in my mother's and my narrative.

As referenced earlier, my experiences in U.S. public schools reflected the historical assimilationist objectives of U.S. schooling of Puerto Ricans, on and outside of the island (Irizarry & Antrop-González, 2007). Educators' indifference to the cultural capital of Puerto Rican students serves to Americanize students by suppressing their cultural expressions and privileging white, middle-class values and ways of being (Negrón de Montilla, 1975, and Solís-Jordán, 1994, as cited in Irizarry & Antrop-González, 2007, p. 40). Irizarry and Antrop-González (2007) argue that most Puerto Rican students exist in segregated educational spaces, and exposed to curriculum that does not reflect their lived experiences. Their schooling, therefore, does not serve to educate and liberate, but to assimilate and subjugate (p. 41). Irizarry and Antrop-González's analysis concerns itself primarily with Puerto Ricans in segregated urban spaces, in poorly funded schools teaching mostly Black children and children of color; my experiences as one of the few children of color in my well-funded, segregated, suburban school resulted in similar feelings of assimilation and cultural suppression.

Some scholars see assimilatory differences as rooted in the migrants' original motivations. Ogbu and Simons (1998) argue that those who migrate to the United States by choice ('voluntary' migrants)—as my family did—and not by force ('involuntary' migrants) have an easier time assimilating to U.S. life. The authors name Puerto Ricans as a quintessential "involuntary minority," a recognition of Puerto Ricans as a colonized people (p. 165). I consider the Puerto Rican experience far too varied for this to be categorically true. Colonization is forced and has impacted how generations of Puerto Ricans think of themselves geopolitically. But the boundary between voluntary and involuntary shifts from generation to generation, and these nuances demand attention.

Ogbu and Simons (1998), arguments on assimilation are useful in contextualizing my mother's narrative, particularly her perspective on hardship. 'Voluntary' minorities, especially first-generation migrants, tend to have a positive, dual frame of reference—one based on their U.S. situation and the other on their situation 'back home,' and view the former as advantageous with respect to the latter. In this view, discrimination is temporary, cultural differences are obstacles to overcome, and hard work defines success (p. 170).

Ariza (2010) emphasizes the need for more focus on the "individual level of analysis that emphasizes the immigrant as an active agent in what he/she brings to the situation,… encounters and… does" (p. 151). I hope to convey that there is no archetypal Puerto Rican migration experience. Latinidad is a kaleidoscope of happenings and decisions, sentiments and philosophies; I claim expertise over nothing but my experience. I highlight two themes in Mami's narrative, interspersed with my own: sacrifice, and the things we tell ourselves to cope with struggle and change.

3.3 Methodology and Data Analysis

This is a narrative-autobiographical study involving my mother and me. I conducted two semi-structured, bilingual interviews with my mother via FaceTime over the course of the semester—transcribed in full—as well as one short follow-up interview that was partially transcribed. I also kept an online journal over two months, tracing important experiences of my life and identity formation, resulting in 12 entries.

It takes a conscious effort to see a mother—or any equivalent figure—as a complete person beyond their caregiving role. Being someone's daughter makes me both vulnerable to bias and privy to their innermost thoughts; I wrestled with this dynamic throughout my conversations with Mami. It was important to me that she knew I was listening, that I wasn't asking her personal questions and recording her answers to vilify her. Upon transcription, I used coding to identify salient themes throughout the two interviews, as well as connections and contradictions with my journal entries. To analyze the data, I used thematic and dialogic/performative analysis, following Riessman's (2008) models.

3.4 Presentation of Narratives and Discussion

In this section, I present and discuss my mother's and my narrative organized around the themes of sacrifice—in this case, cultural and familial dissolution—and the things we tell ourselves, or coping mechanisms, in the face of loss. I provide the English translation for all the excerpts in Spanish.

3.4.1 Sacrificio

"La vida es la escuela del dolor" [Life is the school of pain], repeated Abuela Palmira, not two weeks ago in Yabucoa, Puerto Rico. I was in her hammock, eating the best panas con bacalao [breadfruit with cod] I've ever had. It was a bittersweet reunion. My paternal grandmother passed away a few days earlier. Abuela Palmira's body ages but her spirit is fire. The emotion in her voice as she tells a story, every laugh and animation, is traceable in Mami's own. In that moment, I thought about the circumstances that brought us there, and how time is fickle and cruel and auspicious. That just as I was writing Mami's story, I would be in Puerto Rico for a funeral, and that in visiting my only remaining grandparent, a major character in Mami's life, I would be privy to their rare and distinctive conversations.

Mami talks a lot about loss and compromise. In doing so, she grapples directly with the tension between assimilation and cultural preservation. My father's job granted our family socioeconomic privileges. We were fortunate to live in a peaceful state, in a town with good schools and a strong economy. Those who live transnationally (and transculturally), however, are still a border people, and with that comes a sensation of distance, loss, and transformation. Mami's narrative revealed two manifestations of sacrifice and loss: cultural and familial. Below I call them dissolutions. While Parreñas's (2001) term 'dislocations' is equally applicable, 'dissolution' better captures the sense of loss Mami described. Where Mami speaks to the losses, which to her felt so palpable and inevitable, I speak on the subliminal pressure I felt as a child to disregard them and the helplessness I often feel as an adult to recover them.

3.4.2 Cultural Dissolution

Life begets change. "Yo agarro los cambios como vengan" [I take change as it comes], Mami says more than once in our conversations. It feels like a mantra of hers, a way for her to brace for and cope with difficulty and demonstrate strength. It was change that drew her to Minnesota: "Me gustó los cambios de clima,... los diferentes seasons" [I liked the changes in the weather... the different seasons]. As Mami changes, Puerto Rico changes too. Every time she goes back, it feels farther from what she knew:

> Es triste que a la misma vez porque como ya tú llevas tantos años lejos de una tierra, donde ya nada de lo que era...Hace 18 años, ya todo ha cambiado, pues, ya como que tú no lo ves igual. Ni la gente, ni la cultura, ni la misma topografía física. Porque yo me acuerdo antes, la caña cuando...estábamos en Yabucoa, o eran plátanos. O sea, que ahora hay tantas – han hecho tanta casa y tanta carretera y tanta cosa como que ya no... ya no es—nada es como antes, como lo dejamos hace 18 años.

> It's sad because, at the same time, you spend so many years far away from someplace, where nothing is as it was... Eighteen years ago and now everything has changed. Now you don't see it in the same way. Not the people, not the culture, not even the physical topography. Because I remember, before, the sugar cane when we were in Yabucoa, or they were plantains. That is, now there are so many houses and so many roads and so many things that now, nothing is like it was before, as we left it 18 years ago.

She talks about changes to music, "Ya no hay salsa, ya no hay bolero, ya no hay, este, merengue, ya no hay romantic, ya–balada, ya todo es reggaetón, nada más" [There's no salsa, no bolero, there's no merengue, no romantic (music) like balada, now everything is reggaetón and nothing else]; about the changes to food, "la comida, para mí ya yo le perdí el sabor... no me sabe igual... hasta eso, el paladar está perdiendo uno" [the food, it lost its flavor... it doesn't taste the same... I'm even losing my palette]; and about linguistic changes. Mami uses language interestingly, beyond the Spanglish that so frustrates her. Her speech is dramatic, with repetitive phrases like "Ya no hay..." [Now, there isn't...], and as shown in the above excerpt, "Ni..., ni..." [nor]. Every subsequent "Ni..., ni..." feels like Puerto Rico is slipping away in real time. Mami and I speak and think alike. We play with phrasing and thoughts so long-winded they never seem to end. We struggle with concision—there's so much to say that it feels impossible to convey, but once you start, you can't stop. Mami often stepped outside of her narrative to reference this: "Oh, I got so many things that impact me, Maried. [Laughs] See? ¿Cuán complicada soy?" [How complicated I am?]

During our conversations, I realized for the first time that my family has always been part of Puerto Rican circular migration. The physical and emotional distance between Minnesota and the island made family members' lives seem frozen in time and cultural differences and changes more acute. The cultural dissolution Mami laments is, for her, happening in Puerto Rico, too. In spite of this, she often looks down on American culture, dismayed by its frigidity ("aquí todo es tan soso" [everything is so bland]), and yearns for Puerto Ricans' warmth and enthusiasm. Sometimes she commends gringos for their simplicity and humility, while scorning Puerto Ricans' preoccupation with appearance and wealth.

"[Y]a parezco una gringa aquí yo también" [I seem gringa now too], Mami concedes. Twenty minutes earlier, however, she told me that "[Y]o me siento puertorriqueña, Latina 100%. I'm not gringa" [I feel Puerto Rican. Latina 100%. I'm not American]. This contradiction captures the limbo Mami feels suspended in. "[D]espués de tantos años llevando aquí en Minnesota,…voy a Puerto Rico y ya no me encuentro. I mean, como—yo no me siento ni de Minnesota ni de Puerto Rico. It's terrible. Ya no me siento de ninguno de—que no pertenezco a ninguno de los dos lados. Así me siento últimamente. Ni de allá ni de acá [After so many years here in Minnesota, I go to Puerto Rico and I no longer find myself. I mean, like, I don't feel as if I'm neither from Minnesota or from Puerto Rico. It's terrible. I don't find myself anymore—ultimately, I feel like I don't belong in either place. From neither here nor there].

Ya no me encuentro [I no longer find myself]. I was struck by this phrasing, as if Mami were actively looking for something. As if there were something she'd forgotten or now finds unrecognizable. I can recognize the sadness this stirs. I notice that my journaling about Puerto Rico invokes similar feelings. I refer to my Puerto Rican self in the past tense, as if irrecoverable. What I fail to see is that no person is purely one thing or another, no paradox too bewildering to embody. That Mami feels like she cannot find herself anywhere does not impact how she identifies:

> Maried, yo agarro lo más—lo mejor de cada cosa, lo que me acuerde de cada cosa ese día. Hoy me siento puertorriqueña, pues me hago puertorriqueña. Mañana me siento gringa, pues me hago gringa. That's—así–así lo veo. So, depende de cómo esté el día, lo que venga. Porque como yo te digo, ya voy a Puerto Rico y… it's like, 'I don't belong here.' Sin embargo acá, pues, echas de menos entonces lo que tienes allá, [a] lo que tú estabas acostumbrado hace ya… 18 años—19 van a ser, actually. So ya, realmente, ya te estás acostumbrando a las dos cosas. O te desacostumbraste de lo que estabas acostumbrado en Puerto Rico. Y no te queda otro remedio que adaptarte a lo de acá… A veces, por ejemplo, sacamos nuestra comida Latina, nuestra música Latina, pues eso a la misma vez, pues, te conecta otra vez a tus—a tus raíces. Entonces vuelves y ves que si programas americanos o escuchas música americana. O sea, como que estás allá y acá y allá. Es como una mezcla, un va y ven, va y ven… La realidad es esta. See? Que uno está como dividido… Estoy en el limbo de los dos. No me gusta sentir que no pertenezco allá pero no me gusta sentir que no pertenezco aquí tampoco. Pero a la misma vez, pues tienes que

adaptar—es aceptar lo que está pasando. Porque no puedes cambiarlo. No—¿qué puedes hacer? Como dicen, agarra el toro por los cuernos y just… suck it up.

Maried, I take the best of everything, what I can remember of everything, every day. Today, I feel Puerto Rican—well, I make myself Puerto Rican. Tomorrow, I feel gringa—well, I make myself gringa. That's how I see it. So, it depends on the day, on what comes. Because it's like I said, I go to Puerto Rico, and it's like… 'I don't belong here.' Whereas here, well, you miss certain things that you had there, what you were used to 18 years ago, 19 almost. So, now, in reality, you are accustomed to both things. Or you are becoming unaccustomed to what you were accustomed to in Puerto Rico. And you have no choice but to adapt to what is here… Sometimes, for example, we pull out our Latino food, our Latino music, because this connects us to our roots. And then you turn around and you watch American programs and listen to American music. So like, you're there and here and there. It's like a mixture, a coming and going, coming and going. That's the reality. See? You're like, divided. I'm in limbo between both places. I don't like feeling like I don't belong there but I don't like feeling like I don't belong here either. But at the same time, well, you have to adapt. [To adapt] is to accept what is happening. Because you can't change it. What can you do? It's like the say, grab the bull by the horns and just suck it up.

I'm struck by the intentionality of Mami's biculturalism, how she pieces together the hybridity of her identity. In engaging the two idioms—"agarra el toro por los cuernos and suck it up"—her American and Puerto Rican selves are connecting to advance the process of adaptation and compromise. I see her learning, still, how to operate in both worlds. I think about Arroyo's questions while reviewing this excerpt of Mami's interview: "What do you gain? What is it that you might lose? What do you leave behind? What do you take with you?" (Moreno, 2015a, p. 195). Mami's transformation comes in her attitude as she attempts to resolve this dissolution. She chooses what to engage (music or food), when, and for what purpose. She climbs in and out of her identities on a day-to-day basis, a process forever undergoing calibration.

3.4.3 Familial Dissolution

Migration begets sacrifice, the forfeiture or atrophy of a part of yourself. It is an inexorable pain that academic literature fails to capture. When asked about how migration has impacted our family, Mami said:

[U]stedes prácticamente no tienen familia, más que nosotros cinco. Es la realidad… [N]osotros sacrificamos una cosa por la otra. O sea, sacrificamos… pues, en caso de tu papá fue más importante superación para él en el trabajo.

Además de que nosotros queríamos que ustedes tuvieran una mejor educación porque a saber en qué hubieran terminado en Puerto Rico si nos quedábamos allá. Sabes, por lo menos en aquel aspecto, nosotros pensábamos que acá había mejor educación para ustedes… Pero nosotros, pues, no nos dimos cuenta de que dejando toda la familia atrás, pues, que… la íbamos a perder. Porque prácticamente eso fue lo que hicimos… No sé si tú te sientes así también… Una por la otra.

You [and your sisters] basically don't have a family besides us five. It's the reality. We sacrificed one thing for another. That is, we sacrificed—well, in your father's case, his accomplishment at work was more important. Besides, we wanted you all to have a better education because who knows where you would have ended up in Puerto Rico if we had stayed there. You know, at least in that aspect, we thought that here, there would be a better education for you. But we didn't realize that in leaving our family behind, well, that we would lose it. Because that's practically what happened. I don't know if you feel that way too. One thing for another.

I noticed resignation in Mami's voice. As I wiped the tears from my cheeks, she changed the subject. She understands, but her multitasking reveals nonchalance. To hear what sounds like surrender to our reality yields as much pain as the reality itself. Her reflections always feel so finite compared to mine. In revisiting mine, however, I encounter similar sentiments. From my journal in October 2016:

Me pregunto si hubiera pasado toda la vida en Puerto Rico, si las cosas serían diferentes. Si conocería algo de mis primas, que son tan lindas e inteligentes, de mis tías que son tan talentosas y valientes–todas han criado sus hijos prácticamente solas, algunas se fueron de casa, a los Estados Unidos, de adolescentes. Una viaja el mundo corriendo maratones, otra lo ha viajado por su rol en el ejército. Una perdió el hijo hace unos años, otra tiene una hija con discapacidades, a otra se le quemó el apartamento en Rhode Island. Y todas son como míticas, temas de los chismes que cuenta mi mamá, personajes pasivos en sus memorias y también las mías. No conozco sus personalidades, ni sus gestos, sus preocupaciones o inseguridades, sus gustos ni sus metas. Son desconocidas, íconos de perfil que existen virtualmente y en modo superficial, con las cuales comparto felicitaciones de cumpleaños o de cualquier éxito publicado, pero poco más. Ni tengo fotos con ellas, por lo menos nada reciente. Mi familia es inmensa, vivaz y seguramente amadora, si solo tuviera el privilegio de conocerla por completo.

I ask myself whether things would be different if I had spent my whole life in Puerto Rico. If I would better know my cousins, who are so beautiful and intelligent, and my aunts, talented and brave—most of them have raised their children alone, others left the island for the United States as teenagers, alone. One of them gets to see the world marathon by marathon. Another has seen it as a member of the U.S. military. One lost her youngest son a decade ago. Another has a daughter with an intellectual disability. Another lost her apartment to a fire in Rhode Island. And they're all mythical in a way, subjects of my mother's gossip, passive characters in her memories and mine. I don't know their personalities, their mannerisms, their worries or insecurities, their interests or ambitions. They are strangers, profile pictures that exist virtually and superficially, with whom I share the odd birthday wish or congratulations for a publicized success, but little more. I don't have photos with them, nothing recent at least. My family is immense and vivacious and loving, surely, if only I had the privilege of fully knowing it.

This narrative is a contemplation of a life I never knew, embodying the disconnect of migration, the stressors on families, and that technology can mitigate remoteness but not always compensate for the depth of in-person relationships. Mami's family has never been close. In fact, she argues that a lack of connection to our family has in some ways made it easier for her to adapt to U.S. life. Besides, she often reminds me, we can't complain. Mami chooses to zoom out of a sorrowful situation and point to Puerto Ricans' migratory privileges. While our political status is limiting in some ways, we have freedom of movement and, in our case, the means to regularly visit our relatives on the island.

I chose to write the previous journal entry in Spanish in an attempt to flex a muscle that often feels atrophied—this long-inactive iteration of my voice, a connection to something beyond memories and cultural artifacts. Culture is more than what we wear and speak and eat. I am grateful to Mami and Papi for speaking to us in Spanish, even and especially when I resented them for doing so. Writing in Spanish now, this language that I know was once imposed, feels like resistance, just like Puerto Ricans have transformed it into a version all their own. No, I have not completely forgotten, and what is forgotten can be relearned.

But sometimes it feels like I'm having an out-of-body experience. Like I'm watching our family pull away from puertorriqueñidad in real time, that with each familial death and grudge and out-migration and broken promise, our connection to the island fades. Mami feels it, too, I think. She often worries out loud about how once her mother dies, she won't have a reason to go back. Is this how it happens? Will I soon have to grapple with what it's like to be Puerto Rican without a strong familial connection to the island? Is this the relationship with puertorriqueñidad that my children may know, if they cannot use their place of birth as a crutch to prop up their otherwise empty claim to the culture? ("Is this what you really think about the diaspora?", I ask myself.)

3.4.4 *The Things We Tell Ourselves*

Suburban Minnesota did not expose me to much diversity. As a child, my Latinidad survived by my parents' insistence on speaking to us in Spanish, by *their* Latinx friends, by whitewashed Univision, by my hair and skin and reluctant phone conversations with relatives. I recognize Mami in the lonely midwestern Puerto Ricans in Arroyo's work (Interview with Moreno, 2015a, 2015b), victims of a very particular erasure. I recognize it in myself when, in adulthood, I feel resentful about where I was forced to grow up. Not only are Puerto Ricans in the Midwest caught between the United States and the island as geographical locations, but between the U.S. coasts. Perhaps the town my parents chose exacerbated the split already aggravated by transitioning from island to mainland. For me, this split was quickly normalized, a blip in my life story. As a kid, my puertorriqueñidad was a party trick used (or demanded of me) to feel special among friends. For my mother, the split happened over time, and her words disclose a helplessness to stop it. In spite of this, Mami repeatedly chooses to focus on all that she has gained, whereas as an adult, I tend to focus on what could have been and—when distracted from nostalgia by resolve—what I could possibly do differently now.

I wanted to learn about how Mami experiences or interprets being a Puerto Rican/Latina in the United States to know whether we had reached similar conclusions about existing in spaces that don't reflect our realities, if we had been asking the same questions of our society. Listening to her, I realized that our perspectives on race, ethnicity, and the immigrant experience varied. I also realized that this is due to the time when our lives were most different: childhood. Mami always reminds me that I don't know what it's like to be poor—she grew up in a poor, rural household and I in a Midwestern suburb. I knew no need, hunger, or discouragement from my dreams. It was in leaving home that Mami found safety and opportunity. We tell ourselves different things when coping with discrimination, injustice, and the pressure to conform.

Despite her sacrifices, Mami's attitude toward migration and adaptation has been largely positive. This speaks to the variability in the immigrant experience, not only among Puerto Ricans, but among different generations thereof and Latinxs as a whole. Migration, like the middle-class participants in Aranda's (2007b) study, has yielded mostly positive outcomes for her, contributing to increasing levels of educational attainment and work experiences among our family members, something she feels would have been impossible in Puerto Rico, especially in rural Yabucoa, "donde no hay mucho donde crecer" [where there is not much room for growth].

As I strive for more political and social awareness, accompanied by the desire to act, Mami is content with survival and the comfort of waiting. My educational privilege, as well as my decision to live in a more racially and socioeconomically diverse city, facilitates these pursuits. Mami is more concerned with reacting to change as it comes than worrying about why it happens at all. "[Y]o agarro los cambios como vengan" [I take changes as they come], she says. "[S]i tu vas con esa mentalidad de que todo tiene que ser igual a donde estabas anteriormente, pues entonces te va a tomar tiempo de adaptarte mejor. Pero yo no, yo... me tiro yo donde sea. Los cambios, okay [*slams hand on counter*]: venga!" [If you have the mentality that everything has to be the same as where you were before, well then, it's going to take you time to adapt better. But I don't, I throw myself wherever. Change? Okay, bring it on].With a kitchen surface as percussion, Mami slams her hand on the counter and smiles. I don't typically share her enthusiasm for change or for the discomfort it may bring, nor do I share her faith that all change is good.

Mami's faith in the system can be attributed to her being a voluntary migrant and her positive experiences in the United States: "Nunca tuvimos problemas con nadie" [We never had problems with anyone], she says. She does not, however, trust politicians. This she claims to have learned in Puerto Rico. But in the value of hard work and the merits of individualism, she has unfettered belief; perseverance has always worked for Mami. She worked hard to finish high school, despite her parents' wishes and the absence of role models. She didn't want a love life like her sisters', and in her own time, persevered in marrying someone who respected her as their equal. She desired a life beyond her neighborhood and the poverty and abuse she grew up around, and has one. In spite of this, Mami still expresses helplessness in the face of social problems propped up by political negligence. "There's nothing to be done," she often says. "That will never change." This prompts her to disengage from the problems of her friends or of strangers and adopt a wait-and-see mentality. It is a pain she doesn't feel the need to shoulder.

Mami knows that the true Americans are the indigenous peoples, making her no less an outsider than those with European ancestry. She resists the impulse to self-impose difference. But difference is not inherently negative to her:

> A mí nunca me ha avergonzado ser Latino. Pero tu papá siempre ha dicho, como él dice, él dice, "Yo no quiero que por yo ser de la minoría que me traten diferente." [Lo] que yo puedo percibir es que, él dice, "Yo me quiero sentir como cualquier otro gringo que hay alrededor." A mí no me molesta que me digan que yo soy diferente. A mí no me molesta que me digan, "Mira, mi comida es diferente a la tuya." O "tenemos una costumbre diferente a la tuya." A mi no me molesta… Cuando tú te sientes *cómoda* en tu skin, cuando tú te sientes cómoda con lo que eres… a mí no me importa ser diferente. Otra gente no le gusta que le—"Oh, you're different, oh," que te… vean *físicamente* que tú eres diferente. Porque he aprendido a aceptarme como soy, Maried.Y esto es lo que hay [circles face with her hand], ya no hay forma de cambiar ya esto… Soy Latina, cien por ciento, puertorriqueña. A la orden. No me molesta decirlo… Si yo conozco a alguien diferente, "Oh, where are you from? I like your accent" es lo primero que me dicen. A mí no me molesta, "I'm from Puerto Rico!" [Smiles]. No hay ningún problema.

> I've never been ashamed to be Latina. But your dad has always said, "I don't want to be treated differently because I'm a minority." What I perceive is that

he says, "I want to feel like any other gringo around me." It doesn't bother me when people tell me I'm different. It doesn't bother me when people say, "My food is different from yours" or "We have different customs than yours." It doesn't bother me... when you feel comfortable in your skin, when you feel comfortable with who you are... I don't care about being different. Other people don't like it: "Oh, you're different, oh"; they see *physically* that you're different. But I've learned to accept myself how I am, Maried. This is what there is [circles face with her hand], there is no way to change this. I am Latina, 100% Puerto Rican. At your service. It doesn't bother me to say it.... If I meet someone new, "Oh, where are you from? I like your accent" is the first thing they say. It doesn't bother me. "I'm from Puerto Rico!" [Smiles]. There is no problem.

Through this declaration of agency and confidence, Mami argues that people of color and/or other minoritized people's lack of self-love, pride, and strength contributes to their marginalization. For her, discrimination is only ever temporary. Our actions are more important than the intangibles, which we may or may not be judged by. Nonetheless, Mami acknowledges the fearmongering of the Trump presidency, and that our family has been protected by access to good schools and health care and the impression of safety. Her ability to do away with said intangibles denotes a certain privilege, for those in other communities face tangible consequences (e.g., police brutality, housing discrimination, displacement from ancestral lands) because of the factors Mami merely chooses to rise above. Our differences may not be biological in nature, and our ways of self-identifying innocent, but the perceptions of others impact all of us in very real ways.

Nonetheless, I agreed with Papi for a long time; I didn't want to be treated differently because I was Brown, or because I was Latinx. I, too, criticized affirmative action, misunderstanding its purpose. I, too, wanted to 'blend in.' It doesn't bother Mami when people ask her where she is from, or that her face, which she circles with her finger while talking, implicitly gives others the right to assume she's not 'from here,' and that they're owed an explanation. She answers the question with pride, not shame, as evidenced by her smile: "I'm from Puerto Rico!" It is a pride I have only recently begun to familiarize myself with.

3.5 Reflections and Implications for Education

Today, it remains important for both Mami and me to be attuned to our culture, our traditions and our language, but how we go about anchoring ourselves to those parts of our identities are not always the same, because Mami came here as an adult, and I as a girl, and because she experienced childhood struggles that I didn't, and because I've lived in more places than she has, and because I have different curiosities than she does. There is a lot I have yet to know and learn about myself, about my mother, and about our relationship, and we will never stop trying to figure each other out. There is a lot I have yet to know and learn about Puerto Rico, about Latinidad, and I won't stop searching. I'm not sure that I can. I wish I had the opportunity to learn about Puerto Rico, its history, and its cultures when I was in school. I wish the same for current and future students across the country whose communities and existences are invisibilized or whitewashed, and for students who enjoy representation but are also defrauded when kept from a more complete picture of the world.

In public schools across the country, educators are encountering a diversifying student body and dwindling support in their roles. For Puerto Rican migrants in the rural United States, predominantly white schools filled with white teachers and whitewashed curricula can create isolating and destructive spaces, detrimental to our identity development and self-concept. My predominantly white school in my predominantly white neighborhood reminded me every day that all that mattered were my grades, and my parents were its enforcers, and I knew nothing but compliance. An increased focus on culturally responsive and sustaining practices that affirm the identities of minoritized students and the wholeness of a child's being, and the policies that uphold them, are of critical importance.

The other day, out of curiosity, I googled my high school and came across this year's registration guide. To my surprise, my school (no less white now than it was then) now offers courses like Hispanic Studies, African-American History, and Multicultural Perspectives, among others—knowledge unavailable in my time. I want to say that I felt proud and glad, but I didn't. I felt angry, resentful, like I was robbed of something. My eyes welled up; my throat crackled. I deserved access to that information then, just as students do now. As a professional, I now understand that this seemingly simple act—adding a couple of electives to the curriculum—could have offered me a mirror in a building enveloped by windows (thank you, Dr. Rudine Sims Bishop). Opportunities to engage in an archaeology of the self (thank you, Dr. Yolanda Sealey-Ruiz) or other critical reflective practices could have illuminated my (and my teachers') racial identity development and the racial inequity and bias in which my school and home and national cultures were steeped. Collaborative, project-based, and student-led approaches to learning could have been opportunities for continued social-emotional development; I could have seen my teachers and peers and the subjects of our learning as whole people, with emotional lives and unique knowledge, not just as arbiters of goodness or badness, or competitors, or obstacles to productivity, or as a means to a grade or test score.

I could have learned history, art, science, mathematics, and literature through a race-conscious social justice lens—not a colorblind one, but from the perspectives of writers and thinkers and activists spanning multiple racial, socioeconomic, sexual, gender, spiritual, ability, and generational identities. I could have learned to see the world for what it is from the very beginning; I could have learned the tools to critique it and practiced how to transform it. I could have taught my teachers something if I knew I had something to contribute. I could have understood that my education is not just for me, to facilitate my 'success' or socioeconomic mobility, but that it is part of a whole, and that it comes with a mandate. I could have realized I was not, by any stretch of the imagination, alone. In other words, even my education—as a traditionally 'successful' student—demanded a culturally responsive and sustaining approach.

As more Puerto Ricans migrate to the mainland after Hurricane María and the ongoing economic crisis, schools in major destinations like Florida and the Northeast corridor will continue absorbing Puerto Rican students and educators. Schools nationwide must be prepared for their arrival, and their infrastructural and pedagogical capacities bolstered to care for students and families who may have experienced trauma and interrupted education (Save the Children, 2018). My parents were unfamiliar with the U.S. education system. They swam with the tide. They did their best with the information that they were given, and I am fine. I will be a very different parent when my child is in school because of my educational and professional background, which I owe in large part to their sacrifices. I will know which questions to ask, who to ask, what to look for, where I can find it, and how to advocate for it. Every caregiver deserves the same caliber and clarity of information, the same level of care and respect, in order to help them make the best decisions on behalf of their children.

Students and their families deserve educators who are able to leverage pedagogies of the home and student/family funds of knowledge in order to engage caregivers in their children's education. Positive school changes would include more culturally responsive and sustaining family engagement opportunities grounded in relationship-building that harness family interest and commitment to their children's education, whatever they may look like. It would involve the creation of family-inclusive spaces that are welcoming, not intimidating—including interpreters and flexibility with families' schedules and outside responsibilities (and those of their children). It would involve engagement with families' deep cultures—their values, beliefs, and ways of being and knowing—not just their dress or their food or their languages (thank you, Dr. Zaretta Hammond). We know that students benefit from teachers who look and sound like them; hiring teachers, administrators, and staff of color, especially if bi/multilingual, regardless of community demographic, would enrich any school environment and student experience.

Regardless of personnel or student characteristics, all members of a school community should have the tools and institutional support to address and explore their racial, ethnic, and national identity development as a crucial component of child, youth, and adult development. Districts and schools should adopt curricula that challenge traditional U.S. and Eurocentric interpretations of every subject, which bury the existence, experiences, and contributions of minoritized communities in this country. Administrative and classroom practices aren't enough, though. Personal and professional resistance to racism and other forms of systemic oppression must also be accompanied by institutional and systemic responses to be successful over time.

In the end, the intricacy of the challenge of creating educational equity, and of drawing reasonable conclusions from the narratives of two women at once from a breezy coastal mountain town in the Caribbean *and* an eerily quiet Minneapolis suburb, speaks to an inescapable truth about human relationships, culture, and identity: all are messy and ever-shifting. No two journeys are alike, no one more important than another. As educators, it is our duty to see and uplift them all.

3.6 Writer's Note

It has been over three years since I first began thinking about and developing this piece. Since then, I've graduated from my master's program and began working directly with teachers, administrators, and families on issues of culture, race, and equity, particularly in early childhood spaces. Puerto Rican resistance to rampant austerity, political corruption, and colonial oppression is alive and well. In reflecting on this piece today, I cannot help but think how differently I would approach this deeply personal inquiry today. In particular, I have spent considerable time reflecting on my childhood and my educational experiences in Minnesota, the racialization of my identity as a Puerto Rican woman, and the impact of those experiences/my race on my identity development as a whole.

In what way(s) did my education, among my primarily white, middle-class teachers and peers, prepare me for or impede me from racially identifying? From truly understanding the societies I was born and socialized into, and the communities that shaped me? How can my inability to racially identify affect how I advocate for equity and anti-racism, both personally and professionally? How do I reconcile my family's and my own progressive assimilation into whiteness with my political principles, along with my fears and anxieties (stubborn artifacts of cultural hegemony), to find a space in the global struggle for liberation? The older I get, the more I understand that the two nations between which I am perpetually suspended are as similar as they are different.

At the risk of making this comment as long as my paper, I'll close by sharing that the fluidity and ephemeral nature of identity can make narrative study as frustrating as it is cathartic. Returning to these words after time away has continually given rise to discomfort, surprise, and more questions than I ever feel capable of processing, let alone articulating. I accept this with gratitude, knowing that such feelings are possible only when one commits to growth. I hope it continues.

References

Aranda, E. M. (2007a). *Emotional bridges to Puerto Rico: Migration, return migration, and the struggles of incorporation*. Rowman & Littlefield.

Aranda, E. M. (2007b). Struggles of incorporation among the Puerto Rican middle class. *The Sociological Quarterly, 48*(2), 199–228.

Ariza, D. (2010). Puerto Rican youth in central Florida: Adaptation and identity. *CENTRO Journal, 22*(1), 128–153.

Berila, B. (2005). Reading national identities: The radical disruptions of *Borderlands/La Frontera*. In A. Keating (Ed.), *Entre mundos/Among worlds: New perspectives on Gloria Anzaldúa* (pp. 121–128). Palgrave Macmillan.

Center for Puerto Rican Studies. (2018). *New estimates: 135,000+ post-Maria Puerto Ricans relocated to stateside* [Data set]. https://centropr.hunter.cuny.edu/research/data-center/data-sheets/new-estimates-135000post-maria-puerto-ricans-relocated-stateside

Cortez, C. (2001). The new Aztlan: Nepantla and other sites of transmogrification. In V. M. Fields & V. Zamudio-Taylor (Eds.), *The road to Aztlan: Art from a mythic homeland* (pp. 358–373). Museum Associates, Los Angeles Museum of Art.

Darder, A. (2011). The politics of biculturalism: Culture and difference in the formation of "warriors for Gringostroika" and "the new Mestizas". *Counterpoints, 418*, 41–60.

Darder, A. (2012). *Culture and power in the classroom: Educational foundations for the schooling of bicultural students* (20th anniversary ed.). Routledge.

De Genova, N., & Ramos-Zayas, A. Y. (2003). *Latino crossings: Mexicans, Puerto Ricans, and the politics of race and citizenship*. Routledge.

Duany, J. (2002). *Puerto Rican nation on the move: Identities on the island and in the United States*. The University of North Carolina Press.

Duany, J. (2010). The Orlando Ricans: Overlapping identity discourses among middle-class Puerto Rican immigrants. *CENTRO Journal, 22*(1), 84–115.

Gómez, M. L. (2010). Talking about ourselves, talking about our mothers: Latina prospective teachers narrate their life experiences. *The Urban Review, 42*(2), 81–101.

Grosfoguel, R., Negrón-Muntaner, F., & Georas, C. S. (1997). Beyond nationalist and colonialist discourses: The *jaiba* politics of the Puerto Rican ethno-nation. In R. Grosfoguel & F. Negrón-Muntaner (Eds.), *Puerto Rican jam: Rethinking colonialism and nationalism* (pp. 1–36). University of Minnesota Press.

Irizarry, J. G., & Antrop-González, R. (2007). RicanStructing the discourse and promoting school success: Extending a theory of culturally responsive pedagogy for diasporicans. *Centro Journal, 19*(2), 37–59.

Keating, A. (2006). From borderlands and new mestizas to nepantlas and nepantleras: Anzaldúan theories for social change. *Human Architecture: Journal of the Society of Self-Knowledge, 4*(3), 5–16.

Martínez-San Miguel, Y. (2014). *Coloniality of diasporas: Rethinking intra-colonial migrations in a pan-Caribbean context*. Palgrave Macmillan.

Minnesota State Demographic Center [MSDC]. (2015). *Minnesota now, then, when… an overview of demographic change*. https://mn.gov/admin/assets/2015-04-06-overview-MN-demographic-changes_tcm36-74549.pdf

Moreno, M. (2015a). Writing the Puerto Rican rural experience in the Midwest: An interview with Fred Arroyo. *CENTRO Journal, 27*(1), 186–205.

Moreno, M. (2015b). The untold midwestern Puerto Rican story: Fred Arroyo's Western Avenue and other fictions. *Studies in American Fiction, 42*(2), 269–291.

Negrón de Montilla, A. (1975). *Americanization in Puerto Rico and the public school system, 1900–1930*. Editorial Universitaria de Puerto Rico.

Ogbu, J. U., & Simons, H. D. (1998). Voluntary and involuntary minorities: A cultural-ecological theory of school performance with some implications for education. *Anthropology & Education Quarterly, 29*(2), 155–188.

Parreñas, R. S. (2001). *Servants of globalization: Women, migration and domestic work*. Stanford University Press.

Portes, A., & Rumbaut, R. G. (1996). *Immigrant America: A portrait.* University of California Press.

Portes, A., & Rumbaut, R. G. (2001). *Legacies: The story of the immigrant second generation.* University of California Press.

Portes, A., & Zhou, M. (1993). The new second generation: Segmented assimilation and its variants. *Annals of the American Academy of Political and Social Science, 530*(1), 74–96.

Prieto, L., & Villenas, S. A. (2012). Pedagogies from *Nepantla: Testimonio,* Chicana/Latina feminisms and teacher education classrooms. *Equity & Excellence in Education, 45*(3), 411–429.

Riessman, C. K. (2008). *Narrative methods for the human sciences.* SAGE Publications.

Save the Children. (2018, March 20). *Puerto Rico's children have lost more than 13 million school days since Hurricane Maria* [Press release]. https://www.savethechildren.org/us/about-us/media-and-news/2018-press-releases/hurricane-maria-update

Solís-Jordán, J. (1994). *Public school reform in Puerto Rico.* Greenwood Press.

Vélez, W. (2017). A new framework for understanding Puerto Ricans' migration patterns and incorporation. *Centro Journal, 29*(3), 126–153.

Zavala Martínez, I. (1994). Entremundos: The psychological dialectics of Puerto Rican migration and its implication for health. In G. Lamberty, & C. García Coll (Eds.), *Puerto Rican women and children: Issues in health, growth, and development* (pp. 29–38). Plenum Press.

4

ARMONÍA CON UNA PALITA DE CONFLICTO

A 'Latino' Relationship as Intercultural

Martha Iris Rosas

Dedicado a mis queridos padres, Estela y Gregorio Rosas.

A few years ago, a Cuban relative took me aside at a family event. "¡Muchacha!" she said, pointing to a glow-in-the-dark rosary I wore tucked under my blouse, "¡Quítate eso, que pareces Puertorriquena!" [Girl! Take that off—you look Puerto Rican!]. This comment created dissonance for me, a dissonance I hadn't felt being raised in a household with a Cuban mother and Puerto Rican father, and resulted in my rethinking my childhood. Comments by extended family came to mind, such as "You need to marry a good Cuban man," making me wonder if I was being claimed for one side of the family. Then, slowly, differences between my mother and father, specifically in the ways they talked, emerged. For the first time, I considered that although my parents were both 'Latino' and, more specifically, Caribbean, I had been raised by an intercultural couple.

Although I prefer the term 'Latinx,' which Salinas and Lozano (2017) explain "has evolved as [a] new form of liberation for those individuals who do not identify within the gender binary of masculinity or femininity and is used to represent the various intersections of gender as it is understood in different ways within different communities of people" (p. 10), including indigenous conceptions of gender, throughout this paper I will use the term 'Latino.' Salina and Lozano explain that the term 'Latinx' should only be used if "participants self-identify as Latinx" (p. 11) and my parents, when they were alive, usually used their respective nationalities or the terms 'Hispano' and 'Latino' to identify themselves. Furthermore, I will be discussing implications for education in the findings of this study and have not yet found instances of the New York City Board of Education using the term 'Latinx' to identify student populations.

Suárez-Orozco and Páez (2008) identify the term 'Latino' as a construct defined within the U.S. context: "Outside the United States, we don't speak of Latinos; we speak of Mexicans, Cubans, Puerto Ricans, and so forth. Latinos are made in the USA" (p. 4). This makes it evident that 'Latinos' from different regions or nations, such as Cuba and Puerto Rico, might identify with distinct cultures. For example, individuals could instead identify their cultures as being Indigenous or from their nation of origin. In this narrative study, I explore my parents' intercultural relationship to determine how they perceived and dealt with issues of cultural difference. Molina, Estrada & Burnett (2004) have explained that "[i]ntercultural couples may need to negotiate their unique cultural landscapes, as well as withstand the pressures of rejecting communities" (p. 142). My research question is as follows: How do individuals in intercultural relationships address intercultural differences?

This study is relevant to educators working with heterogeneous populations of students. By focusing on two individuals who interact closely on a daily basis, I explore types of intercultural differences that may arise when populations from different nationalities come into close contact, as they do in U.S. schools, to determine possible approaches that may be used to address these differences.

4.1 Theoretical Framework and Literature Review

Biculturalism is frequently explored as a phenomena in which individuals and families navigate between a non-majority home culture and a majority societal culture (Barrios & Egan, 2002; Darder, 2011; Montoya, 1994; Olivos, 2006; Pooremamali, Östman, Persson, & Eklund, 2011). This focus, however, usually does not explore the extent to which heterogeneity could be present within the home culture itself; rather, differences focused on are between the home culture and societal culture. Occasionally, biculturalism is explored as a phenomenon in which families and/or couples from two distinct cultures navigate these cultures *within* their relationship, the household, and/or extended family structures (Anderson, 1999; Blount & Curry, 1993; O'Hearn, 2008; Wamba, 1998). More frequently, though, when the phenomenon of couples or families navigating two distinct cultures amongst themselves is explored, the term used to refer to these families or couples is 'intercultural' (Crippen & Brew, 2007; Molina et al., 2004; Silva, Campbell & Wright, 2012). Crippen and Brew (2007), for example, explain that the "term *intercultural* relates to bringing together or the meeting of two different cultural backgrounds into one relationship" (p. 107). Waldman & Rubalcava (2005) expand the definition of intercultural couples to include "[p]artners with the same ethnicity" when they have "issues [which] nevertheless revolve around unconsciously grounded cultural differences" (p. 228). Whether the literature refers to relationships formed by individuals from two distinct cultural backgrounds as 'bicultural' or 'intercultural," however, potential and actual difficulties arising as a result of heterogeneity or difference within their cultures are discussed: misunderstandings related to the motivation behind their partner's actions (Waldman & Rubalcava, 2005), differences in cultural practices (Wamba, 1998), separation between the two sides of the family (Wamba,1998), mistrust of the other culture by extended family members (O'Hearn, 1988), as well as family opposition to the relationship (Molina et al., 2004).

By using narrative research to explore a successful intercultural relationship (i.e., one that persists despite the difficulties encountered as a result of intercultural difference), this study hopes to focus on ways in which difficulties dealing with intercultural differences can be successfully addressed. To use a framework open to the possibility of an intercultural relationship, this narrative study employs aspects of two poststructural theories, Derrida's (1976) theory of deconstruction and Butler's (1993, 2004) theory of performativity, as described by Jackson and Mazzei (2011) in addition to Butler (2008), to explore issues of intercultural difference.

Derrida (1976) uses the concept of the trace to refer to the "absent presence of sometimes imperceptible imprints on our words and their meanings before we speak or write them" (as cited in Jackson & Mazzei, 2011, p. 21). By identifying traces associated with certain signifiers, or words, Derrida allows for the possibility of using a word without "subscribing to its premises" (Spivak, 1976, xviii). This expands words so that other traces, including those not usually associated with these words, can be connected to them, thereby making them more inclusive. Sarup (1989), explaining Derrida's views on language, acknowledges that because meaning "will never stay the same from context to context" (p. 36), language cannot necessarily be considered stable. Looking at traces therefore "prevents a closure of meaning" (Jackson & Mazzei, 2011, p. 28). Deconstruction "unsettles how... categories seek to stabilize identity and arrest meaning in ways that are limiting" (Jackson & Mazzei, 2011, p. 27). In this way, words used to categorize individuals or groups of individuals can be expanded.

Butler's theory of performativity focuses on the enactment of performative responses to undo "normative categories that place rigid structures on how people live out their lives" (as cited in Jackson & Mazzei, 2011, p. 72). Interpellation, defined as "a linguistic act of *hailing*, or calling an individual that initiates her into subjected status and therefore into 'a certain order of social existence'" (as cited in Jackson & Mazzei, 2011, p. 74), recognizes individuals by referring to normative categories that invoke certain social orders. That Butler's conception of normative categories has affinities with Derrida's conception of traces is made evident when Butler (2008) states:

> Although some would likely argue that norms must already be in place for recognition to become possible, and there is doubtless truth to such a claim, it is also true that new norms are brought into being when unanticipated forms of recognition take place.
>
> (p. 31)

Butler believes that norms come into question when individuals are not rec-ognized by them. If interpellation does not recognize individuals in acceptable ways, individuals can enact performative responses to reconstitute themselves. Thus, in the same way words are made more inclusive by associating them with new traces, recognition can be expanded by issuing performative responses.

It is important to note that although postmodern and poststructural the-ories acknowledge that individuals can enact resistance when represented in unfavorable ways, Latinx scholars such as Moya (2002) have pointed out that these theories do not necessarily take into account how these representations influence the development of a more stable sense of identity in individuals of color. Poststructuralism's influence on postmodernism has resulted in the "conventional understanding of identity [being undermined] by discounting the possibility of objective knowledge" (p. 7). By not attending to identity for-mation, postmodern theories of subjectivity "are unable to explain the persis-tent correlation between certain kinds of bodies and certain kinds of identities" (p. 18) and could lead to the legitimacy of marginalized groups' identities (as oppressed) being theorized away. For the purpose of exploring how two non-majority cultures are navigated when aspiring to form a viable intercultural union, the poststructural theoretical constructs I have chosen are helpful because they emphasize how traces and norms can expand to allow for the possibility of an intercultural union. I have, however, been careful to remain focused on interactions between my parents' non-majority cultures and not on interactions between their non-majority cultures and the prevailing majority culture, as I imagine it is during the latter type of interactions that certain types of repre-sentations of non-majority groups, if made by large numbers of majority group members, are likely to influence the development of marginalized identities in non-majority group members. Because—throughout their relationship—my parents were surrounded by family and friends from their respective non-major-ity groups; neither group had a persistent marginalizing effect on the members of the other group.

4.2 Research Design and Methods

This research is designed as a narrative study, primarily focused on my Cuban mother's narrative about her relationship with my Puerto Rican father, and sup-plemented with segments of my father's narrative. I first interviewed my sister, Marisela, to corroborate my experiences with my parents' language differences and extended family's comments distinguishing Cubans and Puerto Ricans. She cited sufficient examples of differences in our parents' vocabulary and comments by extended family members focusing on her being half Puerto Rican and Cuban to confirm my conception of our household as intercultural. Furthermore, dis-tinctions extended to peers' comments: Latinx friends called her a "mutt," and non-Latinx friends asked, "Don't Cubans and Puerto Ricans hate each other?"

This confirmed that peers had dissonant reactions from learning about our parents' different nationalities.

I then conducted two interviews with my mother, followed by one interview with my father, and a combined interview with both parents, transcribing pertinent portions. I employ performance/dialogic analyses following Riessman (2008), as these methodologies are consistent with my chosen theoretical approaches. Specifically, dialogic analysis' focus on hidden voices in texts as a result of which "authority over meaning is dispersed and embedded" is consistent with Derrida's concept of the always present, even if not explicitly so, trace in that both allow researchers to "locate gaps and indeterminate sections in personal narrative" (Riessman, 2008, p. 107). Performance analysis' focus on identities being performed with specific audiences in mind, making them "situated" (p. 106), is consistent with Butler's conception of subjects being constituted in temporal contexts (as cited in Jackson & Mazzei, 2011, p. 72). Actors staging "performances of desirable selves to preserve 'face'" (Riessman, 2008, p. 106) is consistent with subjects employing agency when norms recognize them unacceptably.

Attention to form and language therefore privilege instances in which hidden voices or traces emerge in the narrative (dialogic analysis), as well as instances when these hidden voices or traces are presented as norms that the narrator must counter to be acceptably reconstituted (performance analysis). In order to ensure I reviewed narrative transcripts without assumptions, I used Derrida's (1976) theory of deconstruction to look for "places in the narrative that 'lead elsewhere than the place we were expecting them'" (as cited in Jackson & Mazzei, 2011, p. 24). In particular, I analyze absent-present traces that emerge in connection to signifiers having to do with 'Puerto Rican' and 'Cuban' nationalities in order to determine how these are presented by my parents. In addition, I use Butler's (1993, 2004, 2008) theory of performativity to explore how my mother enacts agency in ways that 'undo normative categories' that sustain versions of reality that limit her choices, i.e., deciding to marry my father. In keeping with dialogic analysis' focus on hidden voices, segments of my father's narrative highlighting or juxtaposing information provided by my mother are included. Also consistent with dialogic analysis, I (as the researcher) include myself and acknowledge my influence on the resulting narrative, as my family experience enables me to ask targeted questions. Finally, because performance/dialogic analyses incorporate elements from other methodological approaches (Riessman, 2008, p. 105), narrative segments are categorized into themes.

4.2.1 Background Context

My mother Estela immigrated to the United States in 1960 soon after Fidel Castro ousted military dictator Fulgencio Batista from power in 1959. Large numbers of Cubans fleeing the Cuban Revolution arrived in the United States during this year (Pérez, 1986, p. 131). Her sister Fidelia and two brothers were already established in Washington Heights, Manhattan, when she arrived. Long before, in 1946, my father Gregorio migrated to New York after serving in World War II. He came at the start of the 'Great Migration Phase' after World War II, when surplus airplanes made "air travel less expensive and more accessible" (Rodríguez, 1991, p. 3). He had an extended network of relatives in Washington Heights, including his cousins Dilia and Dora.

Estela was introduced to Gregorio by Dilia, who lived in her building. At the time, my father was in the process of divorcing his first wife. Estela's brothers strongly opposed the courtship, even writing to their father in Cuba about it, a maneuver that did not stop my parents from dating. Besides speaking Spanish, my parents shared certain values. Both were Catholic. Estela relates how Gregorio impressed her by asking whether she was Catholic when they met. Both were also Democrats. Initially, all Estela's siblings had been Democrats, becoming Republicans only after John F. Kennedy decided not to back the Bay of Pigs invasion. Estela, however, remained a Democrat. Despite these similarities, the couple still encountered differences between the two cultures, which I address in the Findings section.

4.3 Findings

This section is organized around three salient themes that emerged from the narratives and which I organize chronologically based on when events occurred. Narrative excerpts are presented in Spanish, the language used for interviews, followed by their translation to English.

4.3.1 First Theme: Impressions of Future Spouse's Family, Impressions of Future Spouse's Nationality

This theme documents initial impressions my parents discuss having about each other's nationalities. Traces connected to Puerto Rican and Cuban nationalities are identified and analyzed.

In the excerpt below, Estela explains what she thought about Puerto Ricans and Gregorio's family before meeting him.

> Estela: Yo pensé solamente que era otra nacionalidad. Porque en Cuba, habían muchas nacionalidades también… Y, entonces, a mí me pareció bien que eran personas los que yo había conocido (referencia a la familia de mi padre) que eran personas preparadas, personas educadas, porque yo te digo la mayoría del Cubano siempre pensaba que eran como superiores a los Puertorriqueños y eso. Porque la mayoría del Puertorriqueño que había en Nueva York eran personas de campo, tú sabes, y entonces pues, como ahora estos indocumentados que vienen buscando mejor vida acá…
>
> Martha: Pero, por ejemplo, la familia tuya de Cuba era del campo también, ¿verdad? Pues, ¿qué era la diferencia?

Estela: Mayormente, el Cubano siempre ha sido un poquito orgulloso de sí mismo, ¿tú sabes? Y entonces, claro, los que venían para acá ya venían con su visa y todo eso, que a cualquiera no lo dejaban venir para acá, ¿tú sabes? Que tenía que saber, porque ellos investigaban y eso la clase de persona que era, ¿tú sabes? Entonces, todo que venía ya venía con su visa de residencia. Si era un malhechor o un ladrón o eso así, a ese no le daban visa. Pues, ya uno tenía eso de que uno se siente orgulloso de uno mismo, del comportamiento de uno y si ha tenido una base familiar buena, como realmente nosotros en mi casa la tuvimos, gracias a Dios y eso, pues uno se siente realmente orgulloso. Y si uno ve a alguien que habla feo o que esto o lo otro, pues ya tú sabes, uno dice esta o este es de mala calaña… Pero yo, a la familia de él la conocí… Tú sabes que la familia de Gregory es súper religiosa. Solamente de uno oírlos hablar uno sabía que eran personas buenas y eso.

Estela: I thought only that it was a different nationality. Because in Cuba, there were also many nationalities… And, it seemed good to me that those persons I had met (reference to Gregorio's family) were prepared people, educated people, because I tell you the majority of the Cubans always thought that they were superior to the Puerto Ricans and such. Because the majority of the Puerto Ricans in New York were people from the countryside, you know, like the undocumented immigrants that are coming now looking for a better life here…

Martha: But, for example, your family from Cuba was from the countryside, too, right? So, what's the difference?

Estela: Mostly that Cubans have always been a little proud of themselves, you know? And, then, of course, the ones that came here already came with their visa and all that, they just didn't let anyone come here, you know? They had to know, because they would investigate the type of person you were, you know? So then, everyone that came would come with their visa of residency. If you were a wrong-doer or a thief, they wouldn't give you a visa. So, you already had that, that you felt proud of yourself, of your own behavior and if you've had a good family base, like we actually had in our family, thanks to God and all; well, you feel really proud. And if you see someone who talks ugly or this or that, well you already know, you say this one or that one is of bad stock… But I met his family… You know that Gregory's family is super religious. Just by hearing them talk, you knew that they were good people.

Analysis using Derrida's deconstruction theory makes evident that Estela is identifying inferiority as a trace she believes many Cubans associate with Puerto Ricans. The reason cited for this negative trace reveals a further trace: Puerto Ricans are usually considered simple country folk and therefore not educated. Although, by stating that Gregorio's family were "personas preparadas, personas educadas" [prepared people, educated people], she is not associating this trace with his family, I find the attribution of inferiority to Puerto Ricans from rural backgrounds dissonant, given that her family were rural tobacco growers. When I press for clarification, she cites a trace that Cubans associate with the conferral of residency: respectability, determined by a person's 'comportamiento' [behavior]. By explaining that only well-behaved Cubans received visas, Estela associates the trace of respectability with 'Cuban' immigrants, even those with rural provenance. My mother arrived before the Cuban Adjustment Act of 1966, which promised permanent residency to any Cuban arriving in the United States "by any means, legal or illegal" (Abraham, 2015). She also arrived before the Mariel Cuban wave of immigration in 1980 in which many criminal prisoners were included alongside "legitimate political prisoners" (Novas, 2007). Interestingly, a trace usually associated with Puerto Ricans, citizenship, does not surface in Estela's narrative. If the purpose of traveling to the United States is to make a life here, citizenship could be considered superior in status to residency in that it bestows certain rights, such as the right to vote, that integrate a person further into American civil society. However, her emphasis is on Cubans having to be vetted and found acceptable to enter the United States, a process that Puerto Ricans are not submitted to as citizens.

By citing respectability to explain why Cuban immigrants might consider themselves superior, Estela demonstrates an intimate understanding of why Cubans associate certain traces with their nationality. Jackson & Mazzei (2011) make evident that in deconstruction, "an intimate knowledge of the tradition with which one engages" (p. 25) is needed in order to make room for newness. By explaining that Gregorio's family were "personas buenas" [good people], she expands the traces that Cubans associate with Puerto Ricans, so that the positive trace of being well-behaved can now be associated with Puerto Ricans as well as with Cubans. As a result, she makes it possible for individuals from both nationalities to share a common characteristic.

Analysis using Butler's performativity theory makes evident that, for Estela, conferral of residency serves to recognize Cubans as respectable. In subsequent excerpts, it will become evident that respectability has normative significance. Furthermore, by attributing the positive trace of 'well-behaved' to Puerto Ricans, Estela recognizes herself as a Cuban who does not consider herself superior to Latino individuals from other nationalities, thereby also expanding the traces associated with Cubans (i.e., Cubans can be respectable without being superior).

That respectability is not a trace unequivocally associated with Cuban immigrants is made evident in the excerpt below, where Gregorio discusses his impressions about Cubans before meeting Estela.

> Bueno, yo, tú sabes que yo estuve en Nueva York desde, tú sabes, los 20 años. Fui conociendo, poco a poco, gente allí y eso. Entonces, pues entre esos había gente Cubana, tú sabes, que los conocía así y esas cosas. Bueno, te digo una cosa, al principio, los Cubanos tenían mala fama. Decían que

ellos llevaban drogas… Cuando yo conocí a Estela, fue que conocí a más Cubanos, porque yo no tenía tanto contacto con ellos, entiende.

Well, I, you know that I was in New York, you know, since I was 20 years old. Little by little, I began meeting people and such. And, so there were some Cuban people among them, you know, that I knew and such. Well, I'll tell you one thing; at the beginning, the Cubans had bad fame. People said that they carried drugs…When I met Estela, that was when I met more Cubans, because I didn't have a lot of contact with them, you understand.

The trace Gregorio identifies as connected with Cubans at the time is that of "mala fama" [bad fame], or disreputability due to criminal behavior, such as drug dealing. The discrepancy between the traces Estela and Gregorio identify with Cuban immigrants demonstrates that traces individuals associate with their own nationality might not be universally associated with that nationality. Estela's explanation of the trace she identifies demonstrates in-depth knowledge of the Cuban immigrant experience. Gregorio is careful to attribute the trace he identifies to hearsay, thus making clear that he himself has not encountered disreputable Cubans; however, the identification of such a trace brings to light how negative traces based on hearsay might easily be associated with nationalities people have little experience with. It is interesting to note that my mother attaches traces of well-educated and well-behaved to Puerto Ricans once she has interacted with my father's family and witnessed what they were like.

Furthermore, attaching positive traces to an individual's own nationality could end up determining the traces that become associated with another nationality. This is evident when I ask Gregorio whether anyone from Estela's family made derogatory comments about Puerto Ricans in his presence and he responded:

Al contrario, hablaban bien [de los Puertorriqueños], porque, fíjate, ellos tenían que agradecer que llegaron de Cuba y no sabían inglés y esas cosas… Fidelia y ellos no sabían ni gota [de inglés] ni eso, pero allí estaba Dora. ¿Te recuerdas de Dora? Ella los llevaba al doctor, los llevaba aquí, tú sabes, cuántas cosas tenían que hacer en inglés.

On the contrary, they talked well [of Puerto Ricans], because, take into account, they had to appreciate that they came from Cuba and didn't know English and those things… Fidelia and them didn't know a drop [of English] nor that, but there was Dora. Do you remember Dora? She would take them to the doctor, she would take them here, you know, how many things they had to do in English.

Gregorio's response associates a positive trace, that of being English-proficient, with Puerto Ricans that Estela does not. Once this trace is identified, it becomes evident that the opposite trace, that of not having English proficiency, can be associated with Cuban immigrants. Thus, traces associated with one signifier can be dependent on traces associated with another signifier and therefore relative. This is corroborated by Way, Santos, Niwa, and Kim-Gervey (2008), who demonstrate how positive ethnic identities are maintained in a diverse high school by Puerto Rican students as a result of having Dominican students serve as a foil. Because Puerto Rican students had citizenship and were considered to have the 'best hair' and 'fair skin' (p. 65) by the ethnic groups in the school, they developed a positive ethnic identity in part because they considered themselves as having what the Dominican students might not have. Although not a conclusion Gregorio makes, the identification of a trace that Puerto Ricans have and Cubans do not could very well function to position Puerto Ricans as superior to Cubans. This demonstrates that a single trace can be used to position one signifier as superior to another based on the importance a group of individuals attaches to this specific trace. In the case cited by Gregorio, Puerto Ricans can be positioned as superior because they are associated with a language needed for daily interactions in the United States; in the case cited by Estela, Cubans can be positioned as superior because they are associated with respectability through conferral of residency. Thus, each situation in which a different value is emphasized will set up a different configuration of superior and inferior signifiers. That this could be an interminable process is corroborated by Butler's belief that "identity categories are 'continually…made, unmade, and remade'" (Jackson & Mazzei, 2011, p. 81), as a result of which subjects "are never fully constituted" (p. 83), thereby demonstrating the need for performative responses.

4.3.2 Second Theme: Dating Future Spouse, Defending Future Spouse

This theme documents reactions my parents experienced as a result of dating. Performative responses, or the lack thereof, to these reactions are analyzed and discussed starting with my mother's story:

> Pues fíjate que una conocida mía, que cuando ella, yo le dije que mi novio era puertorriqueño, ¿tú sabes que salió a preguntarme? "Chica, ¿y es bueno?" Ay, a mí me dio una roña cuando esa mujer me dijo eso. Digo yo: "Tú me conoces a mí, ¿verdad? ¿Verdad que me conoces a mí? Si no fuera bueno, pues no fuera novia de él." Y así mismo le contesté: "Si no fuera bueno no fuera novia de él." Pero así mismo: "Chica, ¿y es bueno?" Ay, Dios mío.

> Well, take into account that an acquaintance of mine, that when she, I told her that my boyfriend was Puerto Rican, you know what she came out and asked me? "Girl, and is he good?" Oh, I got so angry when that woman told me that. I said: "Girl, you know me, right? Isn't it true that

you know me? If he wasn't good, well I wouldn't be his girlfriend." Just like that I answered her: "If he wasn't good, well I wouldn't be his girlfriend." But just like that: "Girl, and is he good?" Oh, my God.

The trace Estela's Cuban acquaintance connects with Puerto Ricans is that of not being quality partners. Butler's theory of performativity highlights that this trace can be associated with a normative category; this woman is invoking a norm that partners should be people of quality. In questioning whether Gregorio is of quality, this woman is implying that Estela is not adhering to this norm and, by extension, not making good choices. Because both she and Gregorio are recognized in an unacceptable manner, Estela issues a performative response to be acceptably reconstituted. Interestingly, Estela issues this response by appealing to another normative category valued by Cubans: respectability. By asking the woman the rhetorical question, "Girl, you know me, right?" she ensures the woman recognizes her as a respectable person. She then connects Gregorio with this same norm by stating: "If he wasn't good, well I wouldn't be his girlfriend." Invoking this norm puts to rest concerns about her boyfriend being 'good' as, for Cubans, respectability is garnered through good behavior.

Butler's theory of performativity thus highlights how Estela enacts agency while still operating within a normative category Cubans value, thereby enabling her to continue dating Gregorio without being unacceptably recognized. That an intimate understanding of the norms valued by her culture was instrumental in issuing a targeted performative response that successfully reconstituted her relationship with Gregorio as feasible makes evident that this understanding is necessary when navigating normative categories used to delimit options available to people.

Whereas Estela remembers numerous reactions to her courtship with Gregorio, he remembers only one: an admonition from his own mother, narrated in the excerpt below. Estela, who was present during his narration, reveals that his mother admonished her as well.

> Gregorio: Pero siempre mamá me decía las cosas: "Ten cuidado, hijo mío que ya tú tuviste un fracaso (referencia al primer matrimonio), que no vayas [a tener otro]," tú sabes, como no conocía bien a Estela y nada de esas cosas.
> Estela (en el fondo): Y, a mí me dijo: "ten cuidado mijita, que"—nunca se me olvida—"ten cuidado mijita, que los hombres divorciados" y eso...
> Gregorio: A-ha. Y a tu mamá le dijo ella: "Ten cuidado hijita que los hombres divorciados son muy aprovechaos," ¿tú sabes?

> Gregorio: But always my mother would tell me things: "Be careful, my son, you already had a failure [reference to his first marriage], don't [have another one]," you know, since she didn't know Estela well or any of those things.

Estela (in the background): And, to me, she said: "Be careful my child, that"—
I'll never forget it—"be careful my child, that divorced men" and such…
Gregorio: A-ha. And to your mother, she said: "Be careful child, divorced
men are very opportunistic," you know?

The admonishments issued by my paternal grandmother to each person inter-
pellate the other person in a way that does not assume respectability as a given. The
traces emphasized in these admonishments, however, are not tied to nationality-
related signifiers. She does not tell Estela to be careful of Puerto Rican men; she
tells her to be careful of divorced men because *they* are "aprovechaos" [opportunis-
tic]. In this case, it is more difficult for Estela to issue a performative response that
reconstitutes Gregorio and her relationship with him as feasible because she is just
getting to know him. As his mother, my grandmother has intimate knowledge of
Gregorio that might justify her saying this. Because people can't be reduced to one
category (Jackson & Mazzei, 2011, p. 77), how they are recognized can depend on
a variety of norms. This can make issuing a performative response to reconstitute
an individual someone is getting to know more difficult, particularly when the
response has to be issued to someone who is more familiar with the individual. For
Estela, the fact that Gregorio was divorced made deciding whether to marry him
more complicated as she had to deal with concerns, initially from her brothers and
now from his own mother, that this signaled he did not take marriage seriously.

4.3.3 Third Theme: Entering the Intercultural Union, Understanding the Intercultural Intricacies

This theme documents descriptions of my parent's life together after they were
married. How each partner's practices are presented by the other partner is analyzed and discussed.

In the excerpt below, Estela responds to a question about whether her life was
the same or different after marriage.

Bueno, igual porque gracias a Dios que mi marido era una persona que
se—en otra palabras, él era una persona que se relacionaba, él era una
persona que le gustaba tener esto, esa relación, esa amistad de familia, y
eso. Y también, pues por otro lado, yo con la familia de él para mí era
como si fuera mi familia…… Yo hubiera querido que Gregory hubiera
conocido a mi papá y mi papá a él. Yo sé que se hubieran llevado muy
bien, muy bien. Porque más o menos el carácter de mi papá y el carácter
de él, como es, se asemejaban mucho. Únicamente que el carácter de mi
marido era un poquito explosivo (Se ríe y yo me río también) cuando
se enfadaba por algo (Se ríe otra vez)…

Well, the same because thank God my husband was a person that—in other
words, he was a person that liked to have this, that relationship, that

friendship with the family, and such. And also, on the other side, me with his family, for me it was like they were my family… I would have wished that Gregory would have met my father and my father met him. Because pretty much my father's character and my husband's character, how is it, they were very similar. Only that my husband's character was a little explosive (she laughs and I laugh, too) when he got annoyed by something (she laughs again)…

By identifying a value, spending time with extended family, that she and Gregorio share, and then making a connection between Gregorio's way of being and her own father's way of being, Estela recognizes Gregorio as a person who engages in practices and ways of being similar to those of her Cuban family. The specificity of the similarities detailed indicate Estela has developed intimate knowledge of Gregorio as a result of being married. The connections made between Gregorio and Estela's family no longer belong to the general categories (i.e., respectable, well-behaved) used when she first met him. Rather, they detail specific practices and ways of being.

That there are differences between Gregorio and her father is made evident when she makes a distinction between their temperaments. However, because her narrative emphasizes similarities, my parents' union is represented as conforming to normative categories her Cuban family finds important. Having accepted Gregorio as partner, the focus has shifted to recognizing the union as viable. An emphasis on similarities is also evident in her responses below.

Martha: Una diferencia que yo me recuerdo entre Papi y tú es que unas veces decían diferentes palabras para las cosas. ¿Puedes hablar un poquito de eso?

Estela: A, bueno, porque en Puerto Rico hay muchas cosas que tienen un significado, esto, que se le dicen, no que tenga un significado, que se le dicen en otra forma y en Cuba de otra, y eso. En suponer, como la famosa palabra de *eñagotao* [en cuclillas]. (Se ríe.)

Martha: ¿Que quiere decir eso?

Estela: En Cuba, se dice 'agachado,' y eso, o 'agachao' para cortarla, y eso. "Me agaché para coger esto." En Puerto Rico se dice, "me eñagoté para coger eso." Entonces, son diferentes, diferentes palabras pero que significan lo mismo, y eso. Entonces, pues hay eso, muchas otras palabras también…

Martha: Pero habían unas palabras que te molestaban, ¿verdad? Como cuando papi decía: "Dame una *palita* de arroz."

Estela: (se ríe.) No-o, pues, eso no, porque es una palita, digo yo, bueno déjame buscar una pala (las dos se ríen.)… Pero uno después se acostumbra… Se acostumbra, tú sabes, porque, si vamos al caso, es la misma, la misma, el mismo significado con distinta palabra. Eso es las costumbres de cada país y eso.

Martha: One difference that I remember between Papi and you is that sometimes you used different words for things. Can you talk a little about that?

Estela: Oh, because, in Puerto Rico there are many things that have a certain significance, this, that you say, it's not that they have a significance, it's that one says them in another way and in Cuba in another, and such. For example, like the famous word *eñagotao*. [squatting] (She laughs)

Martha: What does that mean?

Estela: In Cuba, you say 'agachado,' and such, or 'agachao' to shorten it, and such. "Me agaché...." In Puerto Rico, you say "me eñagoté..." [to crouch]. And so, they are different, different words but that mean the same thing, and such. And so, there's that, many other words as well...

Martha: But there were words that bothered you, right? Like when Papi said "Give me a *little shovelful* of rice."

Estela: (she laughs) No-o, well, not that, because it's a little shovel, I say, well, let me look for a shovel (they both laugh).... But then you get used to it....You get used to it, you know, because, for that matter, it's the same, the same, the same meaning with a different word.

Estela begins using a descriptive rather than prescriptive approach to speech differences by explaining that each country uses different words. However, reference to "*eñagotao*" as "*la famosa palabra*" [the famous word] indicates a possible underlying value judgment. Because my sister and I both remember Estela objecting to certain of my father's words, I pointedly question her about a phrase he used when asking for more rice: "Dame una *palita* de arroz" [Give me a little shovelful of rice], meaning, give me a spoonful of rice. After poking a little fun at the phrase ('well, let me look for a shovel'), her narrative focuses on getting accustomed to differences because, although the words are different, their significance is the same. My mother goes on to question certain terminology Cubans use (such as 'kilo,' a measure of weight, to refer to currency), thus signaling her objections are not about privileging Cubans speech habits, but rather about ensuring correct terminology is used. By emphasizing the similarity between different terms, her narrative represents her union with Gregorio as harmonious rather than conflicted. Thus, in both excerpts, her narrative functions as a performative response to those who might not think an intercultural union will work.

The excerpt from Gregorio's narrative below is consistent with Estela's approach:

Martha: Y ¿tú encontrabas diferencia entre cómo eran ellos y como eran los puertorriqueños?

Gregory: Bueno, sí también, ciertas cosas del hablar, tú sabes, que uno dice ciertas palabras y tiene ciertas costumbres.

Martha: ¿Cómo qué?

Gregory: No mucha diferencia, no mucha diferencia.

Martha: Pero, qué costumbres ¿te recuerdas?... No quiere decir que sea malo, nada más diferente.

...

Gregory: Cuando las *Crismas* que ellos hacían eso de las uvitas (Referencia a la práctica de poner doce uvas en una copa de vino en Nochevieja para tener suerte en los próximos doce meses) y esas cosas, eso no lo teníamos nosotros. Y también, este, en Puerto Rico se come lechón asado en vara y ellos lo abren así, tú sabes. Abierto así, lo ponen. Y había distintas comidas. Yo le decía a Estela *mondongo* y ella decía "eso se le da a los puercos" y eso es lo más rico que hay... Nosotros decimos *chiquito* y ellos dicen *chiquitico*. Pero, uno se adapta a eso, tú sabe.

Martha: And did you find differences between how they were and how the Puerto Ricans were?

Gregory: Well, yes, certain things in talking, you know, that one says certain words and has certain customs.

Martha: Like what?

Gregory: Not much difference, not much difference.

Martha: But what customs, do you remember?... It doesn't mean that it's bad, only different.

...

Gregory: During Christmas, they did that with the grapes (reference to practice of putting 12 grapes in a wine glass on New Year's Eve for luck in the upcoming 12 months) and those things, we didn't have that. And also, in Puerto Rico we eat pork roasted on rods and they open it, you know. They put it open, like this. And there were different foods. I would tell Estela *mondongo* (a Puerto Rican dish) and she would say "that's what the pigs eat" when that is the most delicious thing there is... We say *chiquito* and they say *chiquitito*. But you adapt to it, you know.

Both parents cite getting used to, or adapting to, differences as a way to deal with them. That this process of getting used to differences also entails developing an understanding of these differences is made evident by Gregorio explaining the contexts in which Estela's practices are used and Estela explaining the meaning of words Gregorio used. The excerpts in this section therefore make evident that differences are being downplayed and that, in Estela's case, there is a concerted effort to emphasize similarities. Lee (2006) cites the development of a "relational identity," an identity that is co-constructed with a friend (p. 6), as a crucial component of successful intercultural friendships (p. 4). Practices used to develop relational identities in intercultural friendships include educating "each other by introducing their cultures or eradicating previous stereotypes" (p. 14) and emphasizing shared similarities (p. 16) despite the cultural differences commonly encountered. In this way, my mother's narrative is in keeping with practices used to construct a relational identity. Furthermore, by citing this process of getting used to differences, my parents demonstrate that differences can be surmounted in intercultural relationships.

4.4 Conclusions

The progression of themes in this study demonstrates how my parents' knowledge of their partner's nationality developed from initial general impressions not founded in actual experience to nuanced understandings of the practices associated with the other person's nationality. Because my parents were interested in each other when they met, they were disposed to look beyond initial impressions and learn about each other's cultures.

Furthermore, my mother's narrative makes evident that individuals in intercultural relationships have a vested interest in representing their partner positively. That there were differences that probably created some dissonance for her is evident in her allusion to my father's temperament and her reactions to some of his word choices; however, her narrative focuses on emphasizing the positive. During their courtship, having intimate knowledge of the values of her culture allows her to present her boyfriend in a positive light using norms important to her culture. Gaining intimate knowledge of his culture once she is married allows her to explain his practices as well as make important connections to those of her culture.

Partners in intercultural relationships are therefore in a unique position to represent the other culture to members of their own culture. Because they have a deep understanding of their own culture's values and the stereotypes their culture attributes to members of the other culture, they can more effectively operate within normative categories to dispel these stereotypes. Because they have intimate knowledge of the practices of the other culture, they can also accurately portray similarities between the two cultures as well as explain differences.

4.5 Implications for Education

The variety in practices and word usage discussed by my parents makes evident that homogeneity cannot be assumed even when nationalities fall under the same umbrella term, as is the case with the term 'Latinos.' When discussing conditions that support the development of a bicultural voice that takes into account their cultures of origin, Darder (2011) explains that students of color "need critically conscious teachers who come from their own communities, who can speak and instruct them in their native language, who can serve as translators of the bicultural experience, and who can reinforce an identity grounded in the cultural integrity of their own people" (p. 204). Because of the heterogeneity found in cultures identified as 'Latino,' educators who fall under this umbrella term, such as myself, cannot assume that we will always share the same cultural understandings as our 'Latino' students. Therefore, educators, whether they fall under the same umbrella term as their students or not, will need to continually cultivate awareness of the heterogeneity of cultural understandings present in their classrooms in order to help students and their families explore and affirm them in positive ways. In what follows, I will discuss recommendations that all educators can use to work towards this goal.

The different traces my parents attached to the signifiers 'Cuban' and 'Puerto Rican' when discussing their initial impressions of each other's nationalities indicate that individuals might be more aware of the positive qualities of their own nationality than those of other nationalities. Given that attaching positive traces to one group can serve to position individuals from another group as lacking, heterogeneity could have a polarizing effect in the classroom if not adequately acknowledged and addressed. Facilitating students' development of a 'relational identity' (Lee, 2006) with their classmates so that they can teach each other about their cultures and find similarities amongst the cultures should be an objective for all educators working with heterogeneous populations. This can be done by creating classroom spaces where students can learn about the many positive ways they and their peers describe their practices. Using an overarching framework of positive themes (such as resilience, innovation, inquiry, reciprocity, etc.) introduced in succession throughout the year, educators can have students identify and present aspects of their family's practices pertinent to each theme. In this way, all students' household cultures are affirmed, and everyone in the class acquires concrete knowledge about the culture/s of each student, thereby providing opportunities to expand the positive traces that each group associates with its own culture as well as the cultures of their classmates. Moreover, the process of having students choose practices to present that are consistent with particular positive themes not only ensures that their practices are highlighted in favorable ways, but also that students begin to see connections between practices grouped under the same theme but from different cultures.

The differences in terminology my parents used to refer to certain concepts indicate that use of the same language does not necessarily imply homogeneity. Therefore, educators should engage in activities to ensure that language heterogeneity in the classroom, be it as a result of students using different languages or different varieties of the same language, is explored not from a prescriptivist stance but a descriptive and comparative one, without judgement. For example, Baker (2002) has students in her English classes conduct studies of the dialects or "home languages [they]…bring into class" (p. 52) for the purpose of affirming these ways of speaking as well as getting students in the habit of analyzing language patterns and eventually developing understanding of the grammatical rules of "formal language" (p. 59). For the purpose of ensuring students develop positive understandings of the ways that classmates speak, educators can also employ research projects. They could have students explore terms used by their families for particular objects or concepts and then come together under the guidance of the classroom teacher to create semantic maps that help them tease out similarities and distinctions between terms used by each family, as well as the underlying reasons for these similarities and distinctions (for example, in connotations or in context). In the process, students begin to develop a descriptive understanding of language (i.e., that no term or language is considered better than another, but rather a different way of naming something), thus challenging prescriptivist attitudes held by many that certain dialects of a language are "linguistically deficient" (Rolstad, 2005, p. 1996). As my mother understood after marrying my father, it's "the same meaning with a different word"/"el mismo significado con distinta palabra."

Finally, in working to understand the heterogeneity of cultural understandings present in the classroom and finding ways to help build relational identities despite difference, drawing on the expertise already present in intercultural households could prove useful. Literature on cultural brokers has mostly focused on instances in which individuals have introduced aspects of mainstream culture to non-majority groups for the purpose of empowering them to navigate institutions and/or instances in which individuals have explained aspects of non-majority group culture to mainstream institutions for the purpose of ensuring that these minority group members are better supported (Cooper, Denner, & Lopez, 1999; Gentemann & Whitehead, 1983; Martinez-Cosio & Iannacone, 2007; Yohani, 2013). However, individuals in intercultural relationships are capable of serving as cultural brokers in an additional capacity. Because of their intimate knowledge of two non-majority cultures and vested interest in dispelling stereotypes about these cultures, they are well situated to assist educators in cultivating awareness of ways heterogeneity manifests itself in interactions between these cultures. For example, they would be adept at identifying normative categories that members from each cultural group typically ascribe to members of the other group and explaining how these are received by the group being categorized; this information would be particularly helpful in providing context for educators when they are beginning to address the types of heterogeneity present in their classrooms. Individuals in intercultural relationships are also well-suited to assist in spearheading community-building efforts between families from each of these cultures. For example, adult family members can be invited to a session to affirm their own culture and learn more about other cultures present in the school. The session, which would be led in conjunction with a parent who is or has been in a longstanding intercultural relationship, could begin with this parent talking from their own personal experience about normative categories that are usually used to stereotype their own cultural group and the extent to which their own practices diverge from these categories. This would prompt participating family members to start thinking about the stereotypical normative categories that apply to their cultural group. The parent co-leader can then present the stereotypes usually ascribed to their partner's cultural group and explain the positive strengths she has witnessed in that group's practices as a result of interacting with some of its members. Each participant would then be paired with a participant from another cultural group and given instructions to describe to each other the normative categories usually used to stereotype their own cultural group as well as a practice they take part in that diverges from these stereotypes. Time would be provided for participants to ask each other clarifying questions. Each participant would then be asked to describe to the whole group what they learned about the strengths of their pair's culture group from interacting with them. In an effort to promote continuity, the session can conclude by having a group discussion about what participants would tell their children about the culture they learned about if their children were curious about this culture and also what else they wanted to learn about the culture they learned about that day.

References

Abraham, D. (2015, July 23). *The Cuban Adjustment Act of 1966: Past and future.* LexisNexis. https://www.lexisnexis.com/legalnewsroom/immigration/b/immigration-law-blog/archive/2015/07/23/the-cuban-adjustment-act-of-1966-past-and-future.aspx

Anderson, M. (1999). Children in between: Constructing identities in the bicultural family. *The Journal of Royal Anthropological Institute, 5*(1), 13–26.

Baker, J. (2008). Trilingualism. In L. Delpit & J. K. Dowdy (Eds.) *The skin that we speak: Thoughts on language and culture in the classroom* (pp. 49–61). The New Press.

Barrios, P. G., & Egan, M. (2002). Living in a bicultural world and finding the way home: Native women's stories. *Affilia, 17*(2), 206–228.

Blount, B. W., & Curry, A. (1993). Caring for the bicultural family: The Korean-American example. *The Journal of the American Board of Family Practice, 6*(3), 261–268.

Butler, J. (1993). *Bodies that matter: On the discursive limits of "sex".* Routledge.

Butler, J. (2004). *Undoing gender.* Routledge.

Butler, J. (2008). An account of oneself. In B. Davies (Ed.), *Judith Butler in conversation: Analyzing the text and talk of everyday life* (pp. 19–38). Routledge.

Cooper, C. R., Denner, J., & Lopez, E. M. (1999). Cultural brokers: Helping Latino children on pathways toward success. *The Future of Children, 9*(2), 51–57.

Crippen, C., & Brew, L. (2007). Intercultural parenting and the transcultural family: A literature review. *The Family Journal, 15*(2), 107–115.

Darder, A. (2011). Chapter 10: Bicultural identity and the development of voice: Twin issues in the struggle for cultural and linguistic democracy. In A. Darder (Ed.), *A dissident voice: Essays on culture, pedagogy, and power* (pp. 199–212). Counterpoints Series 418. Peter Lang.

Derrida, O. G. (1976). *Of grammatology* (G. C. Spivak, Trans.). Johns Hopkins University Press.

Gentemann, K. M., & Whitehead, T. L. (1983). The cultural broker concept in bicultural education. *The Journal of Negro Education, 52*(2), 118–129.

Jackson, A.Y., & Mazzei, L. A. (2011). *Thinking with theory in qualitative research: Viewing data across multiple perspectives.* Routledge.

Lee, P. W. (2006). Bridging cultures: Understanding the construction of relational identity in intercultural friendship. *Journal of Intercultural Communication Research, 35*(1), 3–22.

Martinez-Cosio, M., & Iannacone, R. M. (2007). The tenuous role of institutional agents: Parent liaisons as cultural brokers. *Education and Urban Society, 39*(3), 349–369.

Molina, B., Estrada, D., & Burnett, J. A. (2004). Cultural communities: Challenges and opportunities in the creation of "happily ever after" stories of intercultural couplehood. *The Family Journal, 12*(2), 139–147.

Montoya, M. E. (1994). Máscaras, trenzas, y greñas: Un/masking the self while un/braiding Latina stories and legal discourse. *Harvard Women's Law Journal, 17*, 185–220.

Moya, P. M. (2002). *Learning from experience: Minority identities, multicultural struggles.* University of California Press.

Novas, H. (2007). *Everything you need to know about Latino history.* Penguin.

O'Hearn, C. C. (1988). *Half and half: Writers on growing up biracial and bicultural.* Random House Inc.

Olivos, E. M. (2006). Chapter two: Bicultural Parents in the Public Schools. In E. M. Olivos (Ed.), *The power of parents: A critical perspective of bicultural parent involvement in public schools* (pp. 13–23). Counterpoint Series, 290. Peter Lang.

Pérez, L. (1986). Cubans in the United States. *The Annals of the American Academy of Political and Social Science, 487*(1), 126–137.

Pooremamali, P., Östman, M., Persson, D., & Eklund, M. (2011). An occupational therapy approach to the support of a young immigrant female's mental health: A story of bicultural personal growth. *International Journal of Qualitative Studies on Health and Well-being, 6*(3), 7084. 10.3402/qhw.v6i3.7084

Riessman, C. K. (2008). *Narrative methods for the human sciences.* SAGE Publications.

Rodríguez, C. E. (1991). *Puerto Ricans: Immigrants and migrants.* AmericansAll.

Rolstad, K. (2005). Rethinking academic language in second language instruction. In J. Cohen, K. T. McAlister, K. Rolstad, & J. MacSwan (Eds.), *ISB4: Proceedings of the 4th International Symposium on Bilingualism* (pp. 1993–1999). Cascadilla Press.

Salinas Jr., C., & Lozano, A. (2017). Mapping and recontextualizing the evolution of the term Latinx: An environmental scanning in higher education. *Journal of Latinos and Education, 18*(4), 1–14.

Sarup, M. (1989). *An introductory guide to post-structuralism and postmodernism.* University of Georgia Press.

Silva, L. C., Campbell, K., & Wright, D. W. (2012). Intercultural relationships: Entry, adjustment, and cultural negotiations. *Journal of Comparative Family Studies, 43*(6), 857–870.

Spivak, G. C. (1976). Translator's preface. In O. G. Derrida (Ed.), *Of grammatology* (pp. ix–lxxxix). Johns Hopkins University Press.

Suárez-Orozco, M., & Páez, M. (2008). Introduction: The research agenda. In M. Suárez-Orozco & M. Páez (Eds.), *Latinos: Remaking America* (pp. 1–38). University of California.

Waldman, K., & Rubalcava, L. (2005). Psychotherapy with intercultural couples: A contemporary psychodynamic approach. *American Journal of Psychotherapy, 59*(3), 227–245.

Wamba, P. (1998). A middle passage. In C. C. O'Hearn (Ed.), *Half and half: Writers on growing up biracial and bicultural* (pp. 150–169). Random House Inc.

Way, N., Santos, C., Niwa, E. Y., & Kim-Gervey, C. (2008). To be or not to be: An exploration of ethnic identity development in context. *New Directions for Child and Adolescent Development, 2008*(120), 61–79.

Yohani, S. (2013). Educational cultural brokers and the school adaptation of refugee children and families: Challenges and opportunities. *Journal of International Migration and Integration, 14*(1), 61–79.

5

UNEARTHING EL ÁRBOL DE MIS RAÍCES AS A FIRST-GENERATION GRADUATE STUDENT

Victoria Hernandez

In my first semester of graduate school as a master's student at Teachers College, Columbia University, exercising my voice and occupying my space was a challenge. While some instructors and peers in my classes perpetuated deficit perspectives about the Latinx community, other professors, administrators, and peers validated my experiences as a Latina first-generation student.

In one of my classes during my first month of graduate school, we were discussing devastating health outcomes, like higher rates of asthma, in working-class communities of color that impact children's performance in school. The professor endorsed the narrative that the parents of these children are to blame for these higher rates of diseases because they lack the formal education and knowledge to seek the appropriate medical attention for their children. The professor did not present an analysis of environmental racism—the reality that toxic facilities are disproportionately concentrated in working-class communities of color, contributing to higher rates of asthma and other chronic diseases. I knew this from my experience as a youth organizer in high school with an environmental justice organization. We engaged with the devastating impact of toxic facilities in Southeast Los Angeles, and I embraced my power to fight for change in my community at a young age. In that class and other spaces at this Ivy League predominantly white institution (PWI), I felt that my funds of knowledge (González, Moll, Tenery, Rivera, Rendon et al., 2005) as a Latina from a working-class immigrant community were not always acknowledged or valued.

My thoughts represented minoritized perspectives given that there were not many Latinx students from working-class backgrounds in most of my classes. Most of my peers were white and from more affluent communities. I often struggled to speak and share my perspectives because they went counter to the dominant narratives that some of my professors and peers perpetuated about communities like mine. I was different from the majority of my peers. My way of speaking and being was different than that of the dominant culture. I was in many spaces that privileged elite, Eurocentric ways of being. Going to class sometimes felt like I was going into battle to defend my voice and represent my community. I frequently felt uncomfortable, anxious, and sick when going to class. I also felt anxious and ill because of a pressure to assimilate into whiteness and adopt other ways of representation and speaking to exist in this institution. I kept going, and merely being present felt like an act of resistance.

I refused to assimilate into someone I was not and found spaces at Teachers College that embraced me and allowed me to be my authentic self. I found professors, peers, and staff that allowed me to share my perspectives that did not align with the dominant viewpoints. In these spaces, I embodied my academic identity, crafted my scholarship, and unearthed my funds of knowledge and pedagogies of the home.

This chapter is a self-narrative qualitative inquiry that examines my *testimonio* as a Latina first-generation student from a working-class community in my first semester of graduate school. The purpose of this critical inquiry is to uncover the funds of knowledge and pedagogies of the home that enabled me to persist through my first semester and eventually thrive in graduate school. The following questions guide my narrative: What personal and educational experiences came with me to Teachers College? How do my lived experiences enable me, a Latina first-generation student from a working-class immigrant family, to persist throughout my first semester of graduate school in an Ivy League PWI?

5.1 Theoretical Perspective: Latina/Chicana Feminist Epistemology

My testimonio is framed by a Latina/Chicana feminist epistemology (LCFE) (Delgado Bernal, 1998, 2002) that allowed me to make sense of my experiences as a Latina first-generation graduate student. LCFE is concerned with the creation of knowledge about Latinas/Chicanas by Latinas/Chicanas. In her seminal work, Delgado Bernal (1998) explained that adopting a Chicana feminist epistemology enables Latinas/Chicanas to "become agents of knowledge who participate in intellectual discourse that links experience, research, community, and social change" (p. 560). This framework centers the voices of Latinas/Chicanas in research and provides analytical lenses to uncover the nuance of our experiences. Using these analytical lenses counters the erasure of our voices within traditional, Eurocentric epistemologies. Delgado Bernal (1998, 2002) and Calderón, Delgado Bernal, Pérez Huber, Malagón, & Vélez (2012) discuss the application of LCFE in education research as resistance to the racism perpetuated through those epistemologies. I highlight central tenets in LCFE—cultural intuition, *nepantla* and borderlands, mestiza consciousness, and pedagogies of the home. I then discuss how Latina/Chicana researchers have used them to frame their narratives.

5.1.1 Cultural Intuition

Adopting a LCFE enables Latina/Chicana researchers to uncover their cultural intuition. Delgado Bernal (1998) argued that Latina/Chicana researchers have unique cultural intuition perspectives, that parallel Strauss and Corbin's (1990) concept of theoretical sensibility, in which their personal experience, existing literature, and professional experience come together in the analytical research process. She built on Strauss and Corbin's understanding by highlighting that community memory, collective experience, and ancestral wisdom—borrowed from Lawrence-Lightfoot (1994)—influence the personal experiences of Latinas/Chicanas. Latina/Chicana feminists have theorized about nepantla, a space of transformation, using their cultural intuition.

5.1.2 Nepantla and Borderlands

LCFE is connected to indigenous knowledge of the Americas. The Nahuatl concept of nepantla is "the space between two bodies of water, the space between two worlds" (Ikas, 2002, p. 13). Existing in nepantla is painful and chaotic, yet the hope remains that the transformation of one's identity, psyche, and reality will arise in this space (Cortez, 2001; Keating, 2006). Nepantla is intricately connected to Anzaldúa's (1987) understanding of the borderlands, "the geographical, emotional, and/or psychological space occupied by mestizas" (Delgado Bernal, 1998, p. 561). Anzaldúa (1987) used self-narrative to share how Latinxs-Chicanxs exist in the borderlands and struggle to straddle multiple cultures. She discussed the perseverance of the languages and knowledges of the borderlands when faced with subjugating forces.

5.1.3 Mestiza Consciousness

Anzaldúa (1987) theorized about mestiza consciousness—a way of thinking, being, and understanding the world—formed in the borderlands, defining it as "the space between the different worlds she inhabits" (p. 42). The mestiza is "in a constant state of mental Nepantilism... la mestiza undergoes a struggle of flesh, a struggle of borders, an inner war" (p. 100). This inner conflict requires the need for coping mechanisms like "a tolerance for contradictions, a tolerance for ambiguity" (p. 101), and the rejection of rigid boundaries in the mestiza's psychological borders. The acceptance of ambiguity and psychological fluidity are pedagogies of the home that Latinas/Chicanas develop in nepantla as we live in between worlds.

5.1.4 Pedagogies of the Home and Funds of Knowledge

Delgado Bernal (2001) materialized mestiza consciousness by discussing the pedagogies of the home—biculturalism, commitment to community, and spiritualities—that Latina/Chicana students implement to navigate PWIs and resist "the daily experiences of sexist, racist and classist microaggressions" (p. 113). Within a LCFE, pedagogies of the home are described as "the communication, practices, and learning that occur in the home and community... [that] often serve as a cultural knowledge base... [and] provide strategies of resistance that challenge the educational norms of higher education" (Delgado Bernal, 2001, p. 113). Pedagogies of the home are connected to funds of knowledge—the bodies of knowledge necessary for survival and resistance (González et al., 2005). Funds of knowledge are "those historically developed and accumulated strategies (skills, abilities, ideas, practices) or bodies of knowledge that are essential to a household's functioning and well-being" (González et al., 2005, pp. 91–92). This knowledge of survival is passed down from generation to generation through testimonio and oral history.

5.1.5 Testimonio

Testimonio is a central decolonizing methodology within a LCFE. Testimonio—with origins in Latin America—is a narrative method and pedagogical tool widely used and ultimately reshaped by Latina/Chicana feminist scholars (Delgado Bernal, Burciaga, & Flores Carmona, 2012). Delgado Bernal et al. (2012) reviewed the work of various Latinas/Chicanas who used testimonios to demonstrate their power as methodological and pedagogical tools. Testimonio centers marginalized voices, alludes to a collective experience, and prompts critical consciousness-raising (Freire, 1973). Testimonio is a process, product, and an approach to sharing knowledge, as well as a bridge between academia and Brown bodies (Delgado Bernal et al., 2012, p. 364). The use of testimonio by Latina/Chicana researchers is a means to capture our stories in writing and reflect upon "collective experiences, political injustices, and human struggles that are often erased by dominant discourses" (Pérez Huber & Cueva, 2012, p. 393). Various Latina/Chicana scholars have used testimonio and interwoven these concepts within a LCFE.

Adopting a LCFE allowed me to ground my self-narrative in the Latina/Chicana experience and led me to construct a testimonio. A LCFE provided me with the understanding to unearth the pedagogies of the home and funds of knowledge that allowed me to persist in graduate school. My testimonio speaks to the collective experiences of Latina first-generation scholars that are often erased from mainstream discourses in academia.

5.2 Literature Review

Sánchez and Ek (2013), Castillo-Montoya and Torres-Guzmán (2012), Prieto and Villenas (2012), and Burciaga and Cruz Navarro (2015) adopted a LCFE to share their testimonios on survival mechanisms that allowed them to overcome challenges in academia. In doing so, they unraveled knowledge that Latinx first-generation students can adopt to be victorious in their scholarly and community-driven passions.

Sánchez and Ek (2013) and Castillo-Montoya and Torres-Guzmán (2012) constructed testimonios to reflect on their experiences as first-generation professors. Sánchez and Ek (2013), two Chicanas with immigrant and working-class roots, uncovered the ancestral paths of resistance and resilience that enabled them to flourish in their doctoral programs at PWIs, where systemic racism and sexism prevailed. They uncovered roles as pathbreakers and access brokers. They highlighted the importance of connecting with other women of color. Castillo-Montoya and Torres-Guzmán (2012), two Puerto Rican women, adopted LCFE and used pedagogies of the home as a lens by which they interpreted their findings—bilingualism, biculturalism, spirituality, *luchas*, and a commitment to communities.

Bilingualism enabled them to pass down *consejos*, "stories, testimonies, or narratives that are a way of transmitting intergenerational knowledge, wisdom, values, and attitudes" (Castillo-Montoya & Torres-Guzmán, 2012, p. 545). Bilingualism also allowed them to frame ideas in multiple ways and not be limited by the confines of one language. Biculturalism, borrowed from Anzaldúa (1987), enabled them to navigate shifting cultures, gain understandings beyond the dominant discourse, and develop a sociopolitical consciousness in the process. They also discuss the role of spirituality as a means of resistance to the racist, sexist, and classist environment found in PWIs. Castillo-Montoya and Torres-Guzmán (2012) found another dimension in their testimonios, lucha—the source of resistance against colonialism. For them, all of these dimensions interact and intersect. Castillo-Montoya and Torres-Guzmán's testimonios emphasized the ability of Latinas to bridge two worlds—academia and Latinx communities. A commitment to Latinx communities kept their scholarship and personal lives grounded.

Also adopting a LCFE, Prieto and Villenas (2012) co-constructed testimonios over the span of two years about their experiences as Latinas training pre-service teachers in PWIs. They created theory out of their practice and uncovered pedagogies from nepantla—*conciencia con compromiso* [consciousness with responsibility/commitment], cultural dissonance, and *cariño*. Conciencia con compromiso emphasizes the immediacy in social justice work, the use of transformative pedagogy, and the development of critical perspectives. Prieto and Villenas conceptualized cultural dissonance, also known as me *retumba la cabeza* [my head resounds], as tensions and contradictions in the academy and family around intersectionalities. They asserted that cultural dissonance can be employed in classrooms to unveil a wealth of knowledge. Lastly, Prieto and Villenas addressed cariño, which refers to an authentic way of caring for each other and their students. Accordingly, they explain that "cariño pays attention to the whole person, including the historical and political struggles in which we are embedded" (p. 424). Cariño in the classroom leads to an embrace of students' personal and collective histories. Prieto and Villenas (2012) highlighted these pedagogies from nepantla in their classroom praxis with the hope of inspiring pre-service teachers to use them with their students.

Similarly, within a different context, Burciaga and Cruz Navarro (2015) reanalyzed their co-constructed narratives and found that educational testimonios can be used as tools for research and critical pedagogy in the classroom. Cruz Navarro, a Latina first-generation college student, took a course with Burciaga, a Latina instructor, in which students were required to reflect on their educational paths through testimonios. They identified educational inequities in their trajectories, helped other students of color understand those inequalities, and as a result, create anti-deficit scholarship. Cruz Navarro recalled the feelings of imposter syndrome and survivor's guilt that also resonated with other first-generation students of color in her class. Her educational testimonio and dialogue with Burciaga and classmates allowed her to identify those feelings and overcome them. Burciaga and Cruz Navarro (2015) redefined mentorship relationships between instructors and students that could be transformative to support first-generation students in academia.

Castillo-Montoya and Torres-Guzmán's (2012) commitment to communities resonates with Prieto and Villenas's (2012) conciencia con compromiso and highlights the centrality that connections to their communities play for first-generation Latinas in academia. Maintaining these strong connections while existing in academia leads to the retumbos de cabeza that Prieto and Villenas (2012) articulate. Their understanding of me retumba la cabeza intersects with the way Cruz Navarro felt like she did not belong in academic spaces while simultaneously feeling guilty for having opportunities in those spaces that were inaccessible to members from her community. Overcoming those feelings facilitated by cariño (Prieto & Villenas, 2012), consejos, and lucha (Castillo-Montoya & Torres-Guzmán, 2012) is part of the resistance that is necessary to persist in academia.

Through the testimonios of these women, I was able to understand collective experiences of Latina first-generation scholars in academia as they relate to me. While there is literature on testimonios of Latina first-generation scholars well into their careers, more self-narratives on first-generation students in the early stages of graduate school are necessary. My testimonio aims to be a contribution to this body of literature.

5.3 Research Design and Methods

I engaged in a self-narrative inquiry and constructed a testimonio that uncovers the funds of knowledge and pedagogies of the home that enabled me to persist through my first semester of graduate school. My qualitative inquiry aligns most with the progressive-radical research tradition (Mullen & Kealy, 2005) because it draws from the work of critical Latina/Chicana scholars that strive to dismantle the power structures that oppress communities of color.

Within this critical narrative inquiry, testimonio is a feminist research method that serves as a tool to bridge the academy and communities of color. It involves self-reflection and a process of sharing knowledge. I constructed my testimonio from journal entries I wrote once a week for eight weeks from September to October in 2016, and personal statements for my college and graduate school applications. I also used a creative work produced in the course "Teaching English in Diverse Social Cultural Environments" as an artifact, which I analyzed with my journal entries.

My analysis consisted of a dialogue with the texts above by Latina/Chicana scholars in the Latina narrative literature. I used thematic analysis to focus on the content of my data because it is a method suitable to examine autobiographies and journal entries (Riessman, 2008). I also implemented a holistic approach (Lieblich, Tuval-Mashiach, & Zilber, 1998) in my analysis to consider my entire narrative. I began by making a note of global impressions, identified salient themes in the text, and recognized emergent patterns. However, a categorical-content approach (Lieblich et al., 1998) was also used to focus the analysis on examining my self-narrative in the contexts of Latina first-generation students in higher education.

5.3.1 Positionality: More About Me

I share more context about myself at the time of this testimonio for the reader to understand my positionality. At the time I started graduate school, I was a 22-year-old mujer from Southeast Los Angeles, California. My mother emigrated from Honduras and my father emigrated from Mexico. I am the youngest of five and the first to earn a bachelor's degree, continue to graduate school, and move away from Los Angeles. My older siblings have earned professional degrees as nurses and attended community college. Growing up, they were not able to focus solely on their studies like I was because they had to help my parents financially. I grew up in a working-class Black and Latinx community of immigrants. Schools in our neighborhood were under-resourced, thus affecting the quality of our K-12 education. I was one of the few among my peers to attend college. I graduated from the University of California, Los Angeles (UCLA), with a degree in International Development Studies and minors in Education and Chicanx Studies. Shortly after graduating, I moved to New York City to pursue a master's degree in International Educational Development with a concentration in Latin American and Latinx Education. I wanted a deeper understanding of the challenges Latinxs face in education and the mechanisms that supported us throughout our educational paths. I hope that my testimonio resonates with other students who may find themselves in similar academic positions.

5.4 My Testimonio

My connection to my ancestors from Mesoamerica, revealed through the conse-jos and cariño my parents passed down to me, gave me the strength and guidance to persist at a PWI. In conversation with texts by Latina/Chicana first-generation scholars, I uncovered the funds of knowledge and pedagogies of the home from my childhood that helped me navigate the labyrinth of academia and find hid-ing places/counterspaces that allowed me to be my authentic self. Subsequently, I found that my ability to navigate the ambiguity of being a Latina first-generation student in academia is based on my experience navigating the space in between worlds—nepantla. One world is the immigrant community I grew up in, and the other is academia—often, where discussions regarding communities like mine are held *about* them instead of *with* them. I discuss these three themes that form my testimonio in the sections that follow, but first I share more about my struggle during my first semester of graduate school.

5.4.1 The Fruits of Engaging in Silence

During my first semester at Teachers College, I did not fully expect nor was I prepared to face the weight of imposter syndrome (Clance & Imes, 1978). I still remember how I felt in my first class on my first day of graduate school. I was one of the only Latinas in a class of mostly white folks with a white professor—a real-ity that led me to question my presence in that classroom. My fellow classmates shared their international work experience. I did not have the luxury of traveling growing up, nor the opportunity to work abroad. I was overtaken with a deep sense that I did not belong there, and I felt like an imposter that was perhaps allowed in that space by mistake. Before I could process that experience, I had to rush to my next class.

I jumped in an elevator that went down to the basement before going up to the third floor where my class was. The doors to the elevator opened and I saw about six or seven Black and Brown custodial workers. We looked into each oth-er's eyes and acknowledged our presence to one another at this institution. I felt seen in a way that I did not in my first class. I could not help but ask myself: Do I belong in the classroom when all the people that look like me at this institution are working with dignity outside of it? I felt heavy by the time I got to my third class for the day and all I wanted to do was run away.

However, my third class for that day was a unique course on "Latina Narratives" where I would ultimately connect with a Latina professor and friends who would embrace me with cariño. These women partnered with me in unearthing the funds of knowledge and pedagogies of the home that helped me realize that my presence at this institution was necessary and not a mistake. This space and others like it at Teachers College provided me with the cariño and tools to process my challenges, bring my full self to the academy, and excavate my testimonio.

One of those tools that allowed me to process the challenges I faced was writing for myself. For the "Latina Narratives" course, I decided to keep a journal to put words to what I was feeling during my first semester of graduate school. On September 29, 2016, I wrote the following:

> I feel silenced, and no one is silencing me except the environment, the system, the institution that sustains white supremacy. White supremacy is invisible to some but hypervisible to me. I'm invisible to the institution. But not to all. Resisting erasure. Silence as a form of resistance?
>
> (Journal entry)

I wrote about feeling silenced and coming face-to-face with white supremacy in higher education. I engaged in a lot of silence during my first semester of graduate school. It was a form of self-preservation and a means to incubate the knowledge I write about on these pages. I was resisting the erasure of my experience, voice, and ultimately, my ancestors.

It is beyond the scope of my testimonio to explain how white supremacy prevails in PWIs because I aspire to decenter whiteness in my work. I am encouraged by Latina/Chicana feminist scholars who built a foundation that allows me to do so. However, I share the point of reference that informed my understanding of white supremacy to help the reader understand my journal entry. Delgado Bernal and Villalpando (2002) helped me understand that "higher education in the United States is founded on a Eurocentric epistemological perspective based on white privilege" (p. 189). I felt that Eurocentric perspectives, white middle-class values, and their forms of expression were privileged and normalized in many spaces at Teachers College, like in that class I shared about in the introduction. It was covert and invisible to many, but it felt violent to me as a young Latina woman from a working-class community because I did not feel safe to express my authentic self in most spaces. To help the reader discern my comprehension of white supremacy in higher education, I borrow from Pérez Huber's (2009) understandings of it:

> White supremacy... goes beyond overt acts of racism and includes the subtle ways whiteness is deemed superior through the acceptance of a racial hierarchy, where whites are consistently ranked above People of Color. This includes the normalization and perceived superiority of Eurocentric beliefs, values, and worldviews.
>
> (p. 651)

I felt that my beliefs, values, and worldviews were deemed inferior in many spaces at Teachers College because it is an institution that I believe was built on Eurocentric worldviews and normalizes them in many ways. At my worst, I felt inferior in those spaces, but I resisted those forces that I felt were pushing me out of the institution, and I engaged in a lot of silence to preserve my being.

It was in my time of silence and prayer that I was emboldened to speak when I needed to share my views. I was encouraged in the spaces created by Black and Latinx women (professors, administrators, and peers) who saw me, resonated with my experience, and affirmed me. I acknowledge that Teachers College is taking steps to decenter whiteness because of the spaces that existed, like my "Latina Narratives" and "Teaching English" course, that equipped me with the tools to write and share.

5.4.2 El Árbol de Mis Raíces y la Lucha de Salir Adelante Poquito a Poquito

Another tool was to engage in deep reflection about my life through creative expression, which allowed me to unearth *el Árbol de mis Raíces*. At the beginning of my first semester, I did a "what do you see in the mirror" creative activity in my Teaching English course (see Table 5.1).

In one of the three images, I drew a tree with deep roots and expanding branches as a symbol of my humbling yet empowering experience of being in graduate school after all the sacrifices of my family in California, Honduras, and Mexico. Later in the semester, I went on to paint an image of the tree I had initially drawn—a cathartic process that allowed me to transcend time and space to feel connected to my ancestors (Figure 5.1).

I named the painting *El Árbol de Mis Raíces y la Lucha de Salir Adelante Poquito a Poquito* (The Tree of My Roots and the Fight to Move Forward Little by Little). As I struggled to claim my space and voice at Teachers College, I continuously reminded myself of who brought me there in the first place. Through deep reflection, prayer, powerful reading, and necessary conversations with women of color at Teachers College, I gained a deeper understanding of myself, my roots, and my journey of becoming an anti-racist educator. Painting this tree during my first semester showed me that through a recognition of my ancestral knowledge and commitment to dive deeper into my past, which shapes my future, I was also on a journey to reignite the fire that brought me there. I realized that my fire is ignited by my ancestors.

TABLE 5.1 The product of the "What do you see in the mirror" creative activity.

What do you see in the mirror?	I see a brown girl, brown eyes, cute glasses
	I see a girl that wasn't supposed to be here but is.
What do you want to tell the girl in the mirror?	You DESERVE to be here! Why is it so hard for you to understand? Your presence in this space is important. Share those hidden treasures.
Draw three images that represent you:	

FIGURE 5.1 The author's painting, titled *El árbol de mis raíces y la lucha de salir adelante poquito a poquito / The Tree of My Roots and the Fight to Move Forward Little by Little.*

My experiences growing up in Southeast Los Angeles and my parents' ancestral past inspired me to pursue graduate school. My father grew up in a poor agrarian family in el rancho del Durazno in the Mexican state of Hidalgo. My abuelita Victoria was unable to provide for all her children, given that my abuelito Benito passed away when my father was two years old. Therefore, at the age of seven, my father was sent to live with my bisabuelos, and they enrolled him in school for the first time. Every day, my father walked a long distance to the nearest primary school to then come home to help my bisabuelos take care of their farm. As my bisabuelos got older, my father had to leave school to work more and help them financially. He studied up to the sixth grade. Nonetheless, he received an education at home. My abuelita Victoria and bisabuelos taught him to always be humble, kind, honest, generous, and hard-working—values that he would later pass down to me and my siblings. At the age of 17, he left el rancho to work in major cities across Mexico. At the age of 23, he decided to embark on the journey north to the United States in search of better job opportunities. His intentions were to work in the United States, save money, and return to Mexico, but then he met my mother and they started a family. Understandably, my father wanted educational opportunities for my siblings and me that were not offered to him growing up. Therefore, my father and mother built a life in Los Angeles to raise us.

My mother grew up in Potrerillos, a small and impoverished (but rich in spirit) town near San Pedro Sula, Honduras. She also had to work from an early age to help my abuelita Rosa, given that my abuelito Martin left them for 11 years. Even though my mother had to work, my abuelita Rosa always emphasized the importance of pursuing a formal education and put my mother through school. Abuelita Rosa taught mami how to hustle and salir adelante with the resources at their disposal. My mother graduated from high school, became a secretary for the Palacio Municipal, and with her earnings, helped my abuelita Rosa put her younger sisters, my tías, through school—a similar feat my older siblings would later do for me. Mami got married in Honduras, had my two older sisters, and ultimately separated from her husband. Mami also embarked on the journey north to the United States in search of a new beginning and economic opportunities to continue supporting my abuelita Rosa and tías, who were going to school to become teachers. Mami met papi, they started a family, and she later sent for my older sisters in Honduras to be brought to the United States. My sisters were very studious and focused on pursuing an education; they were role models for me.

Mami wasted no time and enrolled me in a Head Start program at the age of three. She volunteered at my preschool, and since I can remember, I loved learning and was always very engaged in school. My parents always emphasized the importance of pursuing an education, and they placed their dreams and hopes in me and my siblings. The difference between my siblings and me was that I was the youngest and did not face the same responsibility to help my parents make a living. My job was to *echarle ganas* and do well in school—a sentiment that stays with me until this day. Mami y papi, mis abuelitas, and mis bisabuelos inspired me to persist throughout my education, especially when it became difficult in college. I felt the weight of their dreams and hopes on me, the driving force that fueled me to pursue graduate school.

I did not fully expect to feel uprooted by living so far away from my home and family in Los Angeles. Thankfully, my cultural intuition led me to my "Latina Narratives" course and "Teaching English in Diverse Social Cultural Environments" course. It was in these spaces that I gained a deeper appreciation of my ancestral past and developed a new understanding of home. Anzaldúa (1987) reminded me that my ancestors are with me and that they speak when I speak when she wrote:

> To separate from my culture (as from my family) I had to feel competent enough on the outside and secure enough inside to live life on my own. Yet in leaving home I did not lose touch with my origins because *lo mexicano* is in my system. I am a turtle, wherever I go I carry "home" on my back.
>
> (p. 43)

After meditating on this text, I realized my ancestors from Mesoamerica are with me and led me here. This understanding prompted in me the desire to operate out of the authority that they bestow upon me to speak our truth. It took me going away from home to realize that I carry home on my back. My roots that expand across Mesoamerica come with me. I strived to bring all of who I am and what I represent into an environment that overwhelmingly urged me to assimilate into whiteness. I think I always knew this, but I was not fully operating out of this knowledge during my first semester. I began to set roots in New York City and allowed people in those two courses to be part of my testimonio. I came to the understanding that this land was not intended to have borders, and our movements across the Americas is in my ancestral past, my roots. *El Árbol de Mis Raíces* represents this body of knowledge that was necessary for my survival and resistance at a PWI.

My analysis and deep reflection also revealed how the *dichos* passed down by my family have encouraged me throughout my education. These dichos carry wisdom that has encouraged our family for generations. I want to emphasize one of the dichos that my parents shared ever since I can remember: "Diosito no los abandona, salimos adelante poquito a poquito" [God doesn't abandon us, we move forward little by little]. No matter the obstacles, trials, and tribulations my parents faced, they never lost hope and continued fighting poquito a poquito. This practice of giving consejos is rooted in the funds of knowledge my abuelitas and bisabuelos passed down as they survived. Whereas Prieto and Villenas (2012) address cariño as part of their classroom pedagogy, my testimonio reveals the cariño ancestral that has been passed down through consejos and words of wisdom uttered by mi mami, tías, y abuelita. This fund of knowledge led me to graduate school and enabled me to persist through my first semester. One of the challenges I persisted through was learning how to navigate the labyrinth of academia.

5.4.3 Finding "Hiding Places"/Counterspaces to Navigate the Labyrinth of Academia

My reflections and analysis revealed parallels between what I experienced as a little girl growing up in Southeast Los Angeles and my experience in graduate school. As my cultural intuition guided me to revisit my college application essays, I discovered a pedagogy of the home—finding hiding spaces—that I used to navigate my childhood and graduate school later on. The excerpt below from a college admissions essay I wrote as a 17-year-old provides an example of how the world I come from, of immigrants, informs my ability to navigate graduate school—a different world.

> At seven, I remember running through the mazes created by tall towers of pallets, trying to find hiding places while my father and brothers, ages ten and twelve, worked. I loved the weekends when my brothers would help my father; I would tag along to play in my father's pallet yard. I witnessed how hard they worked. Although it was a time for me to play, I soon began to feel responsible to help. I went around the yard gathering nails from the floor with a magnet and put them in a bucket for my father to recycle. After these work days I felt tired and hungry, yet accomplished and satisfied, as my father did when he would take a moment to admire his and his sons' hard work,

reflected in his truck bed full of tall stacks of pallets. My world showed me that I had to work hard for what I wanted. My father instilled the importance of education in us, and the need for us to take advantage of the opportunities available here, opportunities never offered to him in his home country. I learned that school would take me far in life… I realized, the same way I went around picking up nails with a magnet as a child, I have to pick up different qualities, lessons, and experiences from life and put them in my personal bucket, not just to get into college, but to go to a university of my choice and succeed. I have to keep working hard.

Although I loved my life, I looked for hiding places as a child because it was hard growing up in a household with stress inflicted by scarcity. As I did when I was a child in my father's pallet yard, I tried to find hiding places in graduate school. In these hiding places I felt safe to relax, play, reflect, and not be overwhelmed by my reality. Similarly, during my first semester of graduate school I found counterspaces where I could bring the entirety of who I am and embrace my truest self. I found these spaces working in the Institute for Urban and Minority Education (IUME), in my "Latina Narratives" and "Teaching English" courses, and with the family I gained as a student organizer in the Coalition of Latinx Scholars (CLS). In these spaces, I was treated with cariño and I felt safe and seen.

Meanwhile, in the larger Teachers College environment, I felt anxiety from the lack of acknowledgment of my internal struggles. I dealt with feelings of unbelonging and erasure in a PWI that I believe has been historically racist and classist. The counterspaces I found at Teachers College allowed me to reflect on my identity and the significance of my presence at an institution that I felt did not fully embrace me. It was not created with women of color in mind. These counterspaces gave me the platform to speak and have my voice be heard. I discovered a strong connection to my home and childhood in the hiding places I found within the labyrinth of academia.

The excerpt from my college essay captures a snippet of my childhood and provides insight into the world I come from. It addressed the reality of many immigrant parents from my community, who labored from sunrise to sunset in order to provide for their families in the United States and Latin America. This excerpt highlights the fruits of my father and brothers' labor—the material that would put food on our plates, a roof over our head, and clothes on our backs. Pallet-making is still my father's livelihood and it fueled my aspiration as a student organizer to make tall towers that welcomed other first-generation graduate students of color, all in the hope that the towers I raised in academia would bring visibility to those Latinx families across the United States on whose backs we, Latina students from working-class communities, stand. I stand because of their labor and perseverance. If I brought all of who I am to the forefront, my presence at Teachers College would bring visibility to the stories of immigrant workers, like my parents, who are cast to the shadows. My family is here with me.

Their fight for survival continues with me. A deep understanding of my life growing up gave me the willingness to persevere and fight to continue my studies at Teachers College. The sense of responsibility to continue my education that I felt as a child came with me and kept me in graduate school.

I partnered with IUME and CLS to create more spaces for other first-generation students of color to feel supported at Teachers College. I soon realized that I was not grappling with feelings of unbelonging and erasure alone but that other students of color felt similarly. We exercised our agency and committed to transforming the institution poquito a poquito by advocating for the needs of students of color and supporting the marriage of our cultural identities and academic identities (meanwhile decentering whiteness). We shared resources and partnered with staff at Teachers College to bridge the divide between communities like mine and academia. We created spaces that centered cariño and celebrated our funds of knowledge and pedagogies of the home. In doing so, we carved out more spaces to unapologetically integrate them into our scholarship and the fabric of Teachers College.

My parents were never fully embraced in this country and they learned how to traverse that reality. However, this country embraced me to a further extent and provided me with opportunities to pursue my education that would not be offered to me in Mexico or Honduras. Growing up, my family was always in a state of uncertainty because of financial instability. There was also a constant state of ambiguity as we bridged Mexican, Honduran, and U.S. cultures. I learned to navigate that constant uncertainty and ambiguity during childhood, which helped me navigate graduate school. Through this reflective process, I also discovered the central role of biculturalism in my educational trajectory and my existence in nepantla.

5.4.4 Becoming at Home in Nepantla, the Borderlands

A profoundly embedded mestiza consciousness and biculturalism enabled me to navigate nepantla and build mechanisms that bridged my world growing up and the world of academia. As I dove into the literature by Latina/Chicana feminists (Anzaldúa, 1987; Castillo-Montoya & Torres-Guzmán, 2012; Delgado Bernal, 2001), I found the language and understanding to make sense of my biculturalism—a pedagogy of the home used by other Latinas to navigate academia. Growing up in Los Angeles, I had to navigate Honduran, Mexican, and U.S cultures. Going to college was my first extensive experience outside of the Latinx bubble I grew up in. At UCLA, Latinxs were part of the minority. I realized that my biculturalism allowed me to navigate multiple cultures at UCLA, graduate, and set myself on a path to graduate education. The excerpt below from my journal reveals the process I underwent to make sense of my biculturalism and existence in-between worlds at Teachers College.

No soy ni de aquí, ni de allá, ni de hasta alla. ¿De donde soy? ¿De donde vengo? ¿Quien soy? ¿Que es mi propósito? Soy de Honduras, soy de Mexico, y soy de California. ¿Y qué es el significado de eso? Sí soy de aquí, y de allá, y de hasta alla!!

I am not from here, nor from there, nor from beyond there. Where am I from? Where do I come from? Who am I? What is my purpose? I am from Honduras, I am from Mexico, and I am from California. And what is the significance of that? Yes, I am from here, and from there, and from beyond there!!

The first few lines illustrate how I felt that I was not from anywhere and that I was lost in between worlds—nepantla, the borderlands (Anzaldúa, 1987). This sentiment originates from never feeling American growing up or fully Honduran and Mexican because I had never been to either place until I was 18. Existing in nepantla was a struggle because I questioned where I came from, who I was, and what my purpose was at an institution where not many people looked like me. I had an existential crisis during my first semester of graduate school. I was far away from my geographical home and family and found myself in an unfamiliar place.

Although I struggled to come to grips with my reality, my journal reflections reveal how I became at home in nepantla and it ultimately served as a bridge between my world and the world of a PWI. As I found counterspaces that allowed me to unearth the funds of knowledge and pedagogies of the home from my community, I was able to bring my full self to Teachers College. This came with embracing my role as a bridge in between worlds. My home transcends space. In nepantla, I find my roots in Honduras, Mexico, across Mesoamérica y Los Angeles, and now New York City. With me come my cultures and experiences from all these geographical locations. In the borderlands, my identity is affirmed along with a confidence and authority in my being.

5.5 Conclusions and Implications

The reading and writing process for my testimonio was a spiritual and healing journey for me that allowed me to deeply understand my experience as a Latina first-generation graduate student. A reflexión of what came with me to Teachers College and enabled me to persist in higher education turned into a deeper connection with my roots and ancestors. On a journey to make sense of my experiences during my first semester of graduate school, I discovered a deeper connection to my funds of knowledge and pedagogies of the home. I realized that my past is in me, runs through me, and is part of my future. This became a testimonio of my educational journey and beyond. Through reading other Latina/Chicana scholars, engaging in reflection, and writing my testimonio, I gained so much clarity about my experiences throughout my life and in graduate school. This process was only possible because of the cariño that Black and Latinx professors, staff, and peers embraced me with within counterspaces, including the classroom.

Testimonios go beyond the self and have a fundamental connection to the communities the researcher comes from. I engaged in this process as an emergent Latina researcher constructing a critical narrative inquiry. I hope that my testimonio is also relevant to other Latina women who identify with the first-generation academic experience. Sánchez and Ek's (2013) testimonios reveal how first-generation women of color in the academy develop mechanisms of resistance and resilience. Similarly, during my first semester of graduate school, I cultivated mechanisms of resistance and resilience, and uncovered my role as a pathbreaker as I partnered with CLS to demystify graduate school for other first-generation students. Testimonio as a method led me to carefully examine the factors that allowed me to persist and resist the factors that I felt were pushing me out of academia.

Professors and teachers serving Latina first-generation college students (aspiring and current) can take away from my testimonio the importance of narrative creation and sharing in their classrooms that unearths their students' funds of knowledge and pedagogies of the home. Narrative writing can reveal to their Latina students the tools that they already possess, perhaps without realizing, that will allow them to persist in PWIs. Narrative writing, by way of a course or unit, allows students' lived experiences to inform the curriculum and also provides space for healing to occur in the classroom for historically marginalized communities. Teachers can center cariño in their classrooms. They can use the work of Latina/Chicana feminist writers to cultivate spaces that allow their Latina students to be empowered to persist and thrive throughout their educational journeys.

References

Anzaldúa, G. (1987). *Borderlands: La frontera.* Aunt Lute.

Burciaga, R., & Cruz Navarro, N. (2015). Educational testimonio: Critical pedagogy as mentorship. *New Directions for Higher Education, 2015*(171), 33–41. https://doi.org/10.1002/he.20140.

Calderón, D., Delgado Bernal, D., Pérez Huber, L., Malagón, M., & Vélez, V. N. (2012). A Chicana feminist epistemology revisited: Cultivating ideas a generation later. *Harvard Educational Review, 82*(4), 513–539.

Castillo-Montoya, M., & Torres-Guzmán, M. E. (2012). Thriving in our identity and in the academy: Latina epistemology as a core resource. *Harvard Educational Review, 82*(4), 540–558.

Clance, P. R., & Imes, S. A. (1978). The imposter phenomenon in high achieving women: Dynamics and therapeutic intervention. *Psychotherapy: Theory, Research & Practice, 15*(3), 241.

Cortez, C. (2001). The new Aztlán: Nepantla (and other sites of transmogrification). In V. M. Fields & Z. Taylor (Eds.), *The road to Aztlán: Art from a mythic homeland* (pp. 358–373). Los Angeles County Museum of Art.

Delgado Bernal, D. (1998). Using a Chicana feminist epistemology in educational research. *Harvard Educational Review, 68*(4), 555–579.

Delgado Bernal, D. (2001). Learning and living pedagogies of the home: The mestiza consciousness of Chicana students. *International Journal of Qualitative Studies in Education*, *14*(5), 623–639.

Delgado Bernal, D. (2002). Critical race theory, Latino critical theory, and critical raced-gendered epistemologies: Recognizing students of color as holders and creators of knowledge. *Qualitative Inquiry*, *8*(1), 105–126.

Delgado Bernal, D., Burciaga, R., & Flores Carmona, J. (2012). Chicana/Latina testimonios: Mapping the methodological, pedagogical, and political. *Equity & Excellence in Education*, *45*(3), 363. https://doi.org/10.1080/10665684.2012.698149

Delgado Bernal, D., & Villalpando, O. (2002). An apartheid of knowledge in academia: The struggle over the "legitimate" knowledge of faculty of color. *Equity & Excellence in Education*, *35*(2), 169–180.

Freire, P. (1973). *Education for critical consciousness* (Vol. 1). Bloomsbury Publishing.

González, N., Moll, L. C., Tenery, M. F., Rivera, A., Rendon, P., Gonzales, R., & C. Amanti. (2005). Funds of knowledge for teaching in Latino households. In N. Gonzalez, L. C. Moll, & C. Amanti (Eds.), *Funds of knowledge: Theorizing practices in households, communities and classrooms* (pp. 89–111). Lawrence Erlbaum.

Ikas, K. R. (2002). *Chicana ways: Conversations with ten Chicana writers*. University of Nevada Press.

Keating, A. L. (2006). From borderlands and new mestizas to nepantlas and nepantleras: Anzaldúan theories for social change. *Human Architecture: Journal of the Sociology of Self-Knowledge*, *4*(3), 5–16.

Lawrence-Lightfoot, S. (1994). *I've known rivers: Lives of loss and liberation*. Penguin Books.

Lieblich, A., Tuval-Mashiach, R., & Zilber, T. (1998). *Narrative research: Reading, analysis, and interpretation*. SAGE Publications.

Mullen, C. A., & Kealy, W. A. (2005). Pathlamp: A self-study guide for teacher research. In C. Mitchell, S. Weber, & K. O'Reilly-Scanlon (Eds.), *Just who do we think we are: Methodologies for autobiography and self-study in teaching* (pp. 154–167). Routledge Falmer.

Pérez Huber, L. (2009). Disrupting apartheid of knowledge: Testimonio as methodology in Latina/o critical race research in education. *International Journal of Qualitative Studies in Education*, *22*(6), 639–654.

Pérez Huber, L., & Cueva, B. M. (2012). Chicana/Latina testimonios on effects and responses to microaggressions. *Equity & Excellence in Education*, *45*(3), 392–410. https://doi.org/10.1080/10665684.2012.698193

Prieto, L., & Villenas, S. A. (2012). Pedagogies from nepantla: Testimonio, Chicana/Latina feminisms and teacher education classrooms. *Equity & Excellence in Education*, *45*(3), 411–429. https://doi.org/10.1080/10665684.2012.698197

Riessman, C. K. (2008). *Narrative methods for the human sciences*. SAGE Publications.

Sánchez, P., & Ek, L. D. (2013). Before the tenure track: Graduate school testimonios and their importance in our profesora-ship today. *Educational Foundations*, *27*(1/2), 15–30.

Strauss, A., & Corbin, J. (1990). *Basics of qualitative research: Grounded theory procedures and techniques*. SAGE Publications.

PART II
Mobilizing Places and Voice
Authoring Linguistic and Academic Identities

6

RECLAIMING LA LENGUA

A Self-Narrative on Language Loss, Learning, and Identity

Marisol Cantú

6.1 The Beginning: Vignette 1

> I am Mexican, I am American, I am Latina. Throughout my life, I did not actually know who I was, second guessing every thought, every action, every lie, every truth because of the society I was born into. The society that stripped my grandmother's tongue and bruised her hand when she tried to use it. The society that imperialized, colonized, and erased, the home of the free and the brave, the United States that is.
>
> —Marisol Cantú

I am Noell Marisol Cantú, born in the San Francisco Bay Area and raised as a Mexican American by my father, Noel Cantú, and mother, Guadalupe Fragozo. On my paternal side, I identify myself as a fifth-generation Mexican American, and on my maternal side, a third-generation Mexican American. After my family being in the United States for five generations, I have come to summarize their historical-sociolinguistic narrative with one sentence: The borders moved on us and erased the Spanish language de mi familia. The linguistic terror or erasure of Spanish, mentioned by Anzaldúa (1987), had crept its way into a small primary school in California.

In 1950, my grandmother stepped into a primary school in California where bilingual education was nonexistent in her district. She attended an English-only school, which prohibited Spanish speaking children from using their only or main form of linguistic communication. When my grandmother spoke Spanish to classmates to gain understanding of content in her classroom, she was punished. In one startling memory, my grandmother recalls being hit on the hand with a ruler by a teacher for using Spanish, changing the course of her language learning trajectory forever. The shared lived experience by other Spanish-speaking children prompted linguistic assimilation from their heritage language of Spanish to the dominant language of English. By the time my grandmother entered middle school, she was forced to only speak Spanish with her parents in the confines of her own home. The relationship between her Mexican identity and the Spanish language had warped into a fully acculturated citizen of the United States. The educational system had succeeded; English became my grandmother's primary mode of communication. Moreover, I paid the price of my grandmother's assimilation as I lost my heritage language and part of my identity along the way.

In this chapter, I share my story of Spanish language loss in my family and subsequently my heritage language learning, both entangled in my bicultural identity. I explore the journal entries I kept over a year during my acquisition of Spanish and a self-written memoir of my paternal grandmother. The research questions guiding my inquiry are: How do the narratives of a granddaughter and grandmother inform the relationship of intergenerational language loss, identity, and erasure in the United States' educational system? Furthermore, how might the process of heritage language learning in educational institutions become a tool to combat erasure? The purpose of the paper is to better understand intergenerational experiences related to identity, language acquisition, and language loss, and how they can be shaped by bilingual pedagogical practices in schools. From my grandmother's experiences of being punished with a ruler by a teacher for speaking Spanish, to my efforts to recover my heritage language, my findings describe how I reclaimed the ruler through language. The results may encourage teachers to build more multicultural, inclusive pedagogies and inform school administrators of the need to support bilingual education, English as a second language, and heritage language programs.

6.2 Theoretical Perspectives

Critical Race Theory (CRT) and Latino Critical Theory (LatCrit) lay the theoretical foundation for this study. Deriving from the field of law, CRT and LatCrit allow researchers to examine the importance of laws within the historical-socio-political context in order to dismantle their racialized underpinnings. I see these frameworks as critical lenses to address the multitude of cultural and linguistic experiences of Latinos within the U.S. educational system.

One example of how the educational system has played an active role in Latinos' language experiences has been their systematic efforts to strip indigenous and minoritized communities of their culture (Spring, 2001). In California, "an 1870 statute required English as the sole language of instruction in both public and private schools," an example of how English-only ideology forces acculturation and assimilation of immigrants and indigenous peoples through the acquisition of English. In 1923, the U.S. Supreme Court decision of *Meyer vs. Nebraska* outlawed the teaching of languages other than English nationally. Consequently, in the 1920s, segregation of Mexican students in California was a common practice due to white parents' fear of the educational retardation of their children (Valdés, Fishman, Chávez, & Pérez, 2006). This practice was justified on linguistic grounds with the reasoning that Mexican children needed special educational programs and specialized instruction for English acquisition (Valdés et al., 2006). Spring (2001), a prominent scholar of the history of education, talks about these processes as deculturalization, "the educational process of destroying a people's culture and replacing it with a new culture" (p. 4).

According to scholars Valdés et al. (2006), the U.S. position has been to continually ignore the non-English-language resources and to "assume that the loss of ethnic languages is part of the price to be paid for becoming American" (p. 2). In essence, English-only schools were responsible for acculturating young Spanish-speaking students through school practices that were demeaning and a form of erasure to students' heritage language practices. Anzaldúa (1987) defines a process that leads to the loss of a person's mother language as linguistic terrorism; this linguistic violence for Latinos in the United States involves the erasure of Spanish. The loss of Spanish has been the source of challenging identity struggles and harsh linguistic experiences for many Mexican Americans amongst other Hispanics/Latino Americans. The lawful but detrimental practices performed within the U.S. educational system to Latino children need to be transformed.

In the 1970s, legal scholars and activists interested in studying and transforming the relationship between race, racism, and power within the United States began Critical Race Theory as a theoretical movement. Within the education field, CRT helps to closely examine racial injustices impacting students of color. Educational research should evoke CRT as a framework because it highlights how the inequalities within the U.S. educational system are historically, racially, and socially constructed. Solórzano (1998) proposes five elements to consider when conducting educational research with a CRT lens. These elements include: the importance of transdisciplinary approaches, an emphasis on experiential knowledge, challenging dominant ideologies of knowledge, the centrality of race and racism and their intersectionality with other forms of subordination, and a commitment to social justice.

An offshoot of CRT is Latino Critical Race Theory (LatCrit). LatCrit elucidates Latinas/Latinos' multidimensional identities and can address the intersectionality of racism, sexism, classism, and other forms of oppression (Delgado Bernal, 2002, p. 108). This intersectionality allows for a unique perspective in examining how race, sex, class, national origin, and sexual orientation intersect and create a multiconsciousness for Latina women (Delgado, Stefancic & Liendo, 2012, p. 57). For this study, I use LatCrit as a way to add dimensionality to the narratives of my grandmother and myself while situating and analyzing them within the historical-sociopolitical context of the U.S. educational system.

6.3 Literature Review

Language and ethnicity are pillars of a person's identity. To lose one's language is to lose one's sense of self. As Balderrama (2011) and Nieto (1992) remind us, language is directly tied to the concepts of identity and individuality. Language ideological discourses shape how minoritized groups develop and negotiate beliefs and attitudes towards the learning and use of a language (Martínez-Roldán & Malavé, 2004, p. 161). Kroskrity, Schieffelin, and Woolard (1998) define language ideology as a concept that characterizes any set of beliefs or feelings about languages as used in their social worlds. Language ideologies inform a person's identity through association of certain types of meanings with a use of a particular language (Kroskrity et al., 1998). Language ideologies thus are the basis for assumptions about language shared by a particular group of speakers. In essence, how one thinks about language will dictate how a person practices it. An educator's beliefs or feelings about language will influence his or her pedagogical practices, thus impacting a student's linguistic identity. In this literature review, I examine how language ideologies directly and indirectly impact the discourse of bilingual practices in the U.S. educational system. The three areas of focus are language loss, identity, and heritage language learning.

6.3.1 Language Loss

Language ideologies function in the context of power struggles among different groups, for instance, immigrants and English-only groups in the United States (Martínez-Roldán & Malavé, 2004, p. 161). English-only ideology is the idea and belief that English is superior to all languages. In the United States, where English-only ideologies are most prevalent, the educational system forces acculturation and devalues Spanish and language varieties spoken by Latinos, including Spanglish and Chicano Spanish (Showstack, 2018). These ideologies manifest into real practices in the classroom and have real consequences for Latino students; English-only ideologies influence bilingual policies. Suárez-Orozco and Suárez-Orozco (2001) state that bilingual education has had strong critics since its initial legislation citing the cost of bilingual programs as too high. They explain that "critics fear that teaching children in a language other than English will undermine the American culture and doom students to academic failure, eventually handicapping them in the job market" (p. 140). The narrative collections in *Words Were All We Had* by Reyes (2011) portray the harsh realities of Latino students being silenced or punished for speaking Spanish in the classroom, as my grandmother was, due to English-only ideologies. One recollection by Mexican-American teacher John Halcón (2011) shares how he was made to stand by a chain fence in 90-degree weather as a punishment for speaking Spanish as a young child. The narratives of Halcón and my grandmother are not isolated events, but mainstream practices by teachers to disarm students of their mother tongue. It is imperative to be aware of and examine the language ideologies and beliefs reflected in our practices as educators because the implications can be severe. One consequence of English-only ideologies that led to language loss has been described as the "third-generation pattern."

The "third-generation pattern" explains the phenomenon of non-English languages in the United States being lost by or during the third-generation of a family. This acculturation pattern was first introduced by sociolinguist Joshua Fishman (1972) as the three-generation process of Anglicization, and he described this language shift as occurring historically in the following ways: The first-generation of immigrants in the United States learn English to 'survive'; however, they prefer to communicate in their native language. The second-generation, children of these immigrants, learn English in school and become bilingual but prefer to speak English. By the third generation, grandchildren of these immigrants are monolingual and have fragmented knowledge of their ancestral language. The largest language shift occurs within this third generation, whose parents are U.S.-born.

According to the Pew Research Center, in a report based on six surveys conducted over the span of four years, the analysis shows 65% of first-generation Hispanic adults say they speak little or no English. By the second-generation, 88% of Hispanic adults say they speak English very well. The amount of Latino adults who speak English very well increases to 94% by the third-generation (Hakimzadeh & Cohn, 2007). In addition, in an analysis of the 1990 and 2000 U.S. Census Data, Alba, Logan, Lutz, & Stults (2002) found a major percentage, 60–70%, of third-generation Hispanics speak only English at home. These findings support the dominant pattern of the third-generational language shift within Spanish-speaking groups. Some factors noted by Alba et al. that lead to this third-generational pattern are parental education, marriage type, and Spanish-speaking relatives in the home. It is critical to consider that this shift in language is not a natural phenomenon but a result of historical-sociopolitical forces at play. One of the driving forces is the dominant discourse in the United States that English is the only way, or English is the "American" way. Unfortunately, school systems perpetuate this vicious pattern of monoglossic language ideology, which impacts a person's identity, as my narrative shows.

6.3.2 Identity

Fanon and Sartre (1963) posit that loss of language disorients those who have lost their language and are forced, by circumstances or violence, to adopt another. Thus language loss involves much more than the loss of a medium of communication and linguistic symbols and codes. Fishman (1991) posits that "The destruction of a language is the destruction of a rooted identity" (p. 4). Individuals have an innate emotional and spiritual connection to their mother or ancestral tongue (Fishman, 1989). According to Ngũgĩ wa Thiong'o (1986), to lose one's language is to lose one's identity because language is a transmitter of a people's culture. He goes on to explain how a people's culture is made of their values, the foundation of their consciousness. The relationship of language and identity, at its core, has psycho-sociocultural dimensions. Language and identity are pillars of a person's social condition. Fishman (1989) states "For most of humanity most of the time, the 'social condition' calls for both language and ethnicity" (p. 48). Losing a language means the potential losing of a philosophy of life and a world-view. It means a potential loss of identity, culture, and social memory.

6.3.3 Spanish as a Heritage Language

Despite the historical and sociopolitical efforts of the United States to discount the diverse linguistic resources of its citizens, Valdés et al. (2006) high-light the increased interest in the teaching of indigenous, immigrant, ancestral, or heritage languages of educators and non-teaching professionals. Heritage language learning is the practice of learning a language (other than the "dominant" language) from those whose family historically spoke the language or from an ethnolinguistic group that traditionally speaks the language (Valdés et al., 2006).

The seminal piece, *Borderlands/La Frontera*, by Anzaldúa (1987) speaks to the transcultural practices of growing up as a Chicana in Texas and how she refused to lose her native language of Spanish. This language maintenance, or continued use of an indigenous or immigrant minority language in a majority context, seeks to reverse the language loss of Spanish; however, the task is a difficult one. Fishman (2006) poignantly states that "if Spanish as an HL [heritage language] is to become what it should be, both for the country as a whole and for the Hispanic community in particular, it needs to become a youth movement rather than just a school course-sequence, and it must seriously pursue, attain, and maintain home, school and community outreach" (p. 9). Clearly, there is a demand for our educational system to invest in bilingual education programs and practices to directly impact how students learn Spanish as a heritage language and develop their linguistic identities. Bilingual practices have the potential to combat language loss, promote Spanish use in the classroom, and impact students' cultural identities.

6.4 Research Methods and Design

The primary source of data in this study is a personal narrative, documented through journal entries, and a written memoir of my grandmother, Lydia Hernandez Cantu. Narratives in research provide a practical means for a narrator to construct and shape their lived experience while making meaning as an active agent. By incorporating a social context, temporality, and reflections, narratives can provide insight into identity construction (Riessman, 2008). Narratives of personal experiences help us understand how the deculturalization process is still taking place in schools and how people are fighting it. The use of a narrative in this research design is intentional because of the power it holds. As Riessman (2008) proposes, individuals use the narrative form to remember, argue, justify, persuade, and engage (p. 8). A narrative is the telling of stories that are situated in a certain time, place, and perspective that allows the research to make connections to larger systemic issues. Riessman posits, "Connecting biography and society becomes possible through the close analysis of stories" (p. 10). Hence, stories help situate a person's meaning-making within historical-sociopolitical contexts that trace larger systemic problems within a society.

6.4.1 Thematic Analysis

For this study, the data was analyzed through thematic and structural analysis. Thematic analysis focuses on what is being told, not how, when, or to whom (Riessman, 2008, pp. 53–54). Riessman (2008) suggests the thematic analysis process involves thoroughly reading through the data set to see if particular themes emerge. The researcher works to isolate stories, organize them, and name those stories. I identified 15 stories in my data and named them as language vignettes. I then created a thematic coding system to analyze the data set. Table 6.1 synthesizes some of these codes and three prominent concepts: language loss, heritage language learning, and identity. To sequence and code the themes, a key word or phrase was located within a single language vignette, then input into the thematic coding chart.

6.4.2 Structural Analysis

I then conducted a structural analysis of the 15 vignettes. The structural-analysis method focuses on the structure of the language being produced and how

TABLE 6.1 Results of thematic analysis coding of 15 language vignettes by the three main themes: language loss, heritage language learning, and identity

Language Loss	Heritage Language Learning	Identity
Spanish	Learning Spanish	Mexican
Spanish Language	Speaking Spanish	American
Español	Reclaiming Spanish	Latina
English as Native Language	New Language	Mexicanness
Language 1	Importance of Spanish	Nationality
Grandmother's Language	Beautiful Language	Gringa
Mother Language		Identity
Erased Language		Identity Crisis
		Becoming
		Transforming

the story is being produced; shifting attention from "the 'told' to the 'telling'" (Riessman, 2008, p. 77). I used Labov's (1973) approach, which identifies sequences and structural parts within a narrative to guide analysis. These structural parts or clauses serve as tools to analyze the narratives' internal structures, the structure of the storytelling, and their relationship with each other. According to Labov, a "fully formed" narrative includes six key elements: abstract, orientation, complicating action, evaluation, resolution, and coda. The "abstract" is a summary of the point of the story; it is why the narrator is telling the story. The "orientation" addresses the time, place, characters, and setting of the story. The "complicating action" represents a specific turning point or crisis that possibly creates a change within the narrative. "Evaluation," or the "soul of the narrative," involves the narrator reflecting about the complicating action. In this study, particular attention was paid to the "evaluation" of my language vignettes to better identify the relationships between the main themes in the narrative. The process of focusing on "evaluations" allows for patterns to emerge and for deeper analysis of a story. The "resolution" focuses on the outcome of the story. The "coda" is when the narrator returns to the present time. I used Labov's classifications as I identified and named the 15 stories listed in Table 6.2. The table summarizes the number of times each story referenced the three main themes: language loss (LL), heritage language acquisition (HL), and identity (ID).

TABLE 6.2 Quantitative summary of the frequency of themes addressed in each language vignette

Story	Language Vignettes	LL	HL	ID
1	The Beginning	3		3
2	Family History	2		1
3	Early Education	1		1
4	First Day of School	1		1
5	From a child			1
6	Clase de Español	1	1	3
7	Becoming	1		2
8	Leaving Noell			3
9	From a teenager			1
10	University	1		1
11	The Decision	1	1	2
12	Americanness			1
13	Mexicanidad	1	1	1
14	Español		2	2
15	Reclaiming Myself		2	2
	Sum of Coding by Themes	12	7	25

6.5 Findings

The most salient aspects of this narrative study are found within the selected vignettes, which address the research questions posited in this study. The following sections are organized around the themes of language loss, heritage language learning, and identity. The first section addresses language loss interwoven throughout nine of the language vignettes. The second section focuses on my heritage language learning, and it is found in five stories; it illustrates my sense of agency in combating my language loss to reconcile my bicultural identity. The last section of the findings concentrates on the concept of identity, a theme present in all 15 vignettes.

6.5.1 Language Loss

6.5.1.1 Becoming: Language Vignette 7

> I remember being told what my name meant by my mother. She would say "Mar is the sea and Sol is the Sun. Your name means the sun and sea." I was in love. I loved how it rolled off my tongue, I loved the meaning, I loved how it was my soft, secret name from my family that others did not understand. I understood my name was in Spanish and that was because I was Mexican but did not understand why I did not speak Spanish. I asked my mother, "Why is my name in Spanish but we do not speak Spanish?" She responded that my father's family did not speak Spanish and so we do not speak Spanish. I was always confused about this during my childhood.
>
> –Marisol Cantú

The importance I place on language in relation to identity is salient throughout my narrative. The thematic analysis shows a pattern of connections between references to language loss and my Mexican-American identity. The analysis of the Language Vignette 7, titled "Becoming," shows the deep connection I felt to Spanish from the onset of my life. From an early age, my Spanish name played a vital role in my identity formation. In Language Vignette 2, I describe how the loss of my "family's primary language, Spanish" created an identity crisis for me, showing also how my linguistic recollections are strongly tied to identity. I reference language loss in 12 language vignettes in total. I reflect about the cause of language loss being the generational language loss passed on from my grandmother to my father and then onto myself. I understand this language loss as a consequence of the United States' efforts at erasing the Spanish language when the 'borders moved on us.' This was also explained by my grandmother, Lydia Cantu, in a memory of not being able to speak Spanish throughout her early education. In her unpublished self-written memoir, she shares the following quote:

> During these times, Spanish was not permitted to be spoken in school and anyone that was caught speaking Spanish was punished. I remember that my teacher hit me on the hand with a ruler because she heard that I was talking in Spanish. I remember my teacher was very mean.

Through the *Meyer vs. Nebraska* (1923) law, teachers were able to discipline children in forms they deemed appropriate when a child spoke Spanish. The law states under Section 1 that "No person, individually or as a teacher, shall, in any private, denominational, parochial or public school, teach any subject to any person in any language other than the English language," which was in practice translated to prohibit students' use of other languages than English at school. This story, however despicable, is not unique, as evident in the book by Reyes (2011), cited earlier, featuring Latino scholars who were corporally punished by their Anglo-Saxon teachers for speaking in Spanish at school. Stories shared in Reyes's edited volume illustrate the cruel and inhumane nature of teachers' practices towards Spanish-speaking children, sanctioned by a schooling system that supported such behaviors. From losing lunch and recess, to having to write 500 lines of "I will not speak Spanish" (Arvizu, 2011), to being hit on the hand, like my grandmother, or being sent to the corner of the classroom (Anzaldúa, 1987), these stories have implications for current educators and practitioners alike. Promoting English-only ideologies in classrooms contradicts and negates the multicultural and diverse heritages of students and subtracts a learning resource from them.

The incorporation of bilingual education and culturally relevant pedagogies at this current time is as needed as before. There are still states in the United States that prohibit or do not make available bilingual education. Furthermore, English-only ideologies still plague many policies, practices, and teachers' mindsets living in the United States. Even when teachers support students to move successfully through school, the covert or overt messages of inadequacy sent to students because of the languages spoken at home can have negative consequences on their students' sense of self and on their academic identities. The story of Spanish language loss in both my grandmother, Lydia, and myself, contextualized within the history of language erasure in the United States, shows the long-term repercussions of English-only ideologies and the complex realities that Mexican Americans have historically endured.

6.5.2 Heritage Language Learning

6.5.2.1 Mexicanidad: Language Vignette 6

> I needed to reclaim the language that was taken away from my grandmother. I remember when she was younger, she told me a story of how she was in elementary school and how they were not allowed to speak Spanish in class, even though that was her native language. She remembers when she was

hit on her hand with a ruler by a teacher for speaking Spanish. This was the beginning of my family's language loss. This was a reason she assimilated and learned English and only spoke Spanish to her parents. She did not want her children to go through the same experiences, so she did not teach my father or tíos Spanish. In one generation, my family's language was lost.

−Marisol Cantú

Throughout the language vignettes, I describe my feelings towards language loss and the subsequent language learning, which help me weave through my bicultural identity. My complex relationship with Spanish is evident throughout my narrative, whether I am referring to language loss or my heritage language learning of Spanish. In Vignette 14, I write about my decision to move to Latin America to reclaim my lost heritage language and to teach English, a decision that reflects my agency to change a situation that had caused so much pain. My grandfather's admiration for Salvador Allende led me to look at Chile for my language learning experience, even when I knew no one from there. My family thought that Chile had a stable government and supported my initiative, even if they didn't understand why I had to travel and why I needed to learn Spanish. By crossing borders and learning Spanish, I was able to begin my reconciliation with my identity and language. The following example in Table 6.3 shows my evaluation of the Language Vignette titled "Español" following Labov's (1972) structural analysis. In particular, the analysis of the "evaluation" component of the structural chart allows me to reflect on emotions or rationalizations of the story (Riessman, 2008, p. 89).

By focusing on the "evaluation" or turning point, I illustrate distinct characteristics of agency through my acquisition of Spanish, such as confidence and 'coming into my own.' I reflect upon a more resolved understanding of who I am in the "resolution" by using Spanish in my narrative while stating 'una Mexicana' instead of 'a Mexican.' This was the first use of Spanish in my personal narrative. I interpret my use of Spanish in relation to my identity as evidence of agency and identity development. To summarize, I used the recovering of my heritage language to fight erasure and create a stronger Latina identity.

6.5.3 Identity

6.5.3.1 The Beginning Continues…: Language Vignette 1

It is not enough that I would be upset when people assumed that I was an immigrant, that I had to prove my own citizenship when my family had been here for 100 years, that I have to explain that the borders moved on us, that my family has been in this land before the United States had to right to claim Texas as a state, and then incorporating it and then colonizing the rest of the West, erasing my people's land, culture, and language along the way. No, it is not enough; I doubt it will ever be.

−Marisol Catú

TABLE 6.3 Structural analysis of language vignette 14, "Español"

Narrative Elements	Lines of the Narrative	Analysis	Theme
Abstract (AB)	After six months of answering questions about not knowing Spanish and teaching English I came to the realization that I was losing time.	Introduces the topic	Language loss Language isolation
Orientation (OR)	I enrolled in Spanish classes and decided to move into a Spanish speaking international house, known as La Casa Nativa.	Provides setting New situation	Spanish speaking
	There were 2 Chilenos living in the house and one Italian woman that spoke Spanish and limited English.	New people	
Complicating action (CA)/ turning point	This is where my Spanish truly flourished. All of my housemates were so patient and helpful with my desire to learn Spanish. They knew how important learning Spanish was to me. I was content listening to my language for hours and hours just trying to make sense of the conversation. Along with the help of intercambios and Spanish classes I finally found my tongue.	Turning point	Agency Resistance Language exposure
Evaluation (EV)	I was able to communicate in the language that was long gone from my past. And I loved every second of it. I was coming into my own in every way I could. I was more confident in my language abilities, in my teaching, as a student learning a new language, but more importantly in my true self.	Soul of narrative	Heritage language learning Second language acquisition Language erasure agency

(continued)

TABLE 6.3 (*Continued*)

Narrative Elements	Lines of the Narrative	Analysis	Theme
Resolution (RE)	I was becoming a woman, a Latina, y una Mexicana.	Outcome	Identity Becoming Transforming
Coda (CO)	This experience changed my life for the better. In ways even to this day I appreciate it.	Present day appreciation	

Interweaving the vignettes of my past, I can see how language loss and heritage language acquisition played important roles in the development of my Mexican-American woman identity living in the United States. In Vignette 1, I contemplate my sense of frustration as my American identity was constantly doubted in the United States, as I felt "that I had to prove my own citizenship when my family had been here for 100 years," in spite of the fact that English was my first language. Along with this constant need to prove myself as American was my need to also affirm my Mexican identity, which led me to commit myself to recovering my heritage language.

Although my experiences in language learning and using language to overcome erasure are intertwined with my dual identities, these struggles are not unique to my experience. The CRT lens explains that every person has potentially conflicting and overlapping identities, loyalties, and allegiances (Delgado et al., 2012, p. 10). The overlap of the Mexican and American identities portrayed in my narratives demonstrates the intersectionality of two different and often opposing cultures. The intersectionality is salient throughout my narratives, as I refer to identity in every language story. In some cases, I mention identity two or three times in a single language vignette (see Table 6.2 above). As seen in Table 6.3, the "resolution" component of Language Vignette 14 made salient the intersectionality of bicultural identity.

In the following, I offer examples from three language vignettes that show the progression of language loss into heritage language acquisition and how identity is woven through each. The examples come from Vignette 6 (Clase de Español), 11 (The Decision), and 13 (Defending My Mexicanness). The analysis of the "evaluations" and the "complicating actions" of the three stories indicate identity confusion early on in my linguistic experiences. For example, the "evaluation" of Language Vignette 6 states "I felt so hurt and angry at myself and my family. I did not understand why we did not speak our mother language." The "evaluation" of Language Vignette 11 illustrates more than one instance where identity is linked to language. My self-reflection of my teaching experience as an American in Chile demonstrates the complexities of my bicultural identity. In my words, "They (my students) did not believe that I was a native English speaker because I looked

Latina and my name was Latina." In that same language vignette, the "complicating action" or turning point in the story, created a new realization: "One student said that I could not identify as Mexican because I was a Gringa." In response to this "complicating action," the "evaluation" was "All of a sudden, everything that I wanted to get away from was blatantly happening to me. It was so very strange." The intersectionality of both of my identities is a major point throughout my language experiences. The feelings and desires of "getting away" from my American identity created confusion, isolation, and shock. These two "evaluations" within one language vignette speak about the tensions involved in navigating my bicultural identity. The last example from Vignette 13, "Defending My Mexicanness," describes my desire to better understand my language loss and reclaim my Spanish tongue. The language learning process of regaining my heritage language ignited a sense of agency and empowerment to fight the language loss inherited through my grandmother's experiences. As quoted in my evaluation:

> As I started telling the story that my Grandmother told me of why she did not speak Spanish, I came to realize how much I needed to learn Spanish even more. I needed to reclaim the language that was taken away from my grandmother.

This vivid quote paints a picture of the criticality that language loss and heritage language acquisition had on my Mexican-American identity. I further express my need for validation by writing about my Chilean students: "Many of my students and the Latinos I encountered outside of the classroom were just as concerned about my loss of language and thought it beautiful that I was learning Spanish again."

My life story is not fully illustrated through this research paper, yet the findings of my linguistic experiences are essential. The interconnectedness of language and identity is clearly present in my 15 language vignettes. Through this narrative analysis, I gained insights into how my stories of language loss and my struggles to affirm my bicultural identity led me to learn Spanish as a source of empowerment.

6.6 Conclusion and Implications

6.6.1 Reclaiming Myself: Language Vignette 15

> This was the first time I was able to use everything I learned in Chile, my new language, the confidence I gained from living abroad, my mind and heart opened to Latin America. I became everything my heart desired; I was a traveler, a teacher, an American, a Mexican, a Latina, a person learning about her heritage that had long been forgotten.
>
> –Marisol Cantú

This narrative study speaks to the inner workings of how generational language loss has led myself, a self-identified Latina, to embrace English as my native language and learn Spanish as my heritage language, and how this process has impacted my bicultural identity. Far from becoming a victim of linguicide, a form of erasure, my narrative explores the linguistic experiences related to what it means to be a fifth-generation Mexican American in a dominantly English society. The narratives capture my strong emotions associated with language loss, my actions of reversing the repercussions of language loss, and how both experiences recreated my Latina identity. Through conducting, analyzing, and reflecting on my linguistic experiences in this self-narrative, I reaffirm who I am as a Mexican-American woman. Through the acquisition of my erased language, Spanish, I portray a powerful stance of resilience and counterstory in an increasingly English-only ideology society. My autobiography illustrates a young Latina woman coming to understand the societal implications on the intersectionality of my identity and linguistic experiences. Language vignettes provide rich and detailed data that depict powerful images and emotions concerning self-growth and cultural identities. In many respects, I am combating language erasure through the acquisition of language; however, there are still many more opportunities to combat erasure within the macro level of society and the micro level of classrooms.

On the macro level, there should be a movement of embracing, not erasing, cultural identities and languages by the promotion of a more respectful and multicultural society. This movement should focus on education, immigration, and welfare reforms, including seminars for educators on immigration policies, language ideologies, and bilingual education policies. While there is an increasing number of bilingual programs at the elementary level, only a minimum of Latino students benefit from those, and there is a great need for promoting bilingual education and bicultural identities in adult and K-12 ESL classrooms. One clear path to multilingualism would be to model the U.S. Educational Policy to reflect that of the European Union (EU) multilingualism policy. The European Commission, run by EU Heads of State, declared an ambitious goal of all citizens learning two foreign languages beginning at an early age. Their rationale, like many scholars, is that multilingualism unites people, strengthens cultural understanding, enhances employability, and enables the EU to compete in the global economy.

On the micro level, some educators work with social workers and immigration workers, and advocate for bilingual daycare programs and family English-language programs that promote bilingual adult and child literacy. Many teachers in K-12 settings implement multiculturalism and bilingual curriculum into their everyday lesson plans. We need more of them. Teachers who engage in these changes understand multicultural curriculum and the sociohistorical experiences of their students and families (Delgado Bernal, 2002). The shift of viewing students' linguistic resources as deficiencies to cultural assets within the classroom, home, and communities has helped ground bilingual educators in more inclusive and diverse theoretical perspectives. Some teachers have adopted bilingual practices in their classrooms, such as translanguaging as a form of communication. Others have integrated storytelling and counterstorytelling. Counterstorytelling serves as a pedagogical tool that allows one to better understand and appreciate the unique experiences and responses of students of color through a deliberate, conscious, and open type of listening (Delgado Bernal, 2002, p. 116). Professors of future educators and administrators of bilingual programs and ESL curricula can also incorporate counterstories to teach the value, importance, and meaning of bilingualism, biliteracy, and bilingual education for working-class Latino immigrant parents (McNee, 2015, p. 122).

Along with communicating with students, teachers who are concerned about involving their students' parents work at effectively communicating with them. These teachers send information, including homework instructions, announcements, and administrative forms, in multiple languages so that non-English speaking parents are able to access the pertinent information as well as become more engaged with their child's learning (Delgado Bernal, 2002). Other pedagogical tools that teachers use include incorporating bilingual literacy in the classroom through the use of books, short films, and movies written by and starring people with various Latino backgrounds. These practices help students to see themselves reflected in their books, their daily work, and in their communities. By hosting guest speakers in the classroom who reflect the students' languages and cultures, teachers also help shape the aspirations and future careers of their students.

The promotion of bilingualism in the public educational system is imperative, as well as more research focusing on the use of bilingualism in adult educational settings and on the integration of bilingual methods in adult ESL community programs. Through these teaching practices, research, and policies, the empowerment and embracement of cultures, identities, and languages will challenge some of the systemic and institutional current issues that could lead to erasure.

References

Alba, R., Logan, J., Lutz, A., & Stults, B. (2002). Only English by the third generation? Loss and preservation of the mother tongue among the grandchildren of contemporary immigrants. *Demography, 39*(3), 467–484. https://doi.org/10.1353/dem.2002.0023

Anzaldúa, G. (1987). *Borderlands/La Frontera: The new Mestiza.* Spinters, Aunt Lute.

Arvizu, S. (2011). Becoming a bilingual cross-cultural educator. In M. de la Luz Reyes (Ed.), *Words were all we had: Becoming biliterate against the odds* (pp. 96–106). Teachers College Press.

Balderrama, M. (2011). Border literacies: Con-textos bilingües. In M. de la Luz Reyes (Ed.), *Words were all we had: Becoming biliterate against the odds* (pp. 71–81). Teachers College Press.

Delgado Bernal, D. (2002). Critical race theory, latino critical theory, and critical raced-gendered epistemologies: Recognizing students of color as holders and creators of knowledge. *Qualitative Inquiry, 8*(1), 105–126. https://doi.org/10.1177/107780040200800107

Delgado, R., Stefancic, J., & Liendo, E. (2012). *Critical race theory: An introduction* (2nd ed.). New York University Press.

Fanon, F., & Sartre, J. (1963). *The wretched of the earth.* Grove Press.

Fishman, J. A. (1972). *Language in sociocultural change.* Stanford University Press.

Fishman, J. A. (1989). *Language and ethnicity in minority sociolinguistic perspective.* Multilingual Matters.

Fishman, J. A. (1991). *Reversing language shift: Theoretical and empirical foundations of assistance to threatened languages.* Multilingual Matters.

Fishman, J. A. (2006). Acquisition, maintenance, and recovery of heritage languages: An "American tragedy" or "new opportunity"? In G. Valdés, J. A. Fishman, R. Chávez, & W. Pérez (Eds.), *Developing minority language resources: The case of Spanish in California* (pp. 1–11). Multilingual Matters.

Hakimzadeh, C., & Cohn, D. (2007). *English usage among Hispanics in the United States.* Pew Research Center. https://www.pewresearch.org/hispanic/2007/11/29

Halcón, J. J. (2011). Obstinate child. In M. de la Luz Reyes (Ed.), *Words were all we had: Becoming biliterate against the odds* (pp. 85–95). Teachers College Press.

Kroskrity, P. V., Schieffelin, B. B., & Woolard, K. A. (1998). *Language ideologies: Practice and theory.* Oxford University Press.

Labov, W. (1973). *Sociolinguistic patterns.* University of Pennsylvania Press.

Reyes, M. de la Luz (Ed.). (2011). *Words were all we had: Becoming biliterate against the odds.* Teachers College Press.

Martínez-Roldán, C., & Malavé, G. (2004). Language ideologies mediating literacy and identity in bilingual contexts. *Journal of Early Childhood Literacy, 4*(2), 155–180.

Meyer v. Nebraska, 262 U.S. 390. (1923). https://www.oyez.org/cases/1900-1940/262us390

McNee, N. A. (2015). *Latina immigrant mothers' counterstories of education: Challenging deficit myths.* [Unpublished doctoral dissertation]. University of San Francisco.

Ngũgĩ, T. (1986). *Decolonising the mind: The politics of language in African literature.* Heinemann.

Nieto, S. (1992). *Affirming diversity: The sociopolitical context of multicultural education.* Longman.

Riessman, C. (2008). *Narrative methods for the human sciences.* SAGE Publications.

Showstack, R. (2018). Spanish and identity among Latin@s in the U.S. In K. Potowski (Ed.), *Routledge handbook of Spanish as a heritage language* (pp. 92–106). Routledge.

Solórzano, D. G. (1998). Critical race theory, race and gender microaggressions, and the experience of Chicana and Chicano scholars. *International Journal of Qualitative Studies in Education, 11,* 121–136.

Spring, J. H. (2001). *Deculturalization and the struggle for equality: A brief history of the education of dominated cultures in the United States* (3rd ed.). McGraw-Hill.

Suárez-Orozco, C., & Suárez-Orozco, M. (2001). *Children of immigration.* Harvard University Press.

Valdés, G., Fishman, J. A., Chávez, R., & Pérez, W. (Eds.). (2006). *Developing minority language resources: The case of Spanish in California.* Multilingual Matters.

7

IT TAKES A VILLAGE

Advocating for a Bilingual Student with Dis/Abilities

Elise Holzbauer Cocozzo

I am a white American female with small-town roots and an elective bilingualism cultivated by extensive study, obsessive love, and missed mail sent to apartments I called home in Argentina and Spain. Now a kindergarten teacher, my profession began as a student teacher in a bilingual, Latinx school in Philadelphia where I met Pedro, a kindergarten student with dis/abilities. Acutely aware of my whiteness and dominance in English, I apprenticed under the expert guidance of Lorena (Pedro's paraeducator), Fermina (his mother), and Victoria (his special education teacher).[1] They welcomed me into their classrooms and homes with an eagerness to share their stories and learn mine. Through a certain kinship with these women and a year under their mentorship, I became more thoughtfully engaged in the complexities of navigating special educational services within a bilingual context. Once I completed my student teaching, we played rounds of email tag to stay in touch; I moved to New York, Pedro went to first grade, and Victoria took a position teaching in a general education class. In graduate school several years later, I visited Pedro's classroom to find it unequivocally changed. The specialists I knew were relocated to neighboring schools and Pedro's specialists now looked and sounded like many of the well-meaning, white, English-monolingual pre-service teachers in my undergraduate program. I sat with the women who taught me so much and began to unpack their newfound realities: This paper tells pieces of the story. Their narratives will attend to the overarching question: How does shifting services from Latina bilingual professionals to white, monolingual professionals impact a bilingual student with dis/abilities and the Latina participants mediating his learning? Confronting structures that fail to capitalize upon community assets, their narratives shed light on some of the critical issues impacting bilingual special education amongst Latinx communities.

7.1 Conceptual Frameworks and Literature Review

In this section, I present two theoretical perspectives that inform my study: Darder's (1995) critical theory of cultural democracy and biculturalism, and Moll, Amanti, Neff, and Gonzalez's (1992) concept of funds of knowledge, followed by a review of relevant literature.

7.1.1 Critical Bicultural Frameworks

By combing through my three mentors' stories with theory, the certainty of power dynamics and linguistic/cultural intersectionality embedded within their narratives led me to employ Darder's (1995) critical theory of cultural democracy and biculturalism as the backbone of my critical analysis. When members of two cultures learn to shift between their divergent cultural codes by reading and reacting to the expected cultural cues of their current space, they engage in an active practice called biculturalism (Benet-Martínez, Leu, Lee, & Morris, 2002). Multiple cultures cohabiting a political arena meet value assignments, typically valuing the culture and language of those in power as the standard at the expense of a group not in power. Eva Hoffman's (1989) narration of her 1959 immigration from Poland describes the cultural absorption that often permeates the navigation of biculturalism for many: "I wanted to figure out, more urgently than before, where I belong in this America that's made up of so many subAmericans… I have to make a shift in my innermost ways. I have to translate myself" (pp. 210–211). In her quest to define an accurate self-referent, she aims to fit into an unarticulated supposed standard of the culturally charged space, one where her "innermost ways" do not suffice. Darder's (1995) view of critical biculturalism describes a normative of dual functionality amongst members of two cultures, a reality marked with continual negotiation by the bicultural person between dominant and nondominant cultures. Cultural differences framed as deficits embedded within assumed social constructs impedes individuals' successful navigation between cultures.

Darder (1995) describes the logistics of biculturalism as a multifaceted, highly political endeavor rooted in observable behaviors and heavily influenced by the "historical amnesia" (p. 1) perpetuated by dominant groups. History often tells its stories from the voices of winners, sometimes later revising the narrative in clarified hindsight. In light of power relations inflicted by these hegemonic histories, Darder describes that hegemony impeding biculturalism works diligently to exist, as does its opposition. Using Gramsci's (1971) theory of contradictory consciousness, Darder argues that nondominant cultures cannot be described as one-dimensional recipients of oppression by the dominant group. Gramsci argues that while hegemonic structures inform orientations, critical insight—including, but not limited to, cultural folklore, scientific ideas, philosophical opinions, and ordinary life experiences—actively competes. This omnipresent human defense engages with external social forces of domination, asserting a natural reaction that challenges oppression by seeking humanization (as cited in Darder, 1995, p. 42). Within these agentic efforts, I see Moll et al.'s (1992) concept of funds of knowledge as a form of critical insight that opposes hegemony. Moll et al. describe funds of knowledge as the historically accumulated and culturally developed bodies of knowledge and skills gained from life experience that serve as families' assets in life (p. 134). I use these theoretical concepts to frame the narratives as stories deeply rooted in hegemonic histories and Lorena, Fermina, and Victoria's choice to engage in discussion as active resistance to normalizing assimilationist discourses in bilingual, bicultural special education.

7.1.2 Literature Review

As the ancient African saying goes, it takes a village to raise a child. A proverb colloquially acknowledged as universal truth, today's teachers, educational specialists, families, and student advocates personify current community villages. Upon entering the arena of American schooling, these supporters meet policies that normalize assimilatory practices and fail to capitalize on the village's collective assets. Albeit there is growing bilingualism and diversity across its student population, the U.S. educational system "is designed and organized to uphold the perspectives and policies of those who are in power" (Vásquez, Alvarez, & Shannon, 1994, p. 194), and does so by providing structures to facilitate assimilation. Although the primary predicator of long-term success in school is academic instruction in a student's first language until at least grade six, complemented with instruction in English for part of the day (Thomas & Collier, 1997, p. 15), evidence-based benefits of dual-language programs seldom reach the students that need them (Cervantes-Soon, Dorner, Palmer, Heiman, Schwerdtfeger et al., 2017). By renaming the "Bilingual Education Act" the "English Language Acquisition Act," No Child Left Behind 2004 affirmed a nationwide policy affirming bilingualism as a reparable deficit and favoring unilateral acquisition over intentional methods of mutual integration (Hakuta, 2011).

I use person-first terminology to highlight the student and not the disability; I use dis/ability with a slash to emphasize the continuum across disability and ability (Martínez-Álvarez, 2018). While culturally and linguistically diverse students (CLD) (Gonzalez, Pagan, Wendell, & Love, 2011) in general education settings confront deficit policies on a national scale, CLD students with dis/abilities constitute a double minority often neglected in research, academia, and political agendas (Mccray & García, 2002). Recent numbers chart that 13.6 million Latinx youth attend American public schools, 12% of whom require special services to reach academic gains (National Center for Education Statistics [NCES], 2018). The critical shortage of special education teachers nationwide (McLeskey, Tyler, & Flippin, 2004) coupled with the lack of Latinx educators in comparison to the rising Latinx student enrollment (Irizarry & Donaldson, 2012; NCES, 2017) results in tangible consequences for Latinx students with dis/abilities.

While bilingual, bicultural education and special education have each seen politically driven changes that negatively impact student learning (Minow, 1985), teacher perceptions of bilingual special education in Latinx settings vary by teacher background. Guzmán's (2008) study across schools in Texas found that Latinx educators viewed programs serving culturally and linguistically diverse students with special needs as less than adequate, citing language loss and cultural silencing as products of institutionalized Anglo-centric models. Alternatively, white colleagues favorably viewed these same programs as fully serving students by providing specialized education within a multilingual school setting. The Latinx educators saw loss to which white educators were blind: experience, and funds of knowledge critically inform sight.

Bilingual special education teachers who utilize the funds of knowledge of their own culturally diverse communities in teaching positively affect student learning and can encourage cultural revitalization in minoritized groups (Bos & Reyes, 1996; Cooper, Denner, & López, 1999). When teachers of diverse backgrounds effectively navigate biculturalism and serve as cultural brokers initiating conversation, they can guide students between cultural and linguistic worlds. Akin to utilizing funds of knowledge within the school, involving families in students' education correlates closely to student accomplishment (Fantuzzo, McWayne, & Perry, 2004). By connecting families of bilingual students with dis/abilities to student progress, a bilingual staff allows for greater trust and communication between specialists and parents (Zehr, 2001). While linguistic commonality bridges gaps, researchers consistently point not to language difference, but "cultural dissonance between the home and school as a contributor to poor educational outcomes" (Cartledge & Kourea, 2008, p. 351) in culturally and linguistically diverse students with dis/abilities.

Because few special educators receive training to effectively teach culturally and linguistically diverse students (Bos & Reyes, 1996), many schools depend heavily on student aides or paraeducators to fill communicative and cultural gaps (Monarrez, 2011). In inclusive settings where students with dis/abilities learn in the general education classroom, paraeducators have become the principal means of support for students with dis/abilities, often having more direct contact with students than teachers or specialists (Chopra & French, 2004). Exploring the relationship between paraeducators and parents of students with dis/abilities through interviews, Chopra and French concluded that communication between paraeducators and parents integrally informs student success because paraeducators' minute interactions offer insight, illuminating students' social and academic realities. It can be thus argued that if paraeducators participate in conversations of pedagogy and strategies alongside teachers and specialists, colleagues would benefit from paraeducators' insights in the same way that parents do.

Paraeducators who come from the same nondominant communities as their students may carry funds of knowledge that can be a vital resource to student success, a reality only helpful when they are empowered to use them as pedagogical tools. In a study investigating one Latina paraeducator's practice, Monzo and Rueda (2003) found that although she held experiences that allowed her to be a sociocultural agent in student learning, numerous factors of the educational system mitigated her from using them effectively in her instruction. When school systems instead choose to "connect paraeducators' funds of knowledge with relevant research and pedagogy to maximize instructional benefits" (p. 91), students benefit and teachers lacking relevant sociocultural experience connected to their students' backgrounds can draw from colleagues' funds of knowledge. The narrative study of Lorena, Fermina, and Victoria will add insights into the consequences of school's choices impacting students with dis/abilities.

7.2 Research Methods

I based this critical qualitative study in narrative methods and first-person methodologies (Riessman, 2008). Narrative interviewing positions storytelling as the purpose of the interview space, shifting the understood roles of interviewer-interviewee or researcher-participant to listener-narrator (Kartch, 2018). Lived experiences become the groundwork for meaning-making within the stories narrators choose to tell, while critical analysis considers the historical and sociopolitical contexts that inform and construct language use. By examining how language in action can "create and reinforce social inequality and hierarchy," critical analysis allows this research "to expose and to challenge taken-for-granted power structures and to offer alternative perspectives to knowledge, theory-building, and social reality" (Holland & Novak, 2018, p. 2). By sharing Lorena, Fermina, and Victoria's stories, their voices offer new insights to bilingual special education.

7.2.1 School Context

The focal public-charter, dual-language school serves an urban community in Philadelphia where 97.87% of students' families self-identify as Hispanic/Latinx and 100% of students qualify for free lunch. Students receive instruction in English and Spanish with a gradual decrease of Spanish each year from Kindergarten until fourth grade, when students receive curriculum equally in both languages until high school. As required by law, students identified as requiring special services receive additional supports inside the general education classroom or through pull-out instruction. While general education classrooms must be bilingual in adherence to the school's bilingual charter agreement, mandated special education services are offered bilingually only when bilingual services are available.

7.2.1.1 Participants

Victoria teaches first grade in a bilingual general education classroom at Pedro's school. When I was a student teacher in Pedro's classroom, Victoria served as

Pedro's main learning specialist and led his pull-out curricula in Spanish. Victoria's narrative voices her changing relationship with Pedro as he navigates new culturally charged social cues. While his services have not changed, Pedro now receives pull-out instruction with new specialists, all of whom are white, monolingual English speakers.

Lorena supports Pedro as his paraeducator, a role she held for two consecutive years at the time of the study. She attends Pedro's classes, assists him in using the bathroom or eating his lunch, and communicates regularly with his parents, whom she considers familia due to the close relationship they developed since Pedro entered kindergarten. Lorena's narrative voices a holistic vantage point of the change in personnel's impact on Pedro and his family.

Fermina emigrated with her husband and young daughter from El Salvador in 2008. Her son, Pedro, was born in the United States after several years living and working in the country. Fermina's narrative addresses the vital relationship between learning specialists and families of students with dis/abilities.

7.2.1.2 Data Collection and Analysis

I conducted five semi-structured interviews of 20–30 minutes in Spanish at Pedro's school, totaling 110 minutes of transcribed data. After coding the data guided by my research question, I encountered repetition of family-centered words across the interviews. I then conducted a holistic-thematic analysis of the narrative data coupled with holistic-structural analysis (Lieblich, Tuval-Mashiach, & Zilber, 1998) that led me to identify the following themes as fundamental constructors of Lorena, Victoria, and Fermina's narratives: (a) cultural erasure, or moments where the new specialists' cultural codes overrode Pedro's; (b) decline in family involvement; and (c) professional "choques," or clashes between colleagues. As part of the structural analysis, I also counted and analyzed repeated speech acts within the coded transcripts, which Miles, Huberman, and Saldaña (2014) propose as a methodological strategy that can add credibility to the thematic findings.

Through critical analysis, findings of narrative research might illustrate "how stories can have effects beyond their meanings for individual storytellers, creating possibilities for social identities, group belonging, and collective action" (Riessman, 2008 p. 54). While narrative research does not aim to propose universal truths, this study aspires to ignite dialogue surrounding current practices of bilingual education for students with dis/abilities.

7.3 Findings

I share Fermina, Lorena, and Victoria's stories in three sections, arranged to highlight impacts thematically. Section one describes the personnel shift's effect on Pedro's family, section two describes cultural micro-shifts Pedro personifies, and section three describes the new professional dynamic between paraeducator and specialist. The excerpts from the interviews will appear in Spanish followed by the English translation.

7.3.1 Decline in Familiar Involvement

Self-assessed as more dominant in Spanish than in English, Fermina chose a bilingual school to benefit her as an informed parent and her children as Spanish speakers, as she explained in the interview:

> Me dijeron sobre una escuela nueva, bilingüe, entonces para… pues, mejor para mí, porque, pues yo voy a entender cuando hablo con las maestras y pues, mi hija hablaba español más que el inglés, y era bueno, una ventaja de que era bilingüe.

> They told me about a new school, bilingual, so I thought for… well, better for me because, well, I will understand when I talk to the teachers and, well, my daughter spoke more Spanish than English, and so it was good, an advantage that it was bilingual.

Now attempting to remain informed on her son's progress, Fermina navigated new communicative waters when Pedro's specialists changed from bilingual to monolingual professionals. She described a shift in her communication:

> Como te digo, siento la diferencia del año pasado a este año. El año pasado con Victoria, yo desde el primer día, empecé a comunicarme con ella. Con la profesora que tiene ahora, la conocí por primera vez en el primer día de report card, eso fue el primer día que yo la vi. Desde que entró a clase hasta report cards, no había ningún tipo de comunicación. Fue como tres meses; septiembre hasta diciembre. Y… eh, pues, entiendo un poquito en inglés; me cuesta pronunciar. Entonces, eh, en el día de los report cards, la, ella me explicó todo, como estaba Pedro avanzando y me dio unos papeles, y pues, desde entonces no la he visto otra vez. O sea, intento saludarla pero es… es otra cosa. Es diferente. Había como una relación con Victoria el año pasado. Y también pienso yo, bueno… puede ser una cosa, el factor de lenguaje, y otra porque el año pasado yo venía por Pedro todos los días, y ahora el viene en el autobús. Sinceramente sí, me gustaría siempre que me mandaran papeles o una nota o algo pero no me envían. El año pasado hablaba por teléfono con las especialistas y… pues, no tengo el teléfono de ella. Y el año pasado, tú sabes, tenía el teléfono de… Pues, de todas. Y ahora pues, no. Creo que tengo su…su correo electrónico, pero… no es lo mismo, tú sabes.

> Like I said, I feel a difference between this year and last year. Last year with Victoria, from the first day, I started communicating with her. With the

teacher he has now, I met her for the first time on report card day; this was the first day that I saw her. From the day he began classes until report cards, there was no type of communication. It was like three months; September through December. And.... Well, I understand a bit of English, the pronunciation is hard for me. So, eh, on the day of report cards, she explained everything to me, how Pedro is advancing, she gave me a few papers, and well, since then I haven't seen her again. I mean, I try to greet her but there's just not a lot of communication with her. There was a type of relationship with Victoria last year. I also think, I think, well… It could be one thing, it could be a factor of language or another because last year, I came for Pedro every day, and now he comes on the bus. Sincerely, I would like them to always send me papers or information or something, but they don't send anything. Last year, I spoke on the telephone with all the specialists and… well, I don't have her telephone number. Last year, you know, I had the telephone of… well, of everyone. And now, well, no. I think that I have her… her email address, but… it's not the same, you know.

In the past, a relationship empowered Fermina to access information. With communication now residing between Pedro's new specialists, those who work most closely with Pedro neglect to invite Fermina to the conversation. Not without consequence, Lorena, Pedro's paraeducator, voiced a new change in Fermina's involvement. During analysis, I encountered repeated speech acts throughout the transcript interviews naming specific family members. While only one question referenced family, Lorena, made 40 references to family members, continuing to bring the conversation back to Pedro's family by mentioning "mamá," "papá," "abuela," "abuelita," "hija," "hermana," "casa," or "familia" regularly across two separate interview sessions. The recurring regularity of family-centered labels throughout the narrative discourse affirms the dynamic role of Pedro's family in his learning; with prompting towards new topics, Lorena continued to bring the conversation back to Pedro's family as a necessity to his success. Lorena explains,

> Por ejemplo te pongo el caso de Pedro, que su mamá es hispana y no se siente cómoda. Porque no hablan español. Y ella siempre estaba pendiente de cualquier cosa de Pedro, venía, tenía el teléfono de Victoria, conversaba, estaba pendiente de cualquier cosa pero ahora es muy inconveniente. Yo sé que si ella viene y pide un intérprete, se lo van a poner, pero ya no es lo mismo. Ahora no hay esa confianza, ya no hay ningún tipo de relación entre ella y la maestra [learning specialist]. ¡Porque fíjate que no vinieron ni para la reunión de Pedro! Y eso es bien preocupante. Porque son padres muy buenos, nunca fue así. Y entonces pues cualquier cosa pues yo le… yo le hablo, casi todo el día nos texteamos, o algo, sí. ¿Pero toda la información que tuve antes? No. No la tengo. Por ejemplo, antes ella tenía como el teléfono de Victoria,

muchas veces también hablaba con Fanny [a Latina specialist who used to work with Pedro] también, pero…la que está por Fanny es una gringa, 100%. La muchacha de lenguaje, Miss Hernández, es maravillosa, divina. Sí, esa sí es hispana y me encanta. Ella me encanta. Y esta otro muchacha, pero pensaba que tuvieron una reunión, una conversación sobre Pedro, pero… no…. La comunicación es menos, ha decrecido, ni me pregunta a mí, eh…. Porque para ella es difícil. Y eso es como, pues ella va a venir aquí, si le hace falta un intérprete se lo van a poner. Pero es un problema como de uno, como es su lugar. Ya uno como… como que no es la misma confianza de que bueno, "toma mi teléfono," y "llámame cualquier cosa." Eso es como era antes.

For example, let me give you Pedro's case: His mom is Hispanic and she doesn't feel comfortable. Because nobody speaks Spanish. And before, she was always in touch about any little thing regarding Pedro; she'd come in, she had Victoria's phone number, they'd chat, she was right on whatever little thing, but now it's very inconvenient. And I know that if she'd come and ask for an interpreter, they'd get one, but it's not really the same. Now there's not this trust, there's not any relationship between her and the teacher. Because, listen to this, they didn't come to Pedro's parent-teacher meeting! This is worrisome. Because they're excellent parents, it was never like this. And so, well, if there's anything I… I tell them, almost every day we're texting or something, yeah. But all the information that I used to have? No. No, I don't have it anymore. For example, last year, Pedro's mom had Victoria's number, a lot of times she'd speak with Fanny [a Latina specialist who used to work with Pedro] too but…. The one who took over for Fanny is a gringa,★ 100%. The language lady, Miss Hernández, she's lovely. Yeah, she's Hispanic and I adore her. And the other lady, well, I thought that they all had a reunion, a meeting about Pedro, but… no…. The communication has decreased, even with me, eh…. Because for her, it's tough. And this is like, well, if she would come here, and there wasn't a bilingual in the room, they'd give her one. But it's a personal problem, like it's one's place. Now one is like… like there's not this same trust or feeling like, alright, "here take my phone number," and "call me with anything." This is how it was before.

In Lorena's narrative, language difference does not prevent communication; instead, power dynamics inherent in knowing "one's place" set the divide between parent and specialist. Fermina's lack of dual functionality (Darder, 1991) in conflicting sociocultural settings hinders communication with Pedro's specialists; her strain to mediate between cultural environments limits contact and thus information. Therefore, power tilts its scale in favor of the informant, in this case actively placing Fermina in "one's place" of subordination.

★"Gringa" refers to a white, English-speaking female, typically American.

7.3.2 Cultural Erasure

Pedro enters the new cultural and linguistic arena of his pull-out sessions with Lorena, who narrates,

> Pero al principio se puso difícil de una manera bien cómico porque [Pedro estaba]… desorientado, por completo. Y ahora, pues está entendiendo más [inglés] porque está todo el tiempo con la maestra gringa. Eso es lo que pasa, que a veces entonces el español, que no queremos que se pierde, se va perdiendo un poquito si no más, obligatoriamente. Pues tengo ansiedades que su español va a decrecer.

> But at first, it was so difficult, it became comical because [Pedro]… was disoriented, completely. And now, he's understanding more [English] because he's spending all his time with the white, English-speaking teacher. This is what happens, sometimes the Spanish, that nobody wants him to lose, he goes on losing it a little, if not a lot, obligatorily. So, well, I'm anxious his Spanish will decrease.

To communicate, Pedro must adopt English at the expense of Spanish in a setting where specialists assume this language structure. If unaddressed, navigation of cultural and social codes in intersecting spaces becomes the responsibility of the code-holders not in power. This often leads to cultural erasure in the minoritized group at the cultural intersection, even if that group constitutes the numerical majority, as in this school. Lorena witnesses Pedro's navigation of his biculturalism in response to white, monolingual specialists' cues:

> Por ejemplo a mí me daba mucha lástima con Pedro en este cambio de este año cuando él venía a abrazarle a la maestra [specialist] nueva como él sabe es [ser] respetuoso, lo dejaba con la mano en el aire, con el abrazo en el aire. Porque se me partía el alma. Porque esta costumbre es de nosotros los latinos y el gringo no es así, el gringo tú tienes que pedirle permiso si le vas a dar un abrazo. Y el pobre se quedaba con la mano en el aire, o iba a tocarla y le decía "no me toque" y para mí tú sabes, fue un poco contradictorio. Piensa que le enseñaba ser respetuoso y con este cambio, es contradictorio. Pero él es bien receptivo, que él va cogiendo las cosas.

> For example, for me, it's such a shame with Pedro, the change this year, when he initially went to hug the new teacher [specialist], as he knows is respectful, they left him with his hands in the air, with his hug in the air. Because this tore my heart. Because this is a Latino custom, gringos aren't like this; with a gringo, you have to ask permission if you're going to give a hug. And poor guy, he was left with his hand in the air, or he's about to touch her and she'd say, "don't touch me," and for me, you know, it was a little contradictory. Just

think, he was taught to be respectful and with this change, it's contradictory. But he's really receptive, he picks up things.

Pedro practiced his normative social code of respect "as he was taught." For his new specialists, hugging upon meeting does not adhere to socially acceptable practices, and they decide, intentionally or subconsciously, to bar physical touch from the norms of classroom conduct. Decisions teachers make "convey assumptions about what is worth knowing, which are typically presented as 'naturally' important to know" (Monzo & Rueda, 2003, p. 72). Therefore, the decision, subconscious or otherwise, to abstain from practicing Latinx cultural norms in a classroom serving Latinx students implies an accepted valuing of non-Latinx social codes.

Consequential cultural omissions can occur for students who struggle to identify, adapt, and adhere to a conversation's assumed social code. Victoria, his former special education specialist, sees the dissonance in Pedro's navigation of divergent social codes:

> Nosotras somos bien cariñosas. Es la Latina de nosotras. Los Hispanos, los Latinos, somos bien cariñosos. Y entonces, Pedro estaba acostumbrado a yo llegar y dame un beso, dame un abrazo; es su cultura. Pero la maestra que tiene ahora [the new specialist] pues no. Entonces tiene una distancia, ¿ves? Entonces pues es difícil, porque yo veo que Pedro no me quiere dar un beso, no me quiere saludar. Y me siento como…como él está cambiando su cultura, y para mí eso me parte el alma. Ahora tengo que pedir un beso, tengo que pedirle un abrazo, y tengo que decir, "Pedro, pero ven acá; ¡salúdame!" Y antes le surgía más… más natural y ahora no. Y me he dado cuenta porque las terapias, la gente que coge afuera son americanas, y la maestra también ahora es americana, y la OT [occupational therapist] que antes era hispana, que ya no es hispana, Americana. Y más que eso, nadie es bilingüe. Eso es difícil porque a veces no le entienden a él. ¿Ves?

> We're very warm. It's the Latina in us. Hispanics, Latinos, we're very loving. And so, Pedro's accustomed to me coming and you know, give me a hug, give me a kiss; it's his culture. And so the teacher [the new specialist] he has now, well, no. So he has this new distance, see? So, you know, it's tough, because I feel like now Pedro doesn't want to give me a kiss, doesn't want to say hello in the Latino way. And I feel like… like he's changing his culture, and for me, it tears my soul. Now I have to ask for a salutatory kiss, I have to ask him for a hug, I have to say, "But Pedro, come here! Say hello!"…. Whereas before, it came more naturally, and now it doesn't. And I realized that his specialists, the ones who do pull-out, are Americans, and his teacher is American, and the OT [occupational therapist], who before was Hispanic, now she's not Hispanic, she's American. And more than this, no one is bilingual. This is tough because sometimes they don't understand him. You see?

As a student who requires repetition and consistency to integrate new information into practice, Pedro's shift in normative action can only derive from deliberate reiteration of what constitutes appropriate behavior. He personifies Darder's (2011) process of biculturalism as he mediates, as others have, "between the dominant discourse of educational institutions and the realities they must face as members of subordinate cultures" (p. 20). In witnessing his cultural dissonance, Victoria personifies Darder's (1991) notion of resistance by resolutely requiring Latino *cariño* in their salutatory interactions. In the case of special education, cognitive challenges complicate the process of cultural mediation described by Darder, making resistance practices like Victoria's crucial in Pedro's process towards biculturalism.

Alternatively, members of the dominant culture can bend towards that of the minoritized group. Non-Latinx specialists can also utilize Darder's notion of biculturalism to actively respond to the existing cultural code created by students; Victoria describes another white, monolingual specialist's approach:

> Porque por ejemplo recuerda Ms. Lancaster, la rubia de educación especial, ella siempre al principio decía que a ella no le gustaba que la abrazaran, besaran, a ella no le gustaba esa proximidad. Y sin embargo ella lleva ya tanto tiempo aquí que, que ella está acostumbrada que cuando empieza la clase o lo que sea que todo el mundo va a abrazarla o algo, y ya ella lo hace e inicialmente era incómodo para ella, todo eso. Yo me doy cuenta, lo noto porque la conozco a ella desde que llegamos, porque llegamos al mismo tiempo. ¿Ves? Entonces ella cambió un poquito. Ahora con esas [new specialists], él está cambiando, Pedrito.

> Because, for example, you remember Ms. Lancaster, the blonde from special education; at the beginning, she said that she didn't like anyone to hug her, kiss her; she didn't like that proximity. And anyway, she's been here so long that now she's accustomed to starting the class or whatever, and everyone's going to hug her or touch her or whatever, and she does it, whereas initially, it made her uncomfortable and all this. I realized, I noticed it because I know her well; we started here at the same time. You see? She changed a little bit. But now with these [new specialists], he's changing a bit. Little Pedro.

Instead of expecting students to assimilate, this non-Latinx specialist navigated Darder's notion of biculturalism and asserted a student-centered pedagogy, personifying culturally responsive teaching in her choice.

7.3.3 *Professional* Choque

Narrative data outlined a shift in professional relationships in lieu of new linguistic or cultural barriers, often producing a professional *choque*, or clash. While

Lorena influenced her professional spaces as Pedro's paraeducator in the past, current *barreras*, or walls, impact her positionality towards power:

> Ahora no hay esa confianza, ya no tenemos ningún tipo de relación. Yo le ayudaba a Victoria muchísimo el año pasado, todo en el salón, haciendo cosas, discutiendo métodos de apoyo con respeto a Pedrito. Pero tú sabes, pues la cultura cambia un montón para él, y pues, también eh… para mí. Por ejemplo, los hispanos, si yo estaba con Victoria, yo ayudaba a ella y todo eso, para ella era bueno y…. Pero las personas anglosajonas tienen esa barrera que como…. como es *su* trabajo. Hay una línea, y es parte de su cultura ¿te parece? Tú eres americana, ¿puede ser eso? ¿te parece? Porque no estoy ayudando ahora en las sesiones, estoy como observando.

> Now there's not this trust; now there's no type of relationship. I helped Victoria a ton last year, everything in the classroom, doing little things, discussing methods to better support Pedro. But you know, well, the culture changed for him, and, well, also, eh… for me. For example, Hispanics, if I would be with Victoria, I would just help her and everything, and for her, it was good, too…But Anglo-Saxons have this wall that's like…. Like it's *their* job. There's a line, and it's part of the culture, do you think? You're American, could this be it? Do you think? Because I'm not really helping in the sessions, I'm, like, observing.

In this instance, Lorena navigated her shift as an active professional to her newly assigned role as a submissive learner. By drawing a line between professional and observer, new specialists fail to capitalize on the resources within the room. Lorena cannot access her funds of knowledge, deep relationship with Pedro's family, and pedagogical expertise as assets to support Pedro's and the specialists' growth towards biculturalism.

Because educational success requires collaboration between multiple parties (Cooper et al., 1999), using colleagues' funds of knowledge and expertise immediately influences Pedro's learning. Lorena describes a scene working alongside Victoria in the past, where their collegial collaboration positively affected Pedro:

> Estaban haciendo un examen de matemáticas para Pedro, con todas las personas en inglés pero con Victoria; era el año anterior. Y Pedro era como, mudo, ni para tras ni para frente. Y yo pensé, ¿pues cómo es posible, si ya sé que él sabe todo conmigo? Y dije a Victoria, cambia la técnica. Hazle el examen en español, todas las explicaciones en español; recuérdate que su mamá habla español, le da todo los repasos en español. Y le cambió todo. Sabía todo, todo, todo. Lo matemática para él se le hace como más fácil en español. Yo pienso que es porque tiene el apoyo en la casa. En español, ¿ves?

We were doing a math test for Pedro, with all these people in English, but with Victoria; this was last year. And Pedro was, like, mute, nothing going in or out. And I thought, well, how is this possible? If he already knows it all with me? And I said to Victoria, change the technique. Do the exam in Spanish, all of the explanations in Spanish; remember that his mom speaks Spanish, she does all of the review in Spanish. And it changed everything. He knew everything, everything, everything. Mathematics for him just comes easier in Spanish. I think it's because of the extra support at home. In Spanish, you see?

Because Lorena participated actively in Pedro's sessions and communicated daily with Fermina, she could provide insight outside assessors could not. While Victoria's presence as a fellow Latinx and bilingual made it easier for Lorena to share her insight to Victoria in Spanish, linguistic commonality cannot be the only environment where voices receive value, because, as Quiroz (2001) states, voice is not synonymous with empowerment, nor is language synonymous with voice. Rather, she adds, "language is merely the tool through which voice is expressed. For voice to be empowering, it must be heard, not simply spoken" (p. 328).

In this episode of agency, Lorena's words spoken in Spanish in an English-dominant conversation held value because others listened and responded; in this reciprocal relationship, action taken by Lorena's advice established her membership in their professional conversation.

7.4 Conclusions and Implications

Often, educational research written from quiet corner offices point to teachers as the drivers of necessary change. On my subway commute to and from my kindergarten classroom at 6:30am and 6:30pm respectively, I read articles whose conclusions point to implications for teacher change. On the surface, this might seem intuitive—if Pedro's white, monolingual English specialist chose to navigate biculturalism instead of proposing Pedro's assimilation as Ms. Lancaster did, or if Pedro's specialist utilized available funds of knowledge as pedagogical assets, perhaps Lorena, Fermina, and Victoria would have told their stories differently. However, I argue that pointing to teachers as the faces of an institutionalized normative naïvely underscores the structures that create and support teachers to be as we are and do as we do.

For teachers to navigate biculturalism themselves, we must understand the intersectionality of the coexisting cultural and linguistic codes in their classrooms and unpack the systemic power imbalances constructed by alternating hegemonic bricks of privilege and injustice. Ms. Lancaster chose to accept her student's cultural code as her own to passing praise, but she was not trained or structurally encouraged to do so. To move words written by researchers from the pages of journals to the magical trenches of classroom life, teachers must be institutionally supported and critically expected to actualize academically sound pedagogical practices within the sacred walls of their classrooms. To elevate the professional expectations of the field, teachers need to be supported to become researchers themselves in their classrooms by way of time, resources, and professional development. While I initially conducted this study as a full-time graduate student, I reworked the draft numerous times throughout the ensuing years as a first-grade teacher at Avenues: The World School and later as a kindergarten teacher at The Equity Project. To actualize this publication, I strategically took each of my sick days before deadlines because teachers feel lucky when lunch or a restroom break happens over the span of a school day. If we need teachers to be better, we must provide the structures for better to occur.

In this study, I explored the question: How does shifting services from Latina bilingual professionals to white, monolingual professionals impact a bilingual student with dis/abilities and the Latina participants mediating his learning? While the narratives of Fermina, Lorena, and Victoria cannot define the experience of all Latinx students with dis/abilities in the United States, educators might use their narratives to explore "underlying assumptions that [stories] can embody" (Duff & Bell, 2002, p. 207). Inciting a normative of cultural democracy (Darder, 1991), an educational philosophy that affirms students' right to maintain a bicultural identity, would counter the salient findings in Victoria, Lorena, and Fermina's narratives. In order for researched practices to be active classroom realities, policies and institutions designed to support teachers must create structures for teachers to actualize what research consistently validates.

The United States' teaching force employs an overwhelmingly white staff nationwide, a pattern that becomes strikingly more pronounced in urban settings where student populations are not white (Monzo & Rueda, 2003). While federal policies may continue to project deficit mentalities towards linguistic and cultural diversity, I believe that institutions that support teachers' professional growth must resist the assimilatory normatives leading the field by granting access for teachers to assume language and culture as educational rights and resources, and to capitalize upon funds of knowledge to connect more deeply with the communities they serve.

One of my many mentors during my teacher training program, Dr. Althier Lazar, documents how undergraduate coursework inciting critical reflection on policies and practices that impact culturally and linguistically diverse urban classrooms and communities can shift pre-service teachers' attitudes towards teaching in diverse communities (Sharma & Lazar, 2014). If critical social justice conversations can positively affect orientations towards language and culture in pre-service teachers, schools must continue investing in in-service teachers' development as philosophically charged advocates and equip us with the tools to enact research effectively. I propose that instituting structural supports to adopt culturally adept pedagogical approaches and increase professional peer discourse could promote a more just educational experience for students and a more stimulating environment for educators to thrive in as professionals.

Building a village into a town, a town into a city, or a city into a metropolis cannot occur if nearby villages choose to simply coexist or compete in opposition for power. To build bilingual special education students' villages, utilizing the funds of knowledge across their supporters can only benefit students' successes as bilingual, bicultural citizens and teachers' successes as advocates and guiders of student achievement. In doing so families, teachers, paraeducators, and specialists will become valued collaborators in a communal effort to cultivate a new reality where bilingualism and biculturalism thrive within American educational spaces.

Note

1 To protect participants' privacy, all names and identifying details have been changed.

References

Benet-Martínez, V., Leu, J., Lee, F., & Morris, M. (2002). Negotiating biculturalism: Cultural frame switching in biculturals with oppositional versus compatible cultural identities. *Journal of Cross-Cultural Psychology, 33*(5), 492–516. https://doi.org/10.1177%2F0022022102033005005

Bos, C., & Reyes, E. (1996). Conversations with a Latina teacher about education for language-minority students with special needs. *The Elementary School Journal, 96*(3), 343–351. http://www.jstor.org/stable/1001762

Cartledge, G., & Kourea, L. (2008). Culturally responsive classrooms for culturally diverse students with and at risk for disabilities. *Exceptional Children, 74*(3), 351–371. https://doi.org/10.1177/001440290807400305

Cervantes-Soon, C. G., Dorner, L., Palmer, D. K., Heiman, D., Schwerdtfeger, R., & Choi, J. (2017). Combating inequalities in two-way language immersion programs: New Directions for bilingual education. *Review of Research in Education, 41*(1), 403–427.

Chopra, R.V., & French, N. K. (2004). Paraeducator relationships with parents of students with significant disabilities. *Remedial and Special Education, 25*(4), 240–251. https://doi.org/10.1177%2F07419325040250040701

Cooper, C., Denner, L., & López, E. (1999). Cultural brokers: Helping Latino children on pathways to success. *The Future of Children, 9*(2), 51–57. http://www.jstor.org/stable/1602705

Darder, A. (1991). *Culture and power in the classroom: A critical foundation for bicultural education.* Greenwood Publishing Group.

Darder, A. (1995). *Culture and difference: Critical perspectives on the bicultural experience in the United States.* Greenwood Publishing Group.

Darder, A. (2011). *A dissident voice: Essays on culture, pedagogy, and power.* Peter Lang.

Duff, P., & Bell, J. S. (2002). Narrative research in TESOL: Narrative inquiry: More than just telling stories. *TESOL Quarterly, 36*, 207–213.

Fantuzzo, J., & McWayne, C., & Perry, M. (2004). Multiple dimensions of family involvement and their relations to behavioral and learning competencies for urban, low-income children. *School Psychology Review, 33*(4), 467–480. http://eportfoliocathymendoza.pbworks.com/f/Fantuzzo.pdf

Gonzalez, R., Pagan, M., Wendell, L., & Love, C. (2011). *Supporting ELL/culturally and linguistically diverse students for academic achievement* [PDF]. International Center for Leadership in Education.

Gramsci, A. (1971). *Selections from the prison notes* (Q. Hoare & G. Nowell Smith, Eds.). International Publishers.

Guzmán, N. A. (2008). *Culturally and linguistically diverse students at the intersection of bilingual education and special education in Texas* (Publication No. 3315933). [Doctoral dissertation, The University of Texas at San Antonio]. ProQuest Dissertations Publishing.

Hakuta, K. (2011). Educating language minority students and affirming their equal rights research and practical perspectives. *Educational Researcher, 40*(4), 163–174. http://dx.doi.org/10.3102/0013189X11404943

Hoffman, E. (1989). *Lost in translation: A life in a new language.* E.P. Dutton.

Holland, L., & Novak, D. (2018). Critical analysis. In M. Allen (Ed.), *The sage encyclopedia of communication research methods*, (pp. 1–4). SAGE Publications. http://dx.doi.org/10.4135/9781483381411

Irizarry, J., & Donaldson, M. (2012). Teach for América: The latinization of U.S. schools and the critical shortage of Latina/o teachers. *American Educational Research Journal, 49*(1), 155–194. http://aer.sagepub.com/content/49/1/155.full.pdf+html

Kartch, F. (2018). Narrative interviewing. In M. Allen (Ed.), *The sage encyclopedia of communication research methods* (pp. 1–4). SAGE Publications. http://dx.doi.org/10.4135/9781483381411

Lieblich, A., Tuval-Mashiach, R., & Zilber, T. (1998). *Narrative research Reading, analysis, and interpretation.* SAGE Publications.

Martínez-Álvarez, P. (2018). Dis/ability labels and emergent bilingual children: Current research and new possibilities to grow as bilingual and biliterate learners. *Race Ethnicity and Education, 22*(2), 174–193. https://doi.org/10.1080/13613324.2018.1538120

Mccray, A., & García, S. (2002). The stories we must tell: Developing a research agenda for multicultural and bilingual special education. *International Journal of Qualitative Studies in Education, 15*(6), 599–612. http://www.tandfonline.com/doi/pdf/10.1080/0951839022000014330

McLeskey, J., Tyler, N., & Flippin, S. (2004). The supply of and demand for special education teachers: A review of research regarding the chronic shortage of special education teachers. *The Journal of Special Education, 38*(5), 5–21.

Miles, M., Huberman, A., & Saldaña, J. (2014). *Qualitative data analysis: A methods sourcebook.* SAGE Publications.

Minow, M. (1985). Learning to live with the dilemma of difference: Bilingual and special education. *Law and Contemporary Problems, 48*(2), 157–211. Duke University School of Law. http://www.jstor.org/stable/1191571

Moll, L., Amanti, C., Neff, D., & Gonzalez, N. (1992). Funds of knowledge for teaching: Using a qualitative approach to connect homes and classrooms. *Theory Into Practice, 31*(2), 132–141.

Monarrez, R. H. (2011). *Tales of "la lucha": Reflections of latina bilingual educators.* (Publication no. 3436587). [Doctoral dissertation, Claremont Graduate University] ProQuest UMI Dissertation Publishers.

Monzo, L., & Rueda, R. (2003). Shaping education through diverse funds of knowledge: A look at one Latina paraeducator's lived experiences, beliefs, and teaching practice. *Anthropology and Education Quarterly, 34*(1), 72–95. http://ezproxy.cul.columbia.edu/login?url=https://search-proquest-com.ezproxy.cul.columbia.edu/docview/218129807?accountid=10226

National Center for Education Statistics. (2017). *Status and trends in the education of racial and ethnic groups 2017*. U.S. Department of Education Institute of Education Sciences. https://nces.ed.gov/pubs2017/2017051.pdf

National Center for Education Statistics. (2018). *Children and youth with disabilities*. U.S. Department of Education Institute of Education Sciences. https://nces.ed.gov/programs/coe/indicator_cgg.asp

Quiroz, P. (2001). The silencing of Latino student "voice": Puerto Rican and Mexican narratives in eighth grade and high school. *Anthropology & Education Quarterly, 32*(3), 326–349.

Riessman, K. (2008). *Narrative methods for the human sciences*. SAGE Publications.

Sharma, S., & Lazar, A. (2014). Pedagogies of discomfort: Shifting preservice teachers' deficit orientations toward language and literacy resources of emergent bilingual students. In Y. Freeman & D. Freeman (Eds.), *Research on preparing preservice teachers to work effectively with emergent bilinguals* (pp. 3–29). Emerald Group.

Thomas, W., & Collier, V. (1997). *School effectiveness for language minority students* (ED436087). National Clearinghouse for Bilingual Education. https://eric.ed.gov/?id=ED436087

Vásquez, O., Alvarez, L., & Shannon, S. (1994). *Pushing boundaries: Language and culture in a Mexicano community*. Cambridge University Press.

Zehr, M. A. (2001, November 7). Bilingual students with dis-abilities get special help. *Education Week, 21*(10), 22–23.

8

TEACHERS' MENTORING ROLE, OR LACK THEREOF, IN LATINAS' ERASURE OF A STEM IDENTITY

Minosca Alcántara

Latinas are acutely underrepresented in science and engineering fields. In 1988, I was one of only two females who graduated with a degree in Civil Engineering from the Universidad Nacional Pedro Henríquez Ureña in the Dominican Republic. In 1989, again, and to my surprise, I was the only female student in the master's degree program in construction management at George Washington University. Throughout the years working in construction management in the United States, I have consistently been a rarity, one of a handful of women in my field, and more striking, the only Latina in most of my professional settings.

In 2004, I accepted a position at the University of Illinois at Urbana Champaign as an Assistant Director of the Women in Engineering Program. I was shocked to see that 16 years after my graduation, females were still underrepresented in engineering schools. Females in Illinois represented approximately 15% of the engineering student body, and Latinas specifically represented roughly 0.45% of the overall student population (University of Illinois, 2018). When conversing with the few Latina students in the school, it was interesting to see how much we had in common. Our journey to selecting an engineering career could be attributed to two factors: identity and mentoring. Their narratives related to having been great students, particularly excelling in math and science, having science/math teachers or counselors that encouraged them to pursue engineering or who recommended them to join engineering programs in their school. For middle-class Latina students, there was always a relative who had been an engineer and encouraged them to consider those careers. This had been my experience growing up in the Dominican Republic. My father, although a chemical engineer, left the field and became a developer, building residential homes and apartments. My mother received a doctorate degree in pharmacy. Many of my uncles, aunts, and cousins were also scientists or engineers. Thus, I grew up observing my mom mix medicines in her chemical laboratory and watching my dad head to construction sites.

In other ways, our journeys differed. Urban, low-income Latinas spoke about struggles with high school teachers that held low expectations of them, and of confronting ethnic prejudice and racism. Furthermore, they spoke about a low level of academic preparedness that not only disadvantaged them in college, but also almost derailed their college plans due to low ACT and SAT test scores. Many complained that their schools had not prepared them properly for college, much less an engineering career at the University of Illinois. Their level of frustration with their academic struggles, compounded by other factors (i.e., feelings of isolation) would build over time, leading many to transfer out of engineering and, in the most unfortunate scenarios, would lead some to drop out of college.

My interest in trying to understand why Latinas are not pursuing science and engineering careers stemmed from these informal conversations with Illinois students, as well as the hours I invested in creating programs that would reverse this trend. I conducted a study to examine the role schools, teachers, and parents play in erasing Latinas' math and science identities. In this process, I learned that for low-income Latinas, teachers had the most consequential role in their development or erasure of math and science identities. In this narrative study, I focus on the narrative of one of the participants of the larger study, Graciela (a pseudonym), whose interest in math and science was erased. The use of narratives helps me elucidate not only the role teachers and schools played in erasing Latinas' interest in science and engineering careers, but also how Graciela, a low-income first-generation Latina, conformed, contested, and used her agency to navigate limited educational opportunities to excel academically, despite her math hurdles.

8.1 Theoretical Perspectives and Literature Review

I use Holland et al.'s (1998) Sociocultural Theories of Identity as a framework, seeking to understand the institutional and academic practices that impact Latinas' opportunities to self-author themselves as scientists and engineers. Holland et al.'s theory of identity posits that the development of identity takes place within a participatory framework and not in an individual's mind. Within this context, the development of positive math and science self-authoring is situated and involves a process of identity formation, where students not only acquire knowledge and skills, but become a specific type of learner within the figured world of school. Learning becomes a process of becoming; a historical product, intimate and public, produced and reproduced through school practices and the interactions between the person and school actors (Holland et al., 1998).

According to Holland et al. (1998), identity refers to the dense interconnectivity between the self and social practice. Thus, identities develop and evolve as individuals improvise responses to social and cultural openings and impositions while working and reworking the social landscape. These "Practice Identities" are constructs best described by several contexts of activities: *figured worlds* are socially identifiable worlds that provide the frames of meaning that individuals use to interpret human action (i.e., schools). When individuals engage in these worlds, they place themselves as social actors in social arenas in relation to others. *Positionality*, linked to power, status, and rank, refers to individuals' entitlement to social and material resources, and to the higher deference, respect, and legitimacy accorded to the positionalities privileged by society—gender, race, caste, etc. (i.e., Valedictorian student, Varsity Football Captain). *Space of authoring* refers to authorship—how individuals embody identifiable social discourses and practices, arrange them to make them their own, and craft a personal response or identity. Human agency is part of this process. *Making worlds* is a byproduct of individuals' authorship. As individuals author themselves, they might develop new figured worlds, in turn, developing a habitus, which comes to embody the cultural media and the means of expression that are their legacy (Holland et al., 1998).

Of special interest for this narrative study is the figured world of school, as for low-income Latinas, the process of erasure of math and science identities mostly takes place within schools. These figured worlds are cultural models populated by a set of agents (students, teachers, and parents) engaged in a limited range of acts (learn, teach, support, and mentor) motivated by a specific set of forces (success-ful life/enroll in college, career advancement, children are happy/successful lives). Identities become one of the most important outcomes of participating in these figured worlds and learning how to navigate and become successful in them. This process of identity formation relies on the belief that the culturally interpreted figured world has "validity, truth, correctness or rightness" (Holland et al., 1998, p. 120). Figurative identities about these worlds are developed to legitimize their validity (i.e., "If you study hard and excel in school, you will go to a great college and have a successful life").

In the traditional figured world of school, academically successful students are those able to achieve mastery of their academic subjects. Mastery helps them develop a strong sense of confidence (self-efficacy) in their academic capabilities, eventually developing a "good student" identity. Self-efficacy is important because students' beliefs about themselves drive their academic achievement (Bandura, 1986, 1997). In school, for instance, a student's belief about his/her academic capabilities drives the classes they sign up for. Furthermore, students with a strong sense of self-efficacy are more likely to embrace difficult tasks, put forth a high degree of effort to achieve their goals, and recover faster from setbacks (Bandura, 1986, 1997; Pajares, 2005). According to Bandura (1986), self-efficacy beliefs are developed from four sources: *Mastery experience* is the most influential source of self-efficacy. Success typically increases self-efficacy and failure decreases it. However, for a student who has mastered the concepts explained in consecutive math classes, failing a test would not impact their self-efficacy, but almost failing every math class diminishes your confidence in the subject. *Vicarious experience* is the relational positioning or social comparisons students make with others.

Social messages, such as encouragement and discouragement, increase or decrease self-efficacy beliefs. *Physiological states* could also increase students' self-efficacies. A positive mood can increase students' self-efficacy, while anxiety can undermine it. Self-efficacy is paramount to students' self-authoring of identity, as students are more likely to take classes they believe they will do well in and enjoy.

8.1.1 Latinas and Schools

The following review starts by situating Latinas' underrepresentation in Science, Technology, Engineering, and Math (STEM) careers within the larger context of schooling for Latinos. The review then focuses on professional literature of Latinos' cultural and gender socialization, and the role teachers play in their development of good student identities, as well as the self-authoring of student identities. The review illustrates how Latinas develop their identities in the cross-cultural intersection of the values and expectations of the figured world of school transmitted and reconstructed via family, student, and teacher dynamics at home and in school. Significantly, for Latinas coming from low-income families and communities, these cross-cultural perspectives on the role of teachers have a major influence in their construction of their math and science identity formation.

A review of Latinas' underrepresentation in STEM disciplines needs to start by addressing the schools a majority of Latinos attend due to their low socioeconomic status. Approximately 20%, or 11 million, Latinos live in poverty, one of the highest rates in the nation (Semega, Fontenot, & Kollar, 2017). In 2014–2015, nearly half of Hispanic students attended high-poverty schools where at least 75% of students were eligible for free and reduced lunch. These schools were characterized by having the highest rates of teacher turnover (12% vs. 6% at other schools) (National Center of Educational Statistics [NCES], 2016) and low numbers of high-quality teachers as measured by their years of experience in the classroom. While teachers are generally more effective in helping students learn as they gain years of experience, approximately 22% of math teachers and 15% of science teachers in high-poverty middle and high school mathematics were novice teachers (3 or fewer years of experience) (NCES, 2018). To compound this problem, 91% of new mathematics teachers and 90% of new science teachers in high-poverty schools did not participate in student teaching, as compared to 73% and 68% in regular schools, leading to less-confident novice teachers according to the NCES (2018). As teacher-quality is impacted by practical experience (Boyd et al., 2009), these statistics are worrisome.

In addition, teacher educational attainment and professional certification in high-poverty schools for both elementary and secondary schools is also the lowest among all schools—only 41% of science teachers had earned a master's degree compared with nearly 100% of science teachers in non-poverty schools. These statistics are important because teachers play a major role in student achievement;

their effectiveness is additive in students' lives. Students assigned consecutively to ineffective teachers are likely to have a lower level of achievement than those assigned to highly effective teachers (Sanders & Rivers, 1996). Furthermore, teachers' effectiveness in the classroom has been found to be a strong determinant of differences in student learning, far outweighing other important differences such as class size and heterogeneity (American Association of University Women [AAUW], 1991; Sanders & Rivers, 1996; Wright, Horn, & Sanders, 1997).

This lack of access to high-quality teachers impacts Latinas' underrepresentation in the STEM fields, as mastery of math and science knowledge is primary to students' development of positive self-efficacy in math and science. This is crucial because students with positive math self-efficacy are more likely to register in upper-level math classes essential to success and enrollment in STEM majors (Bandura, 1986). Latino students, in particular, fail to register in high school algebra and other advanced math courses (e.g., algebra II and trigonometry, geometry) (Solórzano, Ledesma, Pérez, Burciaga, & Ornelas, 2002); classes that are crucial prerequisites for science and engineering education.

Cultural expectations are also relevant to understand students' success at school. When raising their daughters, many Latina parents follow a collectivistic ideology combined with a patriarchal structure that reinforces traditional gender roles. Many value *familismo* (commitment to family and group), respect (Bámaca, Umaña-Taylor, Shin, & Alfaro, 2005), *simpatía* (harmony and conflict mitigation), and *personalismo* (warmth, closeness, connectedness, and trust) (Marín & Marín, 1991). This Latino emphasis on social relations impacts teacher-student relationships, as Latinos expect a sense of emotional connectedness and dependence between students and teachers (Ho, Holmes, & Cooper, 2004), and high *respeto* between them. Teachers show respect by caring about their students, being kind, having high expectations of them, and by using effective pedagogies of instruction (Alcántara, 2015; Antrop-González & De Jesús, 2006; Valenzuela, 1999).

For Latinas, given the value they place on personal connections and social relations, teachers who understand them and care about them make a substantial difference in their lives, (AAUW, 1991; Gándara & Contreras, 2010). But many American teachers are unprepared to work with students from backgrounds different to theirs, hindering their student engagement and performance, given that when teachers, school staff, and peers demonstrate a lack of cultural sensitivity, students do poorly (National Women's Law Center [NWLC] & Mexican American Legal Defense and Educational Fund [MALDEF], 2009). As relationships and a sense of belonging are very important to Latinas, (Schwartz, 1994), Latina students long for the *cariño* (Authentic Care) they were brought up with—the feelings of caring that came with the loving, serving, giving, and connecting with their families—to prepare them to deal with the outside world within schools. Teachers' fostering of cariño by focusing on the whole person, including the complex historical and political struggles in which Latinas are embedded, produces hope, possibility, and critical consciousness in them

(Prieto & Villenas, 2012). However, when they perceive that their teachers and counselors do not care about them as individuals, their performance in school may suffer, potentially impacting their science and engineering possibilities. Teachers' messages, intentional or not, impact students' self-concept of ability and future career outcomes (Eccles, 1983). For academically talented Latinas, teachers' negative messages are often threatening to their view of themselves as 'smart' and, in some cases, prevent them from assuming math- and science-related identities and STEM careers (Alcántara & Torres-Guzmán, 2016).

8.2 Methods

This narrative study is part of a larger qualitative study conducted for my doctoral thesis (Alcántara, 2015) in which I investigated Latina students' construction or erasure of math and science identities. I interviewed 16 low-income, Latina 12th-graders who selected the most advanced science and math classes available in their high school—honors or advanced placement (AP)—and maintained a B+ average in them. I wanted to ensure that students in the study had the possibility, if they chose to, to join a STEM program; thus, student grades were a criterion considered. The students ranged in age from 17 to 19 and were drawn from three New York City public schools. Seven math and science teachers/instructors as well as five parents/guardians were also participants in the study.

Salient themes identified in the students' collective narratives that impacted their self-authoring of math and science identities included: pedagogy of science (the struggle with ineffective teaching); teachers' evaluations of students that derail their math and science identities; discouraging social messages based on low expectations bordering on racism and sexism; students' perception of teachers as not caring; and the students' own perspectives and stereotypes about scientists and engineers. While all students experienced several of these situations to some extent, those placed in schools with strong math and science teachers and rigorous curricula still ended up choosing a career within the STEM disciplines, as I argue, in spite of these challenges. There were two students, however, that chose not to pursue STEM-related careers. In this chapter, I focus on one of those students to take a closer look at the ways erasure of a STEM-related career choice took place, despite her initial desire to become an astrophysicist. Her schooling experience elucidates some of the issues students face in schools that lead Latina students to reject a math and science identity.

Data collection involved three two-hour in-depth interviews with Graciela. These Spanish and English interviews were transcribed and analyzed. I paid special attention to Graciela's story, seeking for those aspects in her school experience and life that seemed to contribute to her dynamics of math and science erasure. I analyzed her narratives using a holistic-content narrative analysis (Lieblich, Tuval-Mashiach & Zilber, 1998), and used Holland et al.'s (1998) Identity in Practice construct to account for how Graciela placed herself as a social actor within the figured world of school in relation to the characters, events, and inter-actions that occupied those worlds to develop her identity.

Engaging in this research project also brought issues of my own positionality to the forefront. Through my interviews with Graciela and other participants, I came to understand how my own 'insider' identity (as a Latina professional in a STEM field—civil engineer and construction manager) made a difference in my conversations with Graciela and when engaging with the literature.

8.3 Voices from the Margin: A Case Study of Latina Erasure of Math and Science Identity

> I wanted to be an astrophysicist, but wait, I'm stupid, I can't do it. I'm stupid when it comes to math and science.
>
> (Graciela)

What happened to Graciela throughout her schooling trajectory that made her see herself in this negative light? In this section, I focus on Graciela's narrative to understand the role schools and teachers played in erasing her math and science identity. Although her years at school could be characterized as very successful, graduating top of her class and receiving a prestigious national grant upon gradu-ation, Graciela's math experiences derailed her interest in self-authoring a math and science identity, as well as her interests in a science career.

Before exploring this process of erasure, I introduce Graciela through a pro-file constructed from her narrative. Her profile offers a glimpse of another of the figured worlds she inhabits—her home—and in which she coexists, and how she used the pedagogies she learned at home to her advantage, transform-ing them into strengths to self-author a "good student" identity. Her personal profile also offers the contextual circumstances that appeared repeatedly in her narratives.

8.3.1 The Personal Profile of a Luchadora

Graciela is a second-generation Dominican girl with great interpersonal rela-tional abilities and a great sense of humor. Although throughout her life she had to overcome many hurdles (poverty, challenging neighborhoods that lacked services and resources, and near-homelessness), Graciela's narratives show that she did so with a clear sense of purpose and understanding that she would suc-ceed in the end because she had all the characteristics needed to succeed: She was smart, possessed great English teachers who mentored her, and had a good personality and great resolve because she was a tremendous *luchadora,* devel-oping resistance within her oppressive economic and migratory circumstances (Castillo & Torres-Guzmán, 2012); a girl with a passion to succeed and over-come her reality.

When Graciela tells her life story, her intelligence and her love of English, books, and poetry are recurrent themes. She internalized her parents' comments that she was exceedingly smart and that because of it, she would go far in life, making a name for herself and her family: "You are a Pantaleon," her father would always remind her. Her parents also instilled in her a love for reading, particularly her father, who despite only finishing seventh grade, was, according to Graciela, very smart and well-read: a poet and a writer. From him, she and her siblings learned to love poetry. Her mother also values education but never got involved in Graciela's schoolwork or helped with homework. She takes pride in Graciela's academic achievements, always bragging to her friends about her grades in school, and constantly posting on Facebook about her accomplishments.

School seemed to come easy to Graciela, despite not having at home the kinds of academic support and resources that students who are not first-generation usually receive with their assignments. In elementary school, she quickly developed a "good student" identity, always among the top English students in her class and grade. Her "good student" identity continued in middle school, where she scored in the top 2% on the English exam among all New York City students. This honor provided her with the privilege of being accepted to her first high school choice, LF High School (LFHS), and recruited into the Bridge Program, an honors program for academically talented, low-income, minority students with a 90% or higher GPA.

Graciela presents herself as tenacious and savvy enough to transform her financial and social challenges into sources of strength. Having an immigrant mom who was unfamiliar with the American system or language forced her to take the role of family protector early on: "I've always been like the brain at home." This family situation most likely influenced her growth as a self-reliant young woman, self-motivated, resourceful, assertive, confident, and a great leader, as she authored herself through the narratives. She used the *pedagogies of the home* (Delgado Bernal, 2010) that she acquired in her everyday home and community life—i.e., her dad's love for reading; her mother's praises; fending for herself and her family, which allowed her to navigate unfamiliar places successfully; learning to "think outside the box," approaching opportunities, situations, and problems in innovative and different ways; becoming a "positive hustler," not waiting for opportunities to fall in her lap, but creating her own path to help her navigate school successfully. She immersed herself in this world, as shown that by high school, she was spending "12 hours a day at school." She narrated how her days were spent attending classes, participating in leadership activities, after-school tutoring classes, clubs, extracurricular activities, and St. John University and high-school Saturday tutoring classes or college classes. She graduated top of her class in high school with a 3.7/4.0 GPA. She was the only student in her school year that received a Gold medal in English as well as a Posse Scholarship, a four-year, full-tuition scholarship given to students with "extraordinary academic and leadership potential."

8.3.2 Math and Science Erasure

The following discussion of findings is organized around three themes that shaped Graciela's math and science educational experiences: (a) poor-quality schools and tracking practices that denied her a solid math education; (b) inconsistency in the number of effective and experienced math/science teachers; and (c) inconsistency in the number of caring math/science teachers; negative experiences with some math teachers' personalities, lack of professionalism, commitment; and positive, caring experiences with all English teachers.

8.4 Poor-Quality Schools and Tracking Practices

> I live in Carolina (pseudonym), NYC. It's a very low-income neighborhood. I didn't want to be there anymore. Middle school was stupid.
>
> (Graciela)

Graciela attended her local elementary and middle school. These were high-poverty schools serving a large population of Dominican immigrants. Unbeknownst to her, these were poor-quality schools characterized by a high student/teacher ratio and few science and math teachers with a master's degree and with three or fewer years of experience. These schools provided her with a very poor quality of math instruction, as measured by students' dismal performance in math achievement measures and state tests (25%) when compared to their comparison groups at the city, district, and state levels.

Graciela attended the LF High School (LFHS), an elite, co-ed, college preparatory school located in an urban community within the City of New York. Within this school, she was recruited to join The Bridge Program, a precollegiate program whose main goal is to encourage students to continue a successful academic trajectory to place them in the college of their choice. As part of the program, students participated in extracurricular opportunities such as internships, research opportunities, and SAT preparation courses. Understanding the collectivistic perspective of its student body, they also provided students with cohort retreats, field trips, assemblies, and college visits. Parents and guardians were also highly encouraged and welcome to participate in all events.

At the time of her enrollment at LFHS, she would take a test that would determine which track she belonged to. Graciela was placed into the lower math track. This remedial-ability track channeled her into a program that restricted her math educational exposure. These tracks expose students to differential amounts of knowledge, low-rigor classes, and less-effective teachers. Math tracking for Graciela ended up impacting not only her math experiences and derailing the self-authoring of a math identity, but also a science identity and future occupational choice, as she understood the interconnectivity between both fields.

8.5 The Role of Teachers and Students' Definition of Intelligence

Graciela experienced inconsistency in the number of effective and experienced math/science teachers she had in high school, and these experiences influenced her level of engagement with the classes. The bad experiences she had with most math teachers seemed to play a major role in her engagement with math. These experiences were intertwined with stories about insecurities she had developed during her primary schooling about her intelligence for math, insecurities that she had apparently overcome in middle school.

As early as she could remember, Graciela always felt that she "sucked" at math. She relates how, as early as first grade, she already did not understand basic math concepts:

G: I remember in first grade, I would cheat off the girl next to me until my first-grade teacher told me to come up and do 20 plus 12 for her. And I was like, "I don't know"; I was like, "I've been cheating off the girl next to me the entire time." And she showed me, and I'm like, "Oh I get it."

Q: So when they explain it to you, you get it?

G: Yes, but they have to thoroughly explain it; they've got to give me some time.

While this excerpt shows how Graciela struggled with basic math concepts, potentially due to lack of instructional effectiveness or to the large number of students in class, it is important to note how once the teacher took the time to explain the work, she would understand it. Interestingly, as Graciela was starting to develop an understanding of the figured world of school, she started to perceive her need of guided instruction and having the lessons explained in detail, as having a negative connotation. In her mind, "smart" students do not have to place an effort into understanding the subject matter at hand—everything comes easily to them. These misconceptions are important because her perception that intelligent individuals do not have any intellectual struggles may have lowered her self-efficacy beliefs when facing more complicated problems. This may explain why when later on she felt she was "intellectually struggling" in math, she simply started turning away from it and self-authoring an academic identity away from it. These myths are particularly important for math and science because these topics, even for "smart" students, often require significant effort to succeed. It is also important to notice how Graciela's understanding of positionality had already taken hold by first grade. At this early age, she had established a mental ranking of who was good in math class, as mediated by her relational identity established in comparison to her friend, who was better at math. Thus, Graciela started to self-author herself as a struggling math student.

In middle school, her perception of math changed. All of a sudden, it became easier: "Oooh, math was slightly easier in middle school....That was because I had a great teacher.... My eighth-grade teacher did a phenomenal job at teaching the most important things and making them stick."With this excerpt, it became obvious that Graciela could succeed in math when placed with teachers that used effective instructional pedagogies and taught the content well. When placed with a good teacher, her levels of comprehension and performance improved. In middle school, her passion for science also started to develop: "I enjoy science; I enjoy what it means, what it signifies, what it doesn't mean, 'cause you know science doesn't answer everything.... I just love it. I feel that science is so central.... I find it interesting."

Despite her excitement about math and science in middle school, Graciela's potential of self-authoring a math and science identity took a turn for the worse when in high school, she was tracked into remedial math classes after receiving a low score on her placement test. Graciela recounts that in the remedial classes, she had teachers who lacked organizational skills, classroom control, and good communication skills. She started freshman year taking lower-level algebra. In this class, she faced a freshman algebra teacher whom she believed could not teach:

> I think my algebra teacher screwed me up freshman year. She set me down for failure.... She couldn't teach.... She doesn't know how to teach. Her lesson plans were all over the place, she couldn't communicate [with] the class, she didn't know how to handle the class; it was just horrible!

She blamed her not only for her lack of success in the class, but also in the mathematical field overall:

> I blame my freshman algebra teacher for my lack of success in the mathematics field. She was this tiny, scatterbrained woman who had no structure to her math lessons. Parabolas and radicals and quadratic equations were somehow all the same thing in my mind. Her lack of organization and motivation led to my misunderstanding of everything algebra. The only reason I passed my NY State Regents in algebra is because my eighth-grade teacher did a phenomenal job at teaching the most important things and making them stick.

Having a teacher that, according to her, did not provide her with a solid, rigorous education became a source of frustration for Graciela. Her teacher's inability to control the class, effectively organize her lessons, and communicate them properly discouraged her from constructing herself as a capable math student. While in the end she obtained a very low score in the class (65), she showed her spirit of a luchadora and her agency using her eighth-grade notes and by asking for support and guidance from her friends in advanced algebra classes to study for the Regents test, where she received an 85. Her Regents grades were very important to her, as she needed high grades to be a competitive college applicant.

By her junior year, the additive effect of math started to take a toll and Graciela started to fall behind in class. As her many gaps in math compounded, math became a progressively negative experience as she bounced from ineffective teacher to ineffective teacher:

> Yeah, I feel like if I had proper teaching, I'd probably be more comfortable with math, but it's like, in high school, it's cumulative, so if you don't know, if you don't remember and [are] not comfortable with what you learned in the first year, then the second year is going to be harder, and then the third year is going to be harder.

Graciela's lack of mastery in math caught up with her in algebra II and trigonometry, where, as she narrates, once again she was placed with another ineffective teacher. Graciela believed that the fact that she was a new teacher contributed to her performance:

> My trigonometry teacher was new and naïve and had no idea what she was doing. For every three questions she did correct on the board, she'd have one that a student would have to correct HER on. Trig is hard as it is, but it is worse when the person teaching it isn't reliable. To keep it short, I failed my Regents with a 49. On top of that, I scored a 470 in the math section of the SAT. It was bad.

Graciela ended up having to repeat her algebra II and trigonometry class her senior year, which was a horrible experience for her, given her "good student" identity. However, she described her new teacher as excellent, and while not enough to lead her to self-author a math and science identity, her outlook about math changed.

> And then this year, I have a great trig[onometry] teacher 'cause I'm taking it again.... This time, I had a teacher that was 20 years in the game and clearly knew what he was teaching. He was puny, clever, and made the class as interactive and progressive as possible... he's great, he cracks jokes, he keeps everyone awake, he explains thoroughly, he gives out handouts like homework handouts and all of that. I'm doing way better. My highest grade in trig last year was a 65; this year I got an 87, which is a huge jump compared to last year, yeah!

In contrast to math, her science experiences, as well as her experiences in other subjects, were very positive. The Bridge Program provided her with Honors Science classes, taught by first-rate faculty. Even when not understanding a topic, Graciela's attitudes and outlooks of her classes were very positive:

> I could pass the sciences and pay attention 'cause I like science, but I've never really liked math, so even if I didn't get what I was doing in science I'd be

like, "Oh my God! I love this." You should see me in chemistry, I had a song for everything—I had a song about neutrons… I wanted to take AP chemistry, 'cause I love the idea.

Graciela attributed her success and interest in her science classes to her great teachers. In regard to her chemistry teacher, she said, "Well, my teacher was great and she helped a lot, and she was very, very positive. By second period, everyone was down, she would always pick the class back up because she was very cheery and happy…"

In the end, despite Graciela's excitement, interest, great science teachers, and initial interest in an astrophysics career, her numerous negative math experiences had taken a toll. She self-authored an identity not only away from the math fields, but also away from the science fields because she understood science's strong co-relationship with math, as she expressed: "I knew that a lot of science had math in it…. So the math has stopped me from pursuing even things that I like."

8.6 Math Teachers' Lack of Caring

Graciela's negative perception of her math teachers' lack of content knowledge, lack of rigor, inability to communicate clearly, lack of class engagement, and their lack of classroom management, as expressed in her narratives, highly impacted her interest and motivation in math. However, another issue that took an even higher toll with her regard for her math teachers was the lack of caring some of them showed to their students. Graciela experienced inconsistency in the number of teachers caring for her. She narrated very bad memories of experiences with some math teachers' negative personalities and lack of professionalism and commitment to their classes and students. At the same time, she narrated very positive experiences with most English teachers who showed how they cared for her and had high expectations of her. These experiences impacted her relationships with the teachers and seemed to have played a role in her final authoring as a literature major instead of a STEM major. She related the following story that took place with her freshman algebra teacher that left her feeling indignant:

> My freshman year teacher, she acted like she didn't want to be there, as if she had something better to do. I remember one time she was like "I hope you fail"; I was like, "I hope you get fired." She was such a bad teacher!

Graciela's retort in this excerpt was incongruent with her harmonious personality and against her Latina values of respect to elders; teachers, assistant principals, and principals always praised her for respectful attitude towards every adult in the school. Her negative response to this teacher, whom she perceived did not follow a teacher's basic standards of conduct, also shows that her position as a good student had become a disposition, as she perceived this interaction as a threat to her "good student" identity, particularly as this exchange took place in front of her friends. In her figured world of school, teachers valued "good students," and, more importantly, they were expected to be caring and as invested in her education as she was. Graciela's perception of these math teachers' personalities and negative dispositions (i.e., disrespect, rudeness, and belittlement of her) produced a disassociation not only with the teacher, but also with the topic they taught and a potential future career in the STEM fields.

Contrary to Graciela's experiences with some of her math teachers, she only had positive things to say about her English teachers, whom she believed greatly cared about her and greatly mentored her through contemplative activities (Rendón, 2009, p. 27), such as book sharing. She described her English teachers as "amazing" and the most influential in her life:

> My English teachers, they are just amazing. I feel like since I'm a reader, they are always telling me to read these books, and through the books, I get what they want me to know or comprehend or understand and stuff like that, and I'm just very close to them. Like, we are very much alike in the way we think and stuff; like, my AP English teacher, the same teacher I had last year for honors English, and she is so sassy and I'm sassy, and we just got along great.

She also thought highly of her science teachers. Regarding her chemistry teacher in high school, she stated:

> My chemistry teacher was great. She always tried really hard. She made the class fun and engaging.... She helped a lot, and she was very, very positive... so it's [referring to her class] like, second period, everyone was like down, she would always pick the class back up because she was very cheery and happy, so that was great.

Teachers' authentic, caring actions and positive expectations provided the context for her to construct a "good student" identity and grounded her in making and remaking herself as an exceptional English student and a struggling math one.

Despite Graciela's erasure of a math and science identity, her school trajectory ended positively as she agentively made new worlds, creating new possibilities for herself and her family, as she expressed after being selected as a Posse National Scholar: "I'm setting the standard for generations in my family, too, and the younger ones.... So it was a big thing! It was definitely a big thing!"

8.7 Conclusion and Recommendations

Graciela's case study offers a glimpse into the problem of why Latina women are underrepresented in STEM fields. While the lack of resources in schools serving

Latino students represents a major inequity issue, her narratives give credence to findings from other studies that identify key factors related to experiences within the school that contribute to their exodus from STEM careers, namely, tracking practices, ineffective math and science instruction, poor quality of teaching, and low teacher expectations of their students, among others.

Teachers play the largest role in low-income Latina students' self-authoring or erasure of math and science identities and their selection of STEM careers. Math teacher quality (e.g., having experience and being competent) is particularly crucial, as mastery is key for students' development of confidence in the subject matter. Latina students that lack confidence in their math abilities are less likely to select advanced math and science courses and less likely to select STEM careers (Alcántara & Torres-Guzmán, 2016).

This disengagement starts early. Graciela's early negative math experiences failed her because by elementary and middle school, students have already self-authored identities away from the math and science fields. Developing a solid mathematical foundation, particularly in elementary school, is essential for a child's mastery of the fundamentals of mathematics. In addition, mastery is essential to students' confidence/self-efficacy, fundamental to self-authoring positive math identities. These beliefs influence their thinking and attitudes towards mathematics in later years, and also take a large role in their continuous decisions on how they prioritize their math studies.

While numerous studies in K–12 have shown that measurable teacher characteristics, particularly in math and science, such as certification, advanced degrees, and teacher scores on standardized tests can be related to student achievement (Aaronson, Barrow, & Sander, 2007; Kane, Rockoff, & Staiger, 2006), not many math and science teachers in elementary and middle school have degrees in their field of teaching. The National Science Foundation (2018) estimated that in 2012, 96% of elementary math teachers and 65% of middle school math teachers did not have an undergraduate or graduate degree in mathematics or mathematics education. There is a wide disparity in resources devoted to the field of education that needs to be moderated. Districts should mentor teachers on the importance of furthering their knowledge in their fields of study while attracting and retaining teachers for high-needs schools and subjects. Further, they should provide teachers with financial incentives to advance these educational pursuits.

If increasing the numbers of students in the STEM fields is a goal, this trend needs to be reversed, as this case study illustrates. It is in elementary and middle school where students self-author their school identities and where the additive effect of poor math instruction not only decreases students' confidence, but also erases students' ability to self-author math and science identities. Once in high school, it would be critical if the math remedial track functions as laboratory additions to classes, instead of making them core classes. Finally, to increase the number of Latina women in STEM, high-poverty schools should be provided with the resources needed to hire and maintain high-quality teachers, especially math and science teachers.

References

Aaronson, D., Barrow, L., & Sander, W. (2007). Teachers and student achievement in the Chicago Public Schools. *Journal of Labor Economics*, *25*, 95–135.

Alcántara, M. (2015). *Latina high school students figured world of STEM: Identity formation in formal and informal communities of practice*. [Unpublished doctoral dissertation]. Columbia University, Teachers College.

Alcántara, M., & Torres-Guzmán, M. (2016, April 8–12). Latina's selection of STEM careers: Individual social or instructional. Paper presentation American Educational Research Association Annual Meeting, Washington, DC, United States.

American Association of University Women. (1991). *Shortchanging girls, shortchanging America. Executive summary: A nationwide poll to assess self-esteem, educational experiences, interest in math and science, and career aspirations of girls and boys ages 9–15*. https://www.aauw.org/files/2013/02/shortchanging-girls-shortchanging-america-executive-summary.pdf.

Antrop-González, R., & De Jesús, A. (2006). Toward a theory of critical care in urban small school reform: Examining structures and pedagogies of caring in two Latino community-based schools. *International Journal of Qualitative Studies in Education*, *19*, 409–433.

Bámaca, M.Y., Umaña-Taylor, A. J., Shin, N., & Alfaro, E. C. (2005). Latino adolescents' perception of parenting behaviors and self-esteem: Examining the role of neighborhood risk. *Family Relations*, *54*(5), 621–632. https://doi.org/10.1111/j.1741-3729.2005.00346.x

Bandura, A. (1997). *Self-efficacy: The exercise of control*. W. H. Freeman.

Bandura, A., & National Institute of Mental Health. (1986). *Prentice-Hall series in social learning theory. Social foundations of thought and action: A social cognitive theory*. Prentice-Hall, Inc.

Boyd, D., Grossman, P., Lankford, H., Loeb, S., & Wyckoff, J. (2009). Teacher preparation and student achievement. *Educational Evaluation and Policy Analysis*, *31*(4), 416–440. https://doi-org.tc.idm.oclc.org/10.3102/0162373709353129

Castillo-Montoya, M., & Torres-Guzmán, M. E. (2012). Thriving in our identity and in the academy: Latina epistemology as a core resource. *Harvard Educational Review*, *82*(4), 540–558.

Delgado Bernal, D. (2010). Learning and living pedagogies of the home: The mestiza consciousness of Chicana students. *International Journal of Qualitative Studies in Education*, *14*(5), 623–639. 10.1080/09518390110059838

Eccles, J. (1983). Expectancies, values, and academic behaviors. In J. T. Spence (Ed.), *Achievement and achievement motives: Psychological and sociological approaches* (pp. 75–146). W. H. Freeman.

Gándara, P., & Contreras, F. (2010). *The Latino education crisis: The consequences of failed social policies*. Harvard University Press.

Ho, E. S., Holmes, P. M., & Cooper, J. L. (2004). *Review and evaluation of international literature on managing cultural diversity in the classroom*. Hamilton: Migration Research Unit, University of Waikato.

Holland, D., Lachicotte, W., Skinner, D., & Cain, C. (1998). *Identity and agency in cultural worlds*. Harvard University Press.

Kane, T., Rockoff, J., & Staiger, D. (2006). *What does certification tell us about teacher effectiveness? Evidence from New York City* (NBER Working Paper No. 12155). National Bureau of Economic Research: http://www.nber.org/papers/w12155.pdf.

Lieblich, A., Tuval-Mashiach, R., & Zilber, T. (1998). *Narrative research: Reading, analysis, and interpretation.* SAGE Publications.

Marín, G., & Marín, B. V. O. (1991). Research with Hispanic populations. *Applied Social Research Methods Series, 23.* SAGE Publications.

National Center for Education Statistics. (2016). *The condition of education.* https://nces.ed.gov/programs/coe/pdf/coe_slc.pdf

National Center for Educational Statistics. (2018). *The condition of education.* https://nces.ed.gov/programs/coe/analysis/2010-section1a.asp

National Science Foundation. (2018). *Science & Engineering Indicators 2012.* https://wayback.archive-it.org/5902/20170707055205/https://www.nsf.gov/statistics/seind12/c1/c1h.htm#s3

National Women's Law Center & Mexican American Legal Defense of Education Fund. (2009). *Listening to Latinas: Barriers to high school graduations.* https://www.nwlc.org/sites/default/files/pdfs/ListeningtoLatinas.pdf

Pajares, F. (2005). Gender differences in mathematics self-efficacy beliefs. In A. M. Gallagher & J. C. Kaufman (Eds.), *Gender differences in mathematics: An integrative psychological approach* (pp. 294–315). Cambridge University Press.

Prieto, L., & Villenas, S. A. (2012). Pedagogies from Nepantla: Testimonio, Chicana/Latina feminisms and teacher education classrooms. *Equity & Excellence in Education, 45*(3), 411–429.

Rendón, L. I. (2009). *Sentipensante (sensing/thinking) pedagogy: Educating for wholeness, social justice and liberation.* Stylus.

Sanders, W. L., & Rivers, J. C. (1996). *Cumulative and residual effects of teachers on future student academic achievement.* University of Tennessee Value-Added Research and Assessment Center.

Schwartz, S. H. (1994). Are there universal aspects in the structure and contents of human values? *Journal of Social Issues, 50,* 19–45.

Semega, J. L., Fontenot, K. R., & Kollar, M. A. (2017). *Income and poverty in the United States: 2016. Current Population Reports.* United States Census Bureau. https://www.census.gov/content/dam/Census/library/publications/2017/demo/P60-259.pdf

Solórzano, D. G., Ledesma, M. C., Pérez, J., Burciaga, M. R., & Ornelas, A. (2002). *Gaining access to academic enrichment programs.* UCLA Department of Education. http://www.chicano.ucla.edu/press/siteart/LPIB_04Feb2002.pdf

University of Illinois. (2018). *Division of Management Information–UIUC Student Enrollment– New Beginning Freshmen, Fall 2003–"Unofficial" demographic profile.* http://www.dmi.illinois.edu/stuenr/ethsexres/ethsex03.htm

Valenzuela, A. (1999). *Subtractive schooling: U.S.-Mexican youth and the politics of caring.* State University of New York Press.

Wright, S. P., Horn, S. P., & Sanders, W. L. (1997). Teacher and classroom context effects on student achievement: Implications for teacher evaluation. *Journal of Personnel Evaluation in Education, 11,* 57–67.

PART III

Mobilizing Networks of Solidarity

Creating Spaces for Agency

9

FILL A VOID TO CREATE NEW SPACE

The Narrative and Counternarratives of Zoraida Lopez

Eliza Clark

Classroom teachers know the power of a tangible image. Whether with the art-work they use to decorate the classroom, or with the literature they select for read-alouds, culturally responsive teachers use images as moments of connec-tion to empower young minds with the possibilities that every body contains. Teachers showcase stories that students can root in their present and expand into their future, offering an array of selves to see themselves in. These stories form part of the foundation of a young person's healthy and confident identity.

What happens when a story is left out of the discussion, or worse, negatively told? In the United States, the oversimplified history of a society rooted in racism has left out and mangled the stories of many. In this paper, I present the narrative of a young American woman committed to telling her own story and who has made it her life's work to amplify others doing the same. This qualitative research project contributes to the body of Afro-Latina narratives chronicling the erasure of their voices. I ask how the narrative of Zoraida, a self-identifying Afro-Latina artist and activist, addresses the following questions: How does Zoraida's negotia-tion of her racial and ethnic identity affirm and/or disaffirm dominant construc-tions of race and ethnicity in the United States? How much agency does she feel over her positioning in demographic "stories," and what is lost/gained and resisted/accepted in this positioning?

My reading and analysis of this narrative adds to the body of work critiqu-ing delineations of race and ethnicity in the United States. Rather than drawing a hard conclusion, I seek to add complexity to an already divergent body of Afro-Latina narratives by exposing the potential paradoxes that occur within an individual life story. Narrative research is well suited to this task: It values the unique experience of the individual for its deviation from the dominant story, and thus allows previously unheard or erased voices to come through.

Riessman (2008) posits that "Stories that... diverge from established 'truth' can sometimes be the most interesting, indicating silenced voices and subjugated knowledge" (p. 186). In the movement towards a more just society, listening to and valuing voices that break long-held preconceptions of people and events is critical. Teachers play a pivotal role in how these stories are heard and told, as students will bring classroom stories out into the world, incorporating what they've learned at school into lived experience. Here, I reflect on my role as a listener, both for Zoraida and for my students. I hope that this paper highlights the impact that listening can have and above all, that I am able to honor the complexities of Zoraida's voice.

9.1 Theoretical Perspectives and Literature Review

This study draws on poststructural theories, particularly on Derrida's (1997) concept of deconstruction and on Butler's (1988) theories of performativity. These perspectives acknowledge the complexity of the human experience and help describe the negotiation of self in Zoraida's narratives. Theories of deconstruction and performativity resist rigid structures, asking instead that the individual narrative disrupt the dominant. This disruption is relevant to the discussion of Afro-Latina identity, a construct whose very existence destabilizes what is 'Black' and what is 'Latina.' Derrida (1997) writes of deconstruction that "the idea... is to disturb by way of exploring what systematically drops through its grid and, by so disturbing it, to open it up" (p. 77). I employ his theories to examine how Zoraida's articulation of her identity aligns with and interrupts the specific categories of race and ethnicity that dominant society clings to.

With her theory of performativity, Butler (1988) questions the humanistic uses of the word *identity* in regard to gender and suggests that an identity is not an inert possession. Rather, identity is the result of "a stylized repetition of acts" creating "a performative accomplishment compelled by social sanction" (p. 520). Identity categories are unstable and incomplete because what is left out will return to disrupt the coherence that is sought. For example, Zoraida's "repetition" of her Afro-Latina identity generates instability within the discrete social categories of Black, Latino, and white, calling them into question. Though this paper focuses on one individual's Afro-Latina identity, the lens of performativity finds that we are all engaged in the jerky dance of harmonizing conflicting identities. Recognizing this performance can be an effective way for teachers to "listen" to students as they explore their identities in the classroom context.

In the following section, I provide a brief historical context for the term Afro-Latina, grounding it in a number of first-person narratives given by women who self-identify as Afro-Latina. These life-stories highlight the ways Afro-Latinas experience shifting status in different communities because of their location, their nationality and politics, or their linguistic, ideological, and even aesthetic allegiances. Though they share many characteristics, these narratives also highlight the variety of Afro-Latina voices, thus providing a discordant chorus for Zoriada's own narrative to join and disrupt.

The term 'Afro-Latina' emerged in Latin America and the Caribbean as "an assertive self-identification by people of African descent and a clearly articulated condemnation of anti-Black racism" (Jiménez Román & Flores, 2010, p. 2). In the United States, 'Afro-Latina' came into common use in the early 1990s (p. 3), and the unique historical and societal context gave the term a particular significance. Moving between the two regions, Afro-Latinos often find the intricacies of their identity erased in this gap. The Latin American mestizaje, or the mixture of European, Indigenous, and, more recently included, African heritages (Bost, 2000) to create a pan-Latin American ethnicity, clashes with the rigid constructs of race that exist in the United States, highlighting "places of interruption" (Jackson & Mazzei, 2012, p. 16) in both racial discourses.

9.1.1 Location

In her narrative, Hoy (2010) describes an incident that illustrates how Latin American national identities can conflict with racial categories in the United States: While filling out the race section of a U.S. census form, her cousins wrote in 'Costa Rican.' Hoy corrected them, telling them that they looked Black to her, and the cousins replied, "There isn't any such thing in Costa Rica. Everyone is just Costa Rican" (Hoy, 2010, p. 428). Flores (2005) notes that in the United States, many Afro Latinos experience "a pull in two directions—that of the nationality or Latino pan-ethnicity, and that of Blackness and the realities of U.S. African American life." (p. 82).

Many Afro-Latinas describe disorientation when the labels imposed them on because of their 'Afro' features morph across the cultural and political borders of the Americas. Two Afro-Latinas who grew up in Latin America, Modestin (2010) and Vicioso (2010), describe how, after living in the United States, they saw the societies they were born into with changed eyes: After experiencing racism in the United States, they were better able to see how it played out in their Latin American homes. Meanwhile, Chambers (2005) felt excluded while growing up in New York City's Latino community, but eventually found a home in her parents' Panama. And Cruz-Janzen (2001) and Vicioso (2010) both describe experiencing such rejection in their places of birth that they moved as far as the African continent before finding a place where they could fit in.

9.1.2 Exclusion

Facing pressure to deny any trace of African heritage on one side, and an unwavering fixation on anything but their 'African' features on another, Cruz-Janzen (2001) calls Afro-Latinas "a minority within a minority" (p. 168). In her essay *Too Black to be Latino*, Hernández (2003) recalls being told, "You're not Black, like the African

Americans in the United States" (p. 154). Quiñones Riviera (2006) experienced the opposite: "According to U.S. racial polarization, I am Black first and Puerto Rican second" (p. 173). Lambert (2010) adds "I have found that even though you are Black, the fact that you are Latina means that you are of another race" (p. 431)

Some of the women (Bost, 2000; Cruz-Janzen, 2001) employ language as a tool to prove their legitimacy as Latinas. But Cruz-Janzen (2001) recounts the experience of, when speaking her native Spanish, "African-Americans tell me I must be ashamed of my African heritage" (p. 173). She contrasts that with the story of a young Mexican-American Afro-Latina who did not feel accepted in the Mexican-American community because of the darkness of her skin. She "willfully refused to learn Spanish" because she felt that, by speaking imperfect Spanish, her exclusion would be that much more cruel (p. 180).

9.1.3 Affiliation

Many of the narratives I read discuss the communities that have welcomed them. Some narrators find this acceptance in the African-American community (Modestin, 2010). Film director Janicza Bravo was born in the United States but grew up in Panama. She says in an interview, "I don't feel like other Latinos often see me as Latina, which is incredibly painful, but I've also lived in America for a really long time and I have found myself assimilating to African-American culture" (Aguilar, 2017).

Alliances are forged because of (or despite) an Afro-Latina's cultural and ethnic border-crossing. In her narrative, Vicioso (2010) actively rejects the expectations placed upon her as an Afro-Latina woman: She left the Dominican Republic as a teenager to escape what she saw as her fate of getting married at a young age. In New York, she found that she first had to situate herself as a Latin American before she could address "discovering herself as a woman" (p. 263), but that she was considered a 'liberated woman' when she returned to the Dominican Republic, a state that alienated her from other Dominicanas. Describing why she was received with such hostility, she writes, "You are all they cannot be and that must be destroyed for survival" (p. 265).

In a personal online essay, Maya Doig-Acuña (2018) observes that, for the first time in her experience, she is seeing Afro-Latinidad show up in popular television shows, music, and even on T-shirts. As more Latinas openly embrace their own African heritage, Doig-Acuña worries about Afro-Latinidad "turning into a brand." While they are still experiencing the erasures described in the previous narratives, she worries that Afro-Latinas will be erased again as their specific experience is appropriated by a broader culture. She concludes that "Afro-Latinidad is not so much a matter of reclaiming something lost or disputed as proclaiming something *marginalized*" (Doig-Acuña, 2018).

I refer to this array of Afro-Latina experiences as a foundation for my discussion of Zoraida's life story, which is thematically laden with the language of owning who she is in any situation. This chorus provides a backdrop to Zoraida's forging of a solid presentation of self in the face of murky and exclusive outside perceptions.

9.2 Research Design and Methods

This qualitative study (Hatch, 2002) focuses on the narrative and photographic work of Zoraida. At the time of this interview, Zoraida was my roommate, a 32-year-old photographer and student living in New York City. She was born in Connecticut of Panamanian parents, and lived in and around Hartford until she graduated from college in 2003. I chose to interview Zoraida because I knew that she was interested in Afro-Latina narratives and that she would have a lot to say on the topic. I also thought that our decade of friendship would enable me to ask questions that I might have felt uncomfortable asking a stranger.

The first of our two interviews began with a semi-structured set of questions. It took place on a Friday afternoon at a quiet apartment in midtown Manhattan with a view of the Chrysler building. The interview took two hours and was relaxed and conversational. The second interview took place two months later at our apartment, when I asked to include some of Zoriada's photographic work. After looking through a series of her photographs, Zoriada chose two and talked about them.

Because of the nature of the data, and because of my own philosophies concerning the interpretative nature of knowledge, I have approached this project from a radical research tradition (Hatch, 2002; Mullen & Kealy, 2005). The research was done under the assumption that I, as the interviewer, transcriber, and analyst, have brought my own experiences to my interpretation of the data, and that these traces of myself have an impact on my conclusions. Zoraida's life story is not presented here as any kind of 'truth'—I would not like to essentialize her experience. Instead, her stories illuminate the complex process of constructing and deconstructing identity.

I used Jackson and Mazzei's (2012) 'plugging-in' method to analyze the narrative data. With this method, researchers interpret their data through the lens of specific theoretical perspectives. Derrida's (1982) theory of deconstruction and Butler's (1988) theory of performativity lent me tools to interrogate the text of Zoraida's narrative. I learned to pay attention to the "deferred presence" (Derrida, 1982, p. 13) in the data, "the tension between memory, fidelity, the preservation of something that has been given to us and, at the same time, heterogeneity, something absolutely new, and a break" (Derrida, 1997, p. 6).

Additionally, I used the work of Lieblich, Tuval-Mashiach, and Zilber (1998), in which they demonstrate different strategies for reading and analyzing the same data for different purposes. Finally, Riessman (2008) helped me examine data in a variety of ways for different informational outcomes. As with the 'plugging-in' approach, I was curious as to what the different narrative methods would contribute to my understanding of Zoraida's narrative. Exploring different techniques for narrative data analysis could be considered an exercise in listening. As I approached Zoraida's stories with different tools, the stories opened up, and I was able to approach a deeper understanding.

In my first layer of analysis, I looked at the data holistically (Lieblich et al., 1998), to get a feel for the general mood and search for overarching or reoccurring themes. Next, I used two of the approaches described by Riessman (2008) to understand elements of Zoraida's narrative: first, a dialogic/performance analysis, and finally, a visual analysis of two photographs. When a researcher uses dialogic/performance analysis, she looks beyond the 'what' and the 'how' of a story and "asks 'who' an utterance may be spoken to, 'when' and 'why,' that is, for what purposes?" (p. 105). This approach was critical for my analysis given my positionality as an Anglo-American woman. Throughout this study, I was very mindful of the fact that my questions about Zoraida's identity and her responses were perhaps mediated by my own white background. In the dialogic/performance analysis, I interrogate a moment in a transcript where my own presence as researcher becomes embedded in the meaning. In the visual analysis, I examine two of Zoraida's photographs next to her narrative and ask, "How can Zoraida's work as an artist add to her construction of identity?"

9.3 Findings

In my first transcription of the interviews, I tried to preserve as much of Zoraida's speech patterns as possible (this is shown in Excerpt #1). I also included my presence in the conversation in the original transcript. In some of the subsequent excerpts used in this chapter, I have edited out my voice and taken away disfluencies, such as word repetition.

Each of the following three sections offer particular insights regarding my research question, "How much agency does Zoraida feel over her positioning in demographic 'stories,' and what is lost/gained and resisted/accepted in this positioning?" The different methods of analysis were necessary for opening up new insights.

9.3.1 "For a Long Time We Just Didn't Speak": Holistic-Content Analysis

In my first holistic-content approach, I found the tones of Zoraida's narrative positive and bold, with a strong sense of possibility. She described herself as a young artist with a supportive family who had experienced success in her chosen fields. She did not tell her story chronologically, but nevertheless, themes recurred throughout the various anecdotes, namely (a) her relationship with her mother; (b) her defiance of society's confused interpellation of her racial and ethnic background; and (c) having a voice and giving a voice.

In general, Zoraida relates the confusion others have over her or their own ethnicity playfully: "I've totally been with my Latino friends and I've had to say, 'Ok, you're darker than me. That is not from the sun.'" It is when an idea interrupts the positive or playful characterization of the story that Zoraida's voice becomes more assertive. Being accepted as she is and resisting pressure to conform (Theme 2) are salient aspects of her narratives.

In the following excerpt that came up during a conversation about Zoraida's bilingualism, we can see that she admires her mother's efforts to raise her children with the confidence to defy the United States' rigid racial and ethnic categories (Theme 1). Zoraida holds her mother as an example of having pride in oneself. At the same time, as Lieblich et al. (1998) point out, "meaningful components of a life story sometimes manifest themselves through silences, namely, non-elaboration in the narrative. Their force in the story is implied by their lack," (p. 73). After reading this portion of the transcript several times, I started to notice what was not being said.

Excerpt 1

Z: Both of my parents are from Panama, so when they were married, both my brother and I knew Spanish first. And then, they got divorced when—I was, like, in first grade, and my mother started speaking less, so for a long time we just didn't speak.

E: She was speaking less in general or less Spanish?

Z: Less Spanish, less Spanish. Um... I used to stutter really bad when I was little, and then my parents took me to a speech pathologist and just, you know... incredibly incorrect, he said it was because my parents were teaching me Spanish that... and my mother was incredibly offended, and...

E: So what was, how did they react to that?

Z: Ah, you know, my mother does affirmative action work, and she was like, incredibly offended and, you know, took me out of there. But, when we talk about sometimes how, um, people from other countries are viewed in the U.S., it's this attitude of, like, you know, kind of harming, you're harming your child by having them learn Spanish. Especially, this was like the 80s, so...

E: How old were you when you went to this...

Z: Two. She said it was, I was, it was really bad. [laughs]

E: And were you aware of his diagnosis?

Z: No, no. I don't even remember going. Um... So, my mother didn't speak for a while.

Overtly, Zoraida is telling the story of an act of defiance on the part of her mother. Her mother rejected the 'expert's' opinion when his prescription required her to erase an aspect of her and her daughter's identities (namely, the

Spanish-speaking self). She quickly took her daughter out of that speech pathologist's office. Zoraida stresses her mother's activist role in this act of defiance towards the dominant culture, noting that her mother "does affirmative action work" and repeating that she was "incredibly offended." However, the undercurrent of the narrative tells a different story. Jackson and Mazzei (2012) advise that "deconstruction has to do with what is not present; it destabilizes; it snags; it is what remains to be thought; it is excess" (p. 22). In Derrida's (1992) own words, it is "the experience of the impossible" (p. 200). Zoraida, in telling of her mother's rebellion towards mainstream society's harmful attempt to edit her family, is also telling of her mother's reluctant assent. Despite her outrage at being told by a doctor that her daughter's speech impediment was a result of speaking Spanish, the end result of the story is that Zoraida's mother "didn't speak." Zoraida twice leaves the word 'Spanish' out of this phrase, finalizing the anecdote with the impression that her mother was silenced by the speech pathologist's diagnosis.

How can the voice of Zoraida's mother, as portrayed by Zoraida, be both defiant and acquiescent? Perhaps, in this anecdote, 'voice' is a site of Derrida's *différance*, "a sign as a structure of difference, marking both absence and presence" (Jackson & Mazzei, 2012, p. 18). Zoraida is recognizing here how a part of her voice was erased, while acknowledging at the same time the importance of her mother's unwillingness to let her be silenced.

9.3.1.1 Reflection

Looking for the themes in Zoraida's narrative using holistic analysis enabled me to acknowledge the important ways that Zoraida desired her story to be understood. Like Zoraida, our young students give important thematic indicators of how they hope to characterize their own identity narratives. In an educational climate where rigid academic standards deemphasize the cultural identities of students, a student's background is often treated as secondary to their academic success, a stance that ignores research proving that culture is in fact *key* to their success (Nieto, 2010). As a teacher, I am in the position to listen to and support my students' cultural identity. In the case of students like the young Zoraida, I can advocate for their home language, and support mothers like Zoraida's by being familiar with the current research on bilingual/bicultural and multicultural education, offering counterarguments to longstanding misconceptions and biases towards bilingual education.

9.3.2 "Because I'm Not…": Dialogic/Performative Analysis

During our interviews, I wondered how my personal relationship with Zoraida would be integrated into the narrative. How did the fact that I am an Anglo-American woman influence her responses to my questions about her racial and ethnic identities? And, if there is a "subtext of white supremacy" (Hernández,

2003, p. 152) to the construction of a blended pan-racial identity, how does whiteness fit into Zoraida's own racial consciousness?

As the narratives I reviewed above displayed, claiming an Afro-Latina identity comes from a sense of identity affirmation. However, it is also the acknowledgement, in part, of the racism that exists not only in mainstream white American communities, but in both Latino and Black American communities as well. Flores (2005) suggests that "'Hispanic' is a construct that is decidedly nonblack and in significant ways discursively antiblack" (p. 81). The term *mestizaje*, which I have used previously in this paper to represent the celebration of a pan-racial identity that mixes Black, Indigenous, and white heritages in Latin America, is itself critiqued for its usage as a tool to marginalize Blackness and indigenousness, while elevating whiteness (Wade, 2005, p. 249). Hernández (2003) goes so far as to argue that within the field of Latino studies, Blackness itself precludes any claim of access to the Latino label. She points out that "Afro-Latino/as are often positioned as equally foreign as Anglo-Blacks to the portrait of authentic Latino/a identity" (p. 153). This experience, of not being 'Black enough' while also not harmonizing with the Latino 'ideal,' is described by many of the Afro-Latinas in their narratives, as well as by Zoraida herself.

As an Afro-Latina, how does Zoraida position herself in relation to whiteness? To examine this question, I conducted a dialogic/performative analysis (Riessman, 2008). This type of analysis allows the researcher to look at a given narrative as a type of performance by observing the implications of how the participant chooses to perform their story. "We are forever composing impressions of ourselves, projecting a definition of who we are, and making claims about ourselves and the world that we test out and negotiate with others," explains Riessman (2008, p. 106). These words are reinforced by Jackson and Mazzei's (2012) discussion of reality and language: "Language is not a medium for expression—language produces rather than reflects reality" (p. 70). The question is not if the performance is true. The performance, in this case, the narrative, is the construction of reality for that moment, taking into account the many factors at play (the friendship, the differences between interviewer and participant, etc.).

The following is an excerpt of Zoraida's narrative in which she described a visit she made to a prison in Colombia. Prior to this anecdote, Zoraida explained her criticism of salons for catering to a certain straight hairstyle and 'the whitening' that that represents to her. She then switched topics to say, "I really have a problem with calling people 'Negra.' 'Negro' [Black]." The rest of the excerpt is detailed here.

Excerpt 2
    Scene 1
        01 When I was in the prison
        02 I was walking around, I was walking to one of the other buildings
        03 With the guard.
        04 And we were talking about something.

Scene 2

05 And, one of the prisoners, I took a photo of her the day before, and
she wanted to ask me something

06 She was like, "¡Oye, Negra!"

07 And I didn't respond because I was like, "Ok, I know she's not talking to me."

Me: Why?

Scene 3

08 Because I'm not… like…

Scene 4

09 I was talking to my, my mother and I talk about it frequently, and
she's like, "No, people just say that as a term of endearment."

10 And, you know…

Scene 5

11 But nobody says, "Oye, Blanca."

12 You know?

In this excerpt, the context of the story flips, from Zoraida's choice of what
language she uses ("I really have a problem with calling people 'Negra'"), to
her reaction to the language others use towards her. The ambiguity is explained
at the moment I ask her, "Why?" With this utterance, I seem to question the
soundness of Zoraida's self-construction. She begins to respond: "Because I'm
not, like…" What was she going to say? Presumptuously, I imagined how she
would complete the sentence: "Because I'm not Negra," or "Because I'm not
Black." Moving even further away from the words Zoraida was actually saying, I wondered, "What does it mean if Zoraida, a self-identified Afro-Latina,
says, 'I'm not Black'?" Riessman (2008) reminds researchers that "we are forever
composing impressions of ourselves, projecting a definition of who we are, and
making claims about ourselves and the world that we test out and negotiate with
others" (p. 106). Through the reflection that comes with analysis, I eventually
understood this moment in my interview with Zoraida as a "moment of negotiation." I realized the more important question to ask here is: What does it mean
that Zoraida did not complete her sentence during an interview with me?

If I were to minimize my role in this excerpt, I would say that this is a *snag* in
Zoraida's performance of her identity, as explained by Jackson and Mazzei (2012).
They assert that while researchers, "at some level, are always trying to make meaning, even as we resist it with language that is 'twisted and bent,' we are also trying
to snag, to open up, to reveal the imperfections and to purposefully get tripped
up on the loose ends" (p. 31). It is clear from other areas of Zoraida's narrative that
she is a confident woman who proudly embraces all of who she is. This moment
in the interview disrupts that simplicity. As Butler (1996) notes, "If the 'I' is the
effect of a certain repetition, one which produces the semblance of a continuity
or coherence, then… the repetition, and the failure to repeat, produce a string

of performances that constitute and contest the coherence of that 'I.'" (p. 376). Zoraida's 'I' is no longer coherent, but that only makes her more plausible.

However, the interview cannot be read without taking into account my relationship with Zoraida, and this is why I chose to relook at this excerpt with a dialogic/performance lens. After leaving the sentence, "Because I'm not..." unfinished, Zoraida switches into another sphere, the sphere of her mother (Theme 1), where Negra is defined as a term of endearment. Zoraida might be reminding me that, in her life and family, there is no reason to feel ashamed of or to reject her Black heritage. However, she asks, why this word? Why is Blackness always pointed out? Why not "¡Oye, blanca!"?

With a dialogic/performative analysis, instead of seeing a snag in Zoraida's performance, I see a moment of meaning-making between an Afro-Latina woman and an Anglo-American woman. What I see now is Zoraida's recognition of my interpretation of her words, and in response, a pulling back and rephrasing. The difference between the two is drastic: in terms of erasure, my thematic analysis could be construed as a kind of self-erasure. The dialogic/performative analysis, however, shows me that Zoraida's strength is not only expressed as an outright rejection of the obviously repressive, but also through quieter tactics towards more subtle forces of erasure. Indeed, my eagerness to smoothly stir Zoraida's story in with "the Afro-Latina experience" could have led to yet another instance of erasure through generalization.

9.3.2.1 Reflection

It is possible to employ the dialogue/performative style of listening to a classroom context. I think about how my students perform themselves at school, and how my presence impacts their performances. In this part of Zoraida's narrative, I let my assumptions affect how I listened to her story. Though Zoraida knew how to confront me, my young students haven't developed the tools to do this yet. As their teacher, it is important that I be aware of the framework I bring into the classroom, both as an observer and as a presence. Even as a practitioner of bilingual, multicultural education, I must constantly question and evolve the societal schema that I rely upon and invite students to share their expertise. Creating the structure for student-led conversations where I am no longer the only 'expert' invites conversations around identity that create "new cultural categories based on shared experiences, not just shared identities" (Nieto, 2010, p. 201), preserving the space where our internal discrepancies can develop in complexity.

9.3.3 "We're Not What You Expect Us to Be": A Visual Analysis of Zoraida Lopez's Photos

In the fall of 2011, Zoraida spent two months teaching and working in Colombia. She received a grant from the United States embassy to deliver lectures on photography, and as a side project spent a week in a high-security prison outside of Medellín, teaching photography to some of the female inmates. In her narrative,

Zoraida describes her work as an activist and photographer, and her interest in amplifying marginalized voices (Theme 3). In this section, I discuss two of the photographs that were generated out of that project.

Riessman (2008) points out that photographic images were used in the 20th century to illustrate non-Western cultures and to "provide evidence of something seen" (p. 142) without acknowledging the role of interpretation. Narrative analysis asks more of visual data, questioning the 'how' and 'why' decisions behind the creation of an image, as well as bringing in the reaction of the audience. "Photographs are best understood as 'collective assemblages' of photographer, viewer, and photographed subject" (Eileraas, 2003, p. 811). The photographic work of Zoraida on the prison campus in Colombia is very much a joining of these three elements. In her descriptions of the following photographs, Zoraida is aware of her power as an artist, as well as the power she wants her subjects to have, and of the effect she hopes the images will elicit in her various audiences.

Zoraida chose two photographs for me to include in my analysis of her narrative. One was taken by the women in the group, and the other is an image Zoraida took herself. Both of Zoraida's choices are photographs that express the voice of a population she sees as voiceless. Zoraida features these photos in exhibitions to defy and break manufactured assumptions about people, and to humanize those who have been condemned to being 'criminal' and/or 'foreign.' She is critical of traditional images of prison life and of harmful beliefs about the people who reside in the prison system. Below is the first photograph (Figure 9.1) and Zoraida's description:

FIGURE 9.1 Photograph taken by the women in Zoraida's group and orchestrated and chosen by Zoraida.

This photo is of three women who were in my photography class. On the left in the white tank top is Stefania,[1] in the middle is Grace, and on the right is Ruth. They are smiling and running, it's a beautiful sunny day, behind them you can see the wired coiled fence and behind them you can see the prison look-out tower. Behind the beautiful green trees, white clouds, and a blue sky.

Zoraida's description of this photo, an image that she did not take but that was created in circumstances that she orchestrated, uses words like "smiling," "beautiful," "white clouds and a blue sky," emphasizing the pleasant mood of this photograph. It is an image that intentionally disrupts prevailing depictions of gloomy prisoners and bleak prison life. Zoraida goes on to say,

> This was totally their idea. They wanted photos that looked like they were free and happy, and not confined within a prison. You have these three women in a prison, smiling and laughing, and I don't think you will get this composition of women in a U.S. prison. It's interesting because part of it is the prison system in Colombia but this really… challenges the stereotypical view of people in prison. They're saying, "We're not what you expect us to be."

Eileraas (2003) writes that in colonial photography, "subaltern women 'occupy' imagery in order to contest symbolic erasures" (p. 811). In this example, Zoraida has given her students the tools to dramatically shift the dominant perception of prisoners towards a happier, more human reality. The following is her description of the second photograph (Figure 9.2) she selected, one of her own images.

FIGURE 9.2 Photograph captured and chosen by Zoraida in the workshop.

This photograph was taken in the... they call them workshops, they're large rooms where the women have different jobs. And in this particular room, the women make locks and keys that are used in all the other prisons in Colombia. And the excess is sold to hardware stores. So, if you go into a hardware store in Colombia, nine... probably not nine times, maybe like seven times out of ten, the key and lock has come from a prison. I think it's kind of really funny.

The image is of the different tools that are used to make the keys and the locks in the foreground, in the middle is a hammer and a key and a lock, and on the upper third of the image is the woman's hands. She has on gloves, but her index finger is revealed. And she has on a bright fuchsia shiny nail. Colored, colored nail.

It's more of like a work scene. But I think in the same way that the other one humanizes, this one nail totally humanizes this person. It shows that this is a woman who still... I mean, she might be in prison, making keys, wearing these gloves that have gotten... they're white gloves, but they've gotten so dirty with a charcoal dust. But she still has her nails done. She's still, like, when you think of Colombian women, she's still this fashion-y lady. I like the image for that reason.

Once again, Zoraida speaks on her desire to humanize those who have lost their voice, to construct a counternarrative that "breaks the collective silence surrounding shameful events" (Riessman, 2008, p. 146). Zoraida is in control of how these women are seen, and she chooses to pay attention to the way that they see themselves. She added:

I think part of it too is not to continue to produce these stereotypical images that people expect... I mean, like images of men in prison, you expect to see men, photographed in black and white, showing tattoos, it's like a bunch of tattoos, or like bald heads, not smiling... and I think images like that reproduce... really negative opinions and views, and really negative policy.

Zoraida's photographs demonstrate her rejection of a dominant but misconstrued perception of a group of people, or of an individual. The strength of Zoraida's work is in the counternarrative she presents to the world, and it is in her own counternarrative to the tidy racial and ethnic categories that are so rigidly held in U.S. society that she expresses the strength of her voice.

9.3.3.1 Reflection

Images are powerful, especially photographic images, in part because they serve as proof of the existence of what they depict. In this part of her narrative, Zoraida describes harnessing the impact of an image in the name of change. As teachers, we can engender change when we choose the images we present to our students, leading them in meaningful visual analyses of these images. When we showcase characters and leaders with bodies of all colors, languages, sizes, and ages in the books and material that we bring to our students, we offer counternarratives to the harmfully limited scope of mainstream curricula. When we confront the images that mainstream media gives to us of marginalized populations in the classroom, we are teaching our students that they, too, can consume this content with a critical eye. In Colombia, Zoraida acted as both photographer and teacher when she put the image into the hands of her students: They were invited to present themselves to the world as they wanted to be seen. I am inspired by Zoraida's example to give my students affirming tools to create, and recreate, the story they want to tell, and to have told, about themselves.

9.4 Final Thoughts and Implications

Zoraida's narrative gives us the voice of a woman who is not willing to be boxed into convenient categories. Her story does not center around the confusion of being both Black and Latina and therefore neither. Instead, Zoraida's narrative emphasizes her acknowledgement and disregard of a mainstream society's confusion about where it might place her. She replaces that potential void with her own self-definition: "If I'm firm in who I am, then there's less question." Zoraida has the tools to identify the stories that are being told about her and to confront them with her own, self-realized presentation. She is generous with this tool as an activist and photographer, helping others create their own image and tell their own story.

Teachers are entrusted with a space where students' fledgling identities are incubated. With careful listening, teachers can harness this space to support the complicated, often conflicting stories that their students tell about themselves. We can choose to find and tell the stories that upset a dominant narrative, opening cracks so that our students can grow into their full complexity without sacrificing a crucial part of themselves. Zoraida's narrative adds an important note not only the Afro-Latina narrative chorus, but to that of the Black American, the Latino American, and to the loud and complex chorus of the United States. By presenting a story that upsets any convenient understanding of Afro-Latinas or of women or of 'truth,' I hope to destabilize the identity categories that confine and erase the lives and stories of not only Afro-Latina, Black, and Latina women, but anyone who is asked to disregard a piece of themselves to fit into an ill-fitting box.

Note

1 Pseudonyms are used to protect their identities.

References

Aguilar, C. (2017, August 18). *'Lemon' director Janicza Bravo on the lack of Afro-Caribbean inclusion in the Latino community and writing in Spanish again.* Remezcla. http://remezcla.com/features/film/interview-lemon-director-janicza-bravo/

Bost, S. (2000). Transgressing borders: Puerto Rican and Latina mestizaje. *MELUS, 25*(2), 187–211.

Butler, J. (1988). Performative acts and gender constitution: An essay in phenomenology and feminist theory. *Theatre Journal, 40*(4), 519–531.

Butler, J. (1996). Imitation and gender insubordination. In A. Garry & M. Pearsall (Eds.), *Women, knowledge, and reality: Explorations in feminist philosophy* (pp. 371–387). Routledge.

Chambers, V. (2005). Secret Latina at large. In G. B. Ventura (Ed.), *U.S. Latino literature today* (pp. 38–44). Pearson Longman.

Cruz-Janzen, M. I. (2001). Latinegras: Desired women: Undesirable mothers, daughters, sisters and wives. *Frontiers, 22*(3), 168–183.

Derrida, J. (1982). Différance. In A. Bass, (Ed. & Trans.), *Margins of philosophy* (pp. 1–27). University of Chicago Press.

Derrida, J. (1992). Passions: "An oblique offering". In D. Wood (Ed. & Trans.), *Derrida: A critical reader* (pp. 5–35). Blackwell.

Derrida, J. (1997). *Deconstruction in a nutshell: A conversation with Jaques Derrida* (J. Caputo, Ed.). Fordham University Press.

Doig-Acuña, M. (2018, February 6). *On claiming Afro-Latinidad.* Latino Rebels. https://www.latinorebels.com/2018/02/06/on-claiming-afro-latinidad/

Eileraas, K. (2003). Reframing the colonial gaze: Photography, ownership, and feminist resistance. *MLN, 118*(4), 807–840.

Flores, J. (2005). Triple consciousness? Afro-Latinos on the color line. *Wadabegei, 8*(1), 80–85.

Hatch, J. A. (2002). *Doing qualitative research in education settings.* State University of New York Press.

Hernández, T. K. (2003). Response to Silvio Torres-Saillant 'Too Black to be Latino/a:' Blackness and Blacks as foreigners in Latino studies. *Latino Studies, 1,* 152–159.

Hoy, V. C. (2010). Negotiating among invisibilities: Tales of Afro-Latinidades in the United States. In M. Jiménez Román & J. Flores (Eds.), *The Afro-Latin@ Reader: History and culture in the United States* (pp. 426–430). Duke University Press.

Jackson, A., & Mazzei, L. (2012). *Thinking with theory in qualitative research: Viewing data across multiple perspectives.* Routledge.

Jiménez Román, M., & Flores, J. (2010). Introduction. In M. Jiménez Román & J. Flores (Eds.), *The Afro-Latin@ Reader: History and culture in the United States* (pp. 1–15). Duke University Press.

Lambert, A. (2010). We are black too: Experiences of a Honduran Garifuna. In M. Jiménez Román & J. Flores (Eds.), *The Afro-Latin@ Reader: History and culture in the United States* (pp. 431–433). Duke University Press.

Lieblich, A., Tuval-Mashiach, R., & Zilber, T. (1998). *Narrative research: Reading, analysis, and interpretation.* SAGE Publications.

Modestin, Y. (2010). An Afro-Latina's quest for inclusion. In M. Jiménez Román & J. Flores (Eds.), *The Afro-Latin@ Reader: History and culture in the United States* (pp. 417–421). Duke University Press.

Mullen, C. A., & Kealy, W. A. (2005). Pathlamp: A self-study guide for teacher research. In C. Mitchell, S. Weber, & K. O'Reilly-Scanlon (Eds.), *Just who do we think we are?* (pp. 154–167). Routledge Falmer.

Nieto, S. (2010). *Language, culture, and teaching: Critical perspectives* (2nd. ed.). Routledge.

Quiñones Riviera, M. (2006). From Trigueñita to Afro-Puerto Rican: Intersections of the racialized, gendered and sexualized body in Puerto Rico and the U.S. mainland. *Meridians: Feminism, Race, and Transnationalism, 7*(1), 162–182.

Riessman, C. K. (2008). *Narrative methods for the human sciences.* SAGE Publications.

Vicioso, S. (2010). Discovering myself. In M. Jiménez Román & J. Flores (Eds.), *The Afro-Latin@ Reader: History and culture in the United States* (pp. 263–265). Duke University Press.

Wade, P. (2005). Rethinking mestizaje: Ideology and lived experience. *Journal of Latin American Studies, 37*(2), 239–257.

10

TRANSGRESSING PEDAGOGICAL BORDERS OF OPPRESSION

A Poblana Mexicana Indígena-Migrante Praxis

Daniela Conde

10.1 Education as an Avenue for Social Transformation

During these tumultuous times of critical political and social change in the United States, it is important to adhere to our commitment to equity in education. Educators, students, and scholar-practitioners have the potential to contribute to a more socially just world. Education should not be a site of conformity, violence, or erasure. Instead, education should be a space for the practice of liberation for all individuals and the cultivation of humanity (Freire, 1972). A commitment to a liberatory education and good teaching and learning in our K-20 educational institutions is critical to addressing some of the most pressing issues in our society, especially as we witness shifts in political power that have direct material consequences for nondominant communities of color (Boggs & Kurashige, 2011). Therefore, this narrative engages with questions related to the power of pedagogy and the simultaneous contradictions and experiences that an undocumented Latina Indigenous migrant woman, like Dolores Cruz (a pseudonym), navigates through.

The term 'Indígena–Migrante,' or Indigenous migrant, in this chapter refers to Indigenous people of Latinoamérica who have migrated to the United States. More specifically, in this chapter, 'Poblana Mexicana Indígena–Migrante' refers to the Indigenous people who have migrated to the United States from the state of Puebla, México. This is an important identity because Indigenous people from México often face erasure of their Indigeneity under terms such as such as Latinos/xs or Mexicanos due to the inherent colonial history of the term 'Latino/x' and the nationalistic term 'Mexicanos' (Urrieta & Calderón, 2019).

Central to this narrative study are the experiences of Latinx Indigenous migrant students. While there is limited research on this intersecting identity of

Latinx Indigeneity and migration in postsecondary education, there are some studies that shed light on this growing community, as well as migrant students in the United States. For instance, Huizar Murillo and Cerda (2004) articulate that the 2000 census data showed growth in the Native American population nationwide. More specifically, persons who identified as 'American Indian' also identified as 'Hispanic,' with the California population of American Indians of Hispanic origin showing an increase by 146%. A large body of research also highlights the experiences of Latinxs in United States K-20 schooling, including detailing the discrimination and racism students face in educational practices and policies inside and outside of the classroom (Delgado Bernal, 2002; Ladson-Billings & Tate, 1995; Yosso, Smith, Ceja, & Solórzano, 2009). Migrant student populations in the United States also experience marginalization, such as the consequences of living in impoverished neighborhoods, English language learning, and high-stakes testing while also finding support in mentors and teachers (Suárez-Orozco, Suárez-Orozco & Todorova, 2008).

Latinx Indigenous students from México experience a dissonance in the educational systems in the United States, especially when their ancestral knowledge, identities, and languages are erased in the construct of Latinidad (Martinez, 2017; Urrieta & Calderón, 2019). While there is limited research on the Indigenous Mexican migrant students and families, studies such as Casanova's (2012), which focuses on the resilience and agentive practices of Indigenous Mexican migrants, inspires my narrative study (Casanova, 2012; Casanova, O'Connor, & Anthony-Stevens, 2016). Therefore, my research question(s) for this critical narrative study are as follows: How can educational spaces serve as sites of empowerment for an Indigenous migrant woman in Lenni Lenape ancestral lands or New York City? What are some of the possibilities, contradictions, and limitations that arise? How does Dolores Cruz's agency manifest in her life?

10.2 Critical Self-Narrative of the Researcher

Yo soy campesina, Indígena-Migrante, e intelectual, and I became an expert at crossing borders at the age of seven. Borders like the U.S.-México wall militarized my campesina mind, body, and spirit, yet resistance to these political open wounds (Anzaldúa, 1987) unequivocally expanded my humanity. As a child, becoming a professor in a higher-education institution seemed impossible because my situation consisted of being born into a poverty-stricken family in Huaquechula, Puebla, México.

Being Brown and an Indígena-Migrante student as well as an undocumented seven-year-old in a wealthy suburban community on the Kumeyaay Coast in Southern California meant being educated in public schools that centered the project of settler colonialism. I grew up in immigrant enclaves that replicated the poverty of lands, but within miles there existed large mansions and gated communities where my Brown body was interpellated as foreign and dispensable, and as a potential domestic worker at best. At that point in time, I experienced a double-consciousness (Du Bois, 1903), and as an immigrant child, I internalized the colorism and racism towards communities of color that were upheld in the curriculum of the surrounding predominantly white public schools.

My identity as an Indígena-Migrante campesina born in Puebla, México, who grew up in a low-income and single-parent household has contributed to my commitment to educational equity and political activism in my community. As a Gates Millennium Scholar, I was given the opportunity to navigate my undergraduate studies, master's program, and now doctoral program without having to worry about the financial cost of higher education. This privilege has granted me access to spaces of higher education that past generations of my family could not have possibly imagined. However, my passion for educational equity and social justice is rooted in the teachings of my family as well as my work as a community educator. Additionally, my work alongside local grassroots community organizations in San Diego, California, have inspired my approach to research and the methodology of this study, with the intentional act of centering the narrative and experiences of an undocumented Indigenous migrant Latina as a way to disrupt power.

My family, especially my mother, has provided the ultimate inspiration in my educación. Over centuries through their humble labor, in the vast cornfields of Puebla, México, my family laid the foundation for generations. While they worked in the fields in México and in homes, factories, restaurants, and other capitalist enterprises that benefit off of low-wage labor of undocumented folks in the United States, I was given the opportunity to focus on school until the age of thirteen, when I started working menial jobs like my family. Yet, my Má consistently emphasized the importance of a college education and engaged in inspirational *pláticas* and *consejos*, or dialogues and advice, throughout my educational journey, as well as provided a weekly fresh pot of frijoles to sustain me during my time in college. Her tender acts of sustenance did not go unnoticed and are examples of community cultural wealth (Yosso, 2005); my mother's consejos continue to sustain me as I continue in academia as a doctoral student.

I am the first person in my family to graduate from high school, college, and graduate school, and there is undoubtedly immense privilege that comes with being college-educated and a graduate student. At the same time, as an education researcher, my work is also informed by K-2 schooling experiences, some of which include erasure and discrimination in institutional spaces of learning. My goal as a scholar, human, and educator is to practice continuous reflexivity and accountability. In engaging with this chapter, I also invite teachers, professors, and educators to deeply reflect on the ways in which settler colonialism and other systems of oppression show up in the classroom or in educational spaces. By naming and addressing the erasure of Indigenous migrant knowledges, languages, cultures, identities, and lives, as well as working to cultivate equitable spaces of learning, educators can potentially uplift and sustain the lives of students and, by extension, their families and communities.

10.3 Theoretical Frameworks

This study is grounded in the theoretical framework of Latina/Latino Critical Race Theory (LatCrit) (Delgado Bernal, 2002), as well as two tenets from Tribal Critical Race Theory: one, "colonization is endemic to society," and two, "the concepts of culture, knowledge, and power take on new meaning when examined through an Indigenous lens" (Brayboy, 2005, p. 429). Tribal Critical Race Theory also addresses the dimensions of settler colonialism in educational spaces that contribute to the erasure of Indigenous lives.

LatCrit is a framework that counters the deficit models that persist for people of color in education by valuing experiential knowledge and counternarratives, and analyzing the way in which racism permeates society (Delgado Bernal, 2002). LatCrit is an analytic lens that highlights the ways in which educational policies and practices subordinate people of color and specifically Latinx people and students. Using LatCrit and Tribal Critical Race Theory, we can identify the ways in which students of color and Indigenous students persist through experiences of marginalization. Some examples of this marginalization include educational policies that center Western knowledges and ways of learning that do not take into account the identities of students of color or societal injustices that impact their educational pathways.

Additionally, culturally sustaining pedagogies (CSP) (Paris & Alim, 2017), stemming from the seminal work of culturally relevant pedagogy (Ladson-Billings, 1995), demand a response to not just the subject matter, teacher, and students, but also to sustaining linguistic and cultural pluralism. Challenging power and centering the context of the students' lived realities, such as their sociopolitical environments and the historical legacies of systems of oppression, are central to CSP. Additionally, CSP invites inward critiques as a way of continuous reflection of our practices as teachers, students, and communities (Paris & Alim, 2017). Ultimately, CSP aims at enacting practices of equity across race, ethnicity, ability, sexuality, language, and documentation status by sustaining the minds and bodies of nondominant communities. While enactments of asset-based pedagogies, like CSP (Paris & Alim, 2017), remain within the K-12 context, less of CSP and other asset-based pedagogies are found in higher and postsecondary education. CSP is important in this narrative in the ways it can be practiced with and alongside migrant adult students and learners.

10.4 Research Design and Methods: *Comadriando*

This is a narrative study that involves interviews with a migrant, undocumented Latina woman, Dolores Cruz. It is also, in part, a self-narrative.

This critical Latina narrative was accomplished through eight weekly semi-structured interviews within the span of two months, as well as eight weekly handwritten autoethnographic analytic memos. These interviews took place in the comfort of Dolores's home in New York City with *cafecitos* and often *comida*. I call this methodological data collection *comadriando*. Comadriando is modeled after the dialogue I witnessed as a child in Puebla, México, where *comadres*, or the godmother of one's child, engaged in an exchange of food, stories, advice, laughter, plants, and other cultural medicines. While one does not have to be a godmother of one's child to be a comadre, there does have to be a mutual respect, reciprocity, and trust between the people engaging in 'comadriando.' Comadriando is methodology that emerged organically within an already-existing relationship with the participant (Wilson, 2008). Comadriando is also an inherently sacred space of dialogue that nourishes all people involved physically, emotionally, and sometimes even spiritually. Comadriando is not necessarily tied to the gender binary but rather inspired. Dolores, at times, expressed her thoughts, stories, and knowledge while breastfeeding her daughter; therefore she felt a strong sense of trust with me, the researcher. These interviews lasted two to three hours and are the main source of data collection along with the follow-up dialogues regarding the data analysis process. Moreover, the entire paper was read to Dolores; with translation, she helped with editing some of the paper while it was being written and upon completion. Through this approach, Dolores's agency and voice is central to this study.

The questions in the semi-structured interviews included biographical stories of Dolores's experiences in México and the United States, her identity and meaning-making, and her transnational educational experiences. The narrative analysis involved a thematic analysis (Riessman, 2008) of Dolores's responses organized around the four main parts of the interviews: biographical background, migration and identity; education and agency; reflections; and her hopes and dreams for the future. Narrative analysis also requires the researcher to acknowledge their positionality, where reflexivity is important because we recognize the implications of our thoughts that may be occurring within the narrative (Riessman, 2008).

10.5 Dolores Cruz's Counternarrative

Dolores Cruz was born in Puebla, México, in the 1980s. Dolores's family members and ancestors are campesinas/os. The expectations of that time and place were to earn a living doing backbreaking stoop labor in the fields with marriage following soon after one became a teenage girl. This stark reality was one she never accepted, which is why she was determined to migrate to the United States as a young teenager.

During our first interview, I asked Dolores to map out, describe, draw, write, or express in any way about her life. Dolores wrote the passage below.

Mi nombre es Dolores Cruz. Soy de Mexico, hablo dos idiomas, Espanol e Engles. Me gusta mucho bailar, ser ama de casa, cuidar mis hijos y estudiar, seguir aprendiendo cosas nuevas academicas y como ser una persona cada dia mejor. Me gustan los talleres porque aprendes muchas cosas que por siertas circunstancias en el pasado no pudiste, pero nunca es tarde para aprender.

My name is Dolores Cruz. I am from Mexico, I speak two languages, Spanish and English. I really like dancing, being a housewife, taking care of my children and studying, continuing to learn new academic things and how to be a better person every day. I like workshops because you learn many things that due to certain circumstances in the past you couldn't, but it's never too late to learn.

This statement is short but powerful and references her positionality at the time of the interviews. Dolores is in her mid to late thirties during the time of the interviews. She is a mother of three children and lives in New York City. Her goal is to receive her General Educational Development (GED) and continue her education. I reverted back to this passage multiple times during the analysis process of this study as well as in the follow-up dialogue with Dolores; I will address it again in the Findings section.

Dolores disliked school as a young child. She especially despised the way teachers physically reprimanded the students when homework or classwork was done incorrectly. The teachers traveled daily from afar to Dolores's small town in México. Dolores's teachers publicly shamed the students in order to motivate them to do better. They also uplifted the students who excelled and set them as examples for the class. In addition to the strict pedagogical practices of the teachers, Dolores expressed the sadness she felt not being able to afford many of the educational activities. Dolores describes how being one of ten siblings meant that there were limited to no funds for school. During her last year of elementary school, she was selected to be part of a dance performance to the song "La Negra Tomasa." However, her mother did not allow her to perform because they did not have enough money to buy the shoes and dress they needed for the performance.

Moreover, Dolores described the stories of her mother, Doña Luna Cruz (a pseudonym), as formative foundations of knowledge. During one of their mornings together while sipping on a soft cinnamon-flavored dark coffee and dipping their *tlacoyos* into their *salsa de molcajete*, Doña Luna began to reflect on her education—the education she dreamed of and begged her father for. Doña Luna was the oldest of her siblings, which meant that she was not allowed to even think about attending school. Her father also instilled fear and enforced strict gender roles in their household. Participant decided not to share this trauma.

In addition to the many stories Dolores's mother shared with her, she described their Indigenous knowledge that permeated their everyday life. For instance,

Dolores recalled in our interviews that everyone in her small town would continuously talk about the rain, the fields, the growth of crops, the volcano (Volcán Popocatépetl), what to feed the animals, what healer to see, how to keenly cradle corn dough for tortillas and tlacoyos, when to drink mezcal to help with digestion, if the maize was ready for harvesting, what poisonous plants to avoid while taking care of the animals in the fields, what tea to drink when there was a certain pain in the body, and so on. Talks about the land, health, and growing one's own food pervaded almost all conversations. This is important to acknowledge because although this ancestral knowledge is not seen as 'traditional' or 'academic,' or may be questioned or undervalued as 'mundane' through a Eurocentric academic lens, this knowledge is central and encompasses the funds of knowledge of Dolores (Brayboy, 2005; González, Moll & Amanti, 2005). A critical interconnected component of Dolores's ancestral knowledge is that it is tied to the land. In the photo below (Figure 10.1), you can see the Volcán Popocatépetl in Puebla, México. This is Dolores's and my homeland and place of birth.

Nevertheless, the multiple social, political, and economic transnational systems shaping Indigenous communities' working conditions impacted Dolores's family, like many other Indigenous migrant families from México. This included the separation of Dolores's family due to forced migration and the impoverished conditions in México and the United States. Through Dolores's counternarrative and my self-narrative, we are able to witness intergenerational educational inequities and transformative pedagogical experiences, as well as our resistance in educational spaces.

FIGURE 10.1 Photograph of the Volcán Popocatépetl in Puebla, México, Dolores Cruz and Daniela Conde's homeland and place of birth, taken by the chapter author.

10.6 Findings

The findings are organized as follows: the section begins with an analysis of Dolores's narrative, with a closer look at the pedagogical practices enacted by her English as a Second Language (ESL) teacher, which impacted Dolores's activism, followed by a thematic analysis of Dolores's educational trajectory and identity, and a discussion of a Poblana Mexicana Indígena-Migrante Praxis, as well as its implications for teaching and learning.

10.6.1 Pedagogical Analysis of Dolores's Narrative

Nos ayudaba para que nosotros nos ayudáramos.

The narrative I examine is Dolores's retelling of her experience as both a student in postsecondary education and a community leader making changes in the public education of her children.

I paid particular attention to how Dolores's counternarratives of the educational spaces she is part of and the educational inequities in her children's public schools served as catalysts for social change. Dolores expressed gratitude for her GED teachers like Nicole Brown (a pseudonym), who challenged their students and, in some ways, enacted culturally sustaining pedagogies (Paris & Alim, 2017). Nicole Brown was an English teacher that taught free GED classes at an Adult Learning Center in Queens, New York, for an extended period of time. The majority of the students were immigrant parents and adults from all over the world. Nicole Brown, an experienced educator, facilitated dialogues around political issues such as educational injustices while engaging in the English-learning process.

Within these classes, the teaching and learning resembled facets of culturally sustaining pedagogies. Dolores describes Nicole Brown as a good teacher and an impactful educator:

> Nicole Brown fue una maestra de Inglés excelente y con ella aprendí bastante. Ella te enseñaba los temas en una forma que lo entendías, buscaba diferentes maneras de explicarlos, por ejemplo la gramática. Nicole tenía como 50 años, ella enseñó a muchas personas como niños, jóvenes y adultos. Ella hablaba de las injusticias porque sus padres también eran inmigrantes de Italia y ella tuvo que traducir mucho de niña cuando iba a la escuela, entonces tenía experiencia personal y académica. Por ejemplo, para los niños que tenían dislexia (a un papá le pasaba lo mismo) agarraba un papel y le abría una ventanita para ver las letras. Les decía las letras en una forma divertida, como la 'b' tiene una pancita. Nos ayudaba para que nosotros nos ayudáramos.

Nicole Brown was an excellent English teacher and I learned a lot from her. She taught you the subjects in a way that you understood; she found different ways to explain [a concept or lesson], for example, grammar. Nicole was about 50 years old, she taught a lot of people, [she had taught in the past] children, teenagers, and adults. She talked about injustices because her parents were also immigrants from Italy, and she had to translate a lot as a child when she went to school, so she had personal and academic experiences [to relate to us]. For example, for children who had dyslexia (a father in our class also had dyslexia), she grabbed a piece of paper and opened a small window to see the letters. She taught him the letters in a fun way, like the [letter] "b" has a little belly. She helped us so we could help ourselves.

Dolores described the pedagogy enacted by Nicole as one that pays particular attention to the linguistic and cultural pluralism of diverse students. Learning disabilities, such as dyslexia, and immigrant narratives were also at the forefront of the teaching and learning of Nicole's pedagogy. The significance of students' prior knowledge and culture in teaching and learning is connected to the idea that even though teachers can manifest pedagogical content knowledge (Shulman, 2004) such as Nicole's teaching about English grammar, if one is not aware of the students' culture and knowledge or disabilities, such as dyslexia, it can lead to problematic situations because subject matter is framed by the context of the students' backgrounds.

Dolores's teacher, Nicole, had a way of appealing to the immigrant parents by making herself accessible, speaking in a familiar language that people could readily understand, and interacting with them in a way that made them feel they were important to her. Nicole did not use inaccessible language but instead used language that related to their pluralistic experiences, culture, and identities.

My follow-up question for Dolores was: "Mencionó Nicole Brown varias veces, ¿puede contarme de la forma en que enseñaba Nicole? ¿Por qué fue tan importante para usted?" [You mentioned Nicole Brown several times; can you tell me about the way Nicole taught? Why was this so important to you?]. Dolores answered with an extensive response:

Ella [Nicole Brown] era de las personas que no le gustaba las injusticias, y cada [vez] que estaba en las escuela ella decía que los directores no la querían en las escuelas. La sacaban con cualquier pretexto porque a ella no le gustaban las injusticias que cometían con los papás, por ejemplo muchas cosas que en las escuelas tienen que avisarles a los padres, los derechos que ellos tienen, y no lo hacen por obtener los fondos que les dan. Ella nos decía varias cosas, fue hace como cuatro años… ella empezó hablar de los programas que hay [en la escuela], por ejemplo clases de Inglés [para los niños] le llaman ESL, que por ejemplo no lo necesitan y que, las escuelas, por llenar el cupo, el grupo, meten a otros niños para que les den los fondos.

Entonces ella nos dijo que "tú tienes que llenar papeles para que tu niño entre ahí. Las escuelas no pueden nomás meterlo ahí." Ella nos dijo que investigáramos en las escuelas para ver si nuestro hijo estaba y si no lo necesita, debíamos de sacarlos. Porque si tu niño realmente no lo necesita este, para salir de ahí es difícil porque tiene que ir haciendo muchos exámenes y en el futuro los exámenes son más difíciles. Y si no los pasas [los exámenes], ahí te quedas.

Todos nuestros niños iban a esa escuela, entonces todos fuimos a preguntar… como 20 padres…. [Ella nos decía] "Tienen que tener cuidado lo que firman, y si no entienden el idioma, tienen el derecho de pedir traductor. Ellos [la escuela] tiene esa obligación." A partir de ahí, esa escuela, donde iba mi hijo, ya empezó dar la información para informarnos si tu niño necesitaba estar ahí, porque antes no daban esa información de los programas… ella nos decía "Tienen que buscar varios padres… para que la escuela te haga caso. Tienes que buscar un grupo porque si no, [solo] una persona es difícil."

Y sí, sí es verdad. Y también y ahora que ya estoy más involucrada en las escuelas haz de cuenta que también depende del director. Si el director le gusta trabajar no hay ningún problema. Depende de los papás. Ahí me di cuenta que, ahorita que estoy más involucrada, que los padres tienen la voz. Ellos son los que pueden cambiar todo.

She [Nicole Brown] was one of the people who didn't like injustices, and every [time] she was in school, she said principals didn't want her in the schools. They took her out under any pretext because she did not like the injustices they committed against the parents, for example there are many things in schools that they have to notify parents about, the rights they have, and they do not do it to obtain funds. She told us several things, it was about four years ago… she started talking about the programs that are [in school], for example, English classes [for children] called ESL, for example, [some students] they don't need it and that, the schools, to fill the quota, the group, they put children [in these programs] to give them the funds.

Then she told us that "you have to fill out papers for your child to enter there [ESL programs]. Schools can't just put them in there." She told us to investigate in schools to see if our children were in there and if they don't need it, we should get them out. Because if your child really doesn't need it, getting them out of there is difficult because they have to take many exams and in the future, the exams are more difficult. And if they don't pass them [the exams], you stay there.

All our children went to that school, so we all went to ask… about 20 parents…. [She would tell us,] "You all have to be careful with what you sign, and if you don't understand the language, you have the right to ask for a translator. They [the school] have that obligation." From there [after this], that school, where my son was going, started giving the information to inform us if our children needed to be there [in ESL], because before they did not give that information about the programs… she told us "You have to look for several parents… for the school to listen to you. You have to look for a group because if not, [just] one person it's difficult."

And yes, it is true. And also and now that I am more involved in schools, I realize that it also depends on the principal. If the principal likes to work, then there is no problem. It depends on the parents. There, I realized that, right now, that I am more involved, that parents have a voice. They are the ones who can change everything.

Dolores is constructing her counternarrative (Delgado Bernal, 2002) and is positioning herself as a student who values spaces where she was challenged intellectually while learning English and while engaging in activism work with other parents in her class. This event that Dolores describes in which parents organized and confronted the racist xenophobic school policies happened around 2012. Dolores uses repetition and direct speech when she emphasizes what her teacher, Nicole, suggests. This narrative displays the potential of culturally relevant pedagogical practices for parents as a way to make meaning of their education through affirming their own student identities, but also relating the teaching back to how they can contribute to their children's education. It also reveals the institutional inequities that occur with marginalized students, such as first-generation students of color and Latinx students in ESL programs specifically in the public schools of New York City.

Dolores was one of the leaders of the group of parents that organized to fight for an equitable K-12 education for their children by holding the public school accountable for their ESL enrollment. The parents worked to disrupt, locally, the forceful enrollment in ESL classes of Latinx students born in the United States, students of color, and migrant students. Through their local effort, the parents fought against an unjust system of education that sought to track their children into English language learning programs for the purpose of receiving funds rather than supporting the students' English language learning.

10.6.2 Transgressing Borders of Inequality and Redefining Education: Liberatory Schooling

Dolores Cruz came to the United States at the age of 15. Dolores has lived in the United States for over 20 years now; New York City, Lenni Lenape Indigenous land, is now her home. Although she only completed an elementary school education in México and remains undocumented, she has been consistently involved in popular education programs such as workshops on nutrition, legal rights, women's rights and tenant rights, and is pursuing her GED. Dolores currently holds a position as Secretary in her son's middle school Parent Teacher Association (PTA) and is part of a parent Leadership Organization that makes decisions on curriculum and other educational matters. Education is central to the dynamics of her family's life, even though she began the interview reflecting on her negative educational experiences in México.

While Dolores did not receive a formal education in the United States, her ongoing educational trajectory has consisted of a community-based education. Liberatory schooling (Freire, 1972) is grounded in the community, the streets, the land, and the people, and centers individual and collective critical consciousness as well as the disruption of oppressive material conditions imposed upon marginalized people. Moreover, liberatory schooling centers humanizing pedagogies and nonnormative formations of knowledge such as creative manifestations of agency.

Dolores's political consciousness grew out of the multiple programs and educational spaces she was involved in beyond the confines of the traditional classroom. Activism was also an outcome of the teaching and learning facilitated by Nicole Brown but manifested by all of the students through collective action. Dolores identified and articulated the sociopolitical problems, such as discrimination and tracking against young students of color. In doing so, alongside her teacher, she strived to engage parents in educating themselves about local concerns directly tied to educational injustices faced by their children.

She is now fully committed to combating injustices by educating herself and her family and being involved in the PTA and parent leadership at her son's middle school. It is within these realms that empowered people like Dolores cultivate their leadership and make a local impact because they believe in themselves.

10.6.3 Self-Determination Politics

Dolores is recreating herself into the woman she wants to become while centering her family but recognizing her own agency in the process. She rejects patriarchal authority by refusing authoritative male dominance:

> Si estudias, si te educas tú puedes hacer todo. Pues, así de todo lo que he agarrado de todos los maestros, de los talleres de los derechos de las mujeres, así de todo lo que voy agarrando de poquito en poquito. Eso me ayudó. Ahora yo no le tengo miedo nada, ni a los hombres.

> If you study, if you educate yourself, you can do everything. Well, from everything I have grasped from all of the teachers, from the women's rights workshops, as well as everything I am gaining, little by little. That helped me. Now I am not afraid of anything, not even men.

An extension of this self-determination is exemplified in Dolores standing up against gentrification initiatives that have tried to intimidate her to evacuate her apartment in New York City. For Dolores, it is necessary to acknowledge, respect, and create spaces for women to actualize their education, leadership, and joy. Her efforts encompass the principles of self-determination.

Dolores's activism entailed creating local leadership with the parents in her GED classes as well as garnering involvement from parents in her role in the PTA organization. Dolores consistently creates spaces of self-worth and self-determination, and brings others with her.

10.6.4 A Poblana Mexicana Indígena-Migrante Praxis: Dolores Cruz and Daniela Conde's Shared Raíces

Grace Lee Boggs, an Asian-American organizer and philosopher, calls for a radical reimagination of conceptions of social change when she writes about the need to heal ourselves and the planet through decolonizing our imaginations (Boggs & Kurashige, 2011). Rather than attempting to bring change using existing systems and conventions, it is important to reimagine and build worlds that sustain our lives. This project of creation requires the exploration of new theories, alternative knowledge systems, and the centering of counternarratives that can be found in the lives of women such as Dolores Cruz.

As Indigenous migrant communities in urban environments, our dehumanization has occurred through global processes of settler colonialism, racialized capitalism, and white supremacy (Brayboy, 2005; Urrieta & Calderón, 2019). However, I argue that Dolores is forming a way of surviving and thriving in New York City through a Poblana Mexicana Indígena Migrante Praxis.

All four of my grandparents raised me, and all four of them were still alive when this study was conducted. I cried and begged to go back to México the first time I came to the United States. I am not as in tune with my grandparents' every breath as I was before, yet I have seen their presence manifest in every space I am part of. They raised me with a love for the land and my community. They taught me how to live resiliently and fiercely, but with my mind, body, and spirit attentive to the vibrations of the earth. Their teachings about our relationship to land and people and living beings have nurtured me into a human being who does not and will not give up in the face of oppression, just like Dolores. However, detailing the nuances in my upbringing also highlights some important contradictions; these contradictions call for an 'inward critique' (Paris & Alim, 2017) of internalized oppression. The following passage was part of one of my autoethnographic writings:

> As a child, without any critical, deep understanding of gender roles, gender expressions, or sexuality, I would avoid any activities that would render any 'weakness.' I preferred sitting alongside my Abuelito Abraham while he sang

corridos or norteñas with his compadres. I preferred drawing, painting, playing in the garden instead of sewing or cooking; I preferred listening to adult dialogues about life in el campo, la cosecha, and stories of *el norte*. I preferred writing poetry or letters to my parents, who were both in the United States at that time, while I was in Puebla with my Abuelita Gloria. Now, as an adult, I am proudly learning how to sew, cook, and create healing remedies from all of the women in my *familia*. I am especially moved by my Abuelita Lucila's stories of how she would sew hundreds of servilletas and sell them to her comadres to help pay for the education of one of her daughters. Now I see cooking, sewing, and other activities I once thought of as not 'powerful' as pedagogical tools as well as actions of resistance, protest, survival, and sustenance.

Counternarratives and Indigenous ancestral knowledge are anti-colonial because they resist Eurocentric epistemologies and instead expand our understanding of the world (Brayboy, 2005; Wilson, 2008). Yet, close detailing of these counternarratives also help us see the power dynamics and the ways in which oppression is internalized, such as how I viewed gendered activities like sewing and cooking as 'weak' and therefore avoided them until later on in my life.

The years with my grandparents are still quite vivid and their teachings remain with me. Through these one-on-one interviews and autoethnographic writings grew dialogues of our ancestral knowledge; from Dolores's narrative and my self-narrative arises the Poblana Mexicana Indígena-Migrante Praxis.

Dolores is part of a dance collective of women of color, primarily migrant Mexicana women, in Queens, New York City. For Dolores, dance is a way to engage in the process of movement that is nourishing for her mind, body, and spirit. Her dance collective of migrant women meet twice a week and engage in multilingual music, dancing, and community-building. A Queer Latinx dance leader, who is a motivational figure, leads this dance collective. They actively take up space in the built environment, in a public park in the middle of a track field where many people surround the location. During these gatherings, they also dialogue about their children's educational experiences throughout their time together. Dolores described this experience as central to her survival, identity development, and self-care. Therefore, Dolores and I call this a Poblana Mexicana Indígena-Migrante Praxis that is educational at its core while transcending the boundaries of a traditional educational space by bringing it back to the communities and inciting embodied collective knowledge, and centering the mind, body, and spirit.

A Poblana Mexicana Indígena Migrante Praxis bridges our understanding of liberatory schooling grounded in the community and a politics of self-determination. This place-based and collective praxis is deeply relational and sustains both of our lives as Indigenous migrant women navigating educational spaces and beyond. This praxis centers liberatory forms of schooling or education with a politics of self-determination deeply embedded in an Indigenous migrant identity. These concepts are put into action through the dance collective and activism in educational spaces. This praxis does not seek to generalize or romanticize the experience of Indigenous migrant women, nor does it seek to be a prescriptive way of addressing the needs of Indigenous Mexican migrant adult learners, but rather it validates the way in which non-dominant communities theorize through embodied collective practices. In other words, this is us, myself and Dolores, thinking together and naming our theory and practice, albeit to the best of our abilities, as a way to disrupt settler colonialism in educational spaces.

The dance collective of migrant women is an embodiment of this praxis. It is an educational space that sustains the literacies, cultures, and valued practices of the collective of migrant women. The dance collective is also an educational space that visibly centers the bodies of nondominant communities. Their presence in a public space with an intentional incorporation of music that has strong cultural ties to the women's lived experiences is an example of collective resistance to assimilation in urban geographies. The dancers also share energy in the movement of their bodies in a collective rhythm of prayer as well as engage in dialogue about their livelihoods and futures. They are engaging in change-making and living out their collective survival, healing, and resistance.

10.7 Conclusion and Implications

Educational spaces can be sites of transformation; however, educational spaces that center white middle-class norms can also contribute to the erasure of nondominant identities, languages, cultures, and knowledges. In this narrative study, intergenerational counternarratives reveal educational inequalities that impact the educational experiences of Indigenous migrant students. Moreover, Dolores's liberatory schooling, outside of the classroom in her dance collective, brought together not only her politics of self-determination but centered her Indigenous migrant identity and ways of being. A Poblana Mexicana Indígena-Migrante Praxis thus names this specific way of being, living, and resisting in the United States as a migrant woman that encounters multiple forms of oppression both within the Latino/x community and in the larger society of the United States (Urrieta & Calderón, 2019).

Sustaining Indigenous migrant futures requires a paradigm shift in the purpose of education in the United States. Sustaining Indigenous futures invites us to reflect on these and many other questions: How can we, as educators, continue to destabilize settler colonialism in classroom practices and curricula that silence the lives of Indigenous students, especially in American Indian communities? What transformative and humanizing teaching and learning already exist in our communities? How can we support the learning and, by extension, lives of Native and Indigenous migrant students in the United States? How are we collectively dismantling systems of oppression in K-20 schooling?

This critical narrative study details the ways in which Dolores Cruz, both a student and parent, manifests her agency in her educational trajectory. Nevertheless, this work does not do enough to highlight the local Tribal Nations and Indigenous communities in Lenni Lenape ancestral territory (New York City); further research hopes to highlight the relationships or lack there of between Indigenous peoples in the United States and Latinx Indigenous communities. From Dolores's narrative we learn that cultivating spaces for Indigenous migrant parents' learning and holistic empowerment can lead to parental advocacy. However, this requires facilitators and teachers that see Latinx and Indigenous migrant parents in a non-deficit manner, center their funds of knowledge, critique systems of oppression, and historicize local and national schooling practices and policies. Seeing parents as valued members of classrooms can greatly contribute to teaching and learning that supports heterogeneous ways of knowing as well as sustains students' cultures, languages, and identities. These narratives bring to light the resistance that is happening through localized educational spaces, yet this is an ongoing, urgent, and long-term struggle that demands our collective commitment as scholars, community members, and educators.

Final Note: I would kindly like to express my gratitude and love to my family, elders, and ancestors from Puebla, México and to my mother, Ildefonsa and my three sisters: Yvette, Gabby, and Karen Conde.
A special thank you to Dra. Carmen M. Martínez-Roldán for this opportunity.
Thank you to Dolores Cruz for her willingness to participate and engage in this co-constructed research study.
I continue to be inspired by her story, life, and resilience.

Dolores Cruz's hopes and dreams:
Mis sueño[s], míos, mis sueños es ver a mis hijos [ob]tener su degree. Los tres. De la universidad. Y el otro [sueño], algún día, [yo quiero] terminar mi GED también.

References

Anzaldúa, G. (1987). *Borderlands: The new mestiza = La frontera*. Spinsters/Aunt Lute.

Boggs, G. L., & Kurashige, S. (2011). *The next American revolution: Sustainable activism for the twenty-first century*. University of California Press.

Brayboy, B. (2005). Toward a tribal critical race theory. *The Urban Review, 37*(5), 425–446. https://doi.org/10.1007/s11256-005-0018-y

Casanova, S. (2012). The stigmatization and resilience of a female Indigenous Mexican immigrant. *Hispanic Journal of Behavioral Sciences, 34*, 375–403. https://doi.org/10.1177/0739986312449584

Casanova, S., O'Connor, B. H., & Anthony-Stevens, V. (2016). Ecologies of adaptation for Mexican Indigenous im/migrant children and families in the United States: Implications for Latino studies. *Latino Studies, 14*, 192–213. https://doi.org/10.1057/lst.2016.4

Delgado Bernal, D. (2002). Critical race theory, Latino critical theory, and critical raced-gendered epistemologies: Recognizing students of color as holders and creators of knowledge. *Qualitative Inquiry, 8*(1), 105–126. https://doi.org/10.1177/107780040200800107

Du Bois, W. E. B. (1903). *The souls of black folk*. A. G. McClurg.

Fox, J., & Rivera-Salgado, G. (2004). *Indigenous Mexican migrants in the United States*. Center for U.S.-Mexican Studies, UCSD.

Freire, P. (1972). *Pedagogy of the oppressed*. Herder and Herder.

González, N., Moll, L. C., & Amanti, C. (2005). *Funds of knowledge: Theorizing practice in households, communities, and classrooms*. Erlbaum Associates.

Huizar Murillo, J., & Cerda, I. (2004). Indigenous Mexican migrants in the 2000 US Census: "Hispanic American Indians". In J. Fox & G. Rivera-Salgado (Eds.), *Indigenous Mexican migrants in the United States* (pp. 311–333). University of California, San Diego.

Ladson-Billings, G. (1995). Toward a theory of culturally relevant pedagogy. *American Educational Research Journal, 32*(3), 465–491.

Ladson-Billings, G., & Tate, W. F. (1995). Toward a critical race theory of education. *The Teachers College Record, 97*(1), 47–68.

Martinez, R. A. (2017). Dual language education and the erasure of Chicanx, Latinx, and Indigenous Mexican children: A call to re-imagine (and imagine beyond) bilingualism. *Texas Education Review, 5*, 81–92.

Paris, D., & Alim, H. S. (2017). *Culturally sustaining pedagogies: Teaching and learning for justice in a changing world*. Teachers College Press.

Riessman, C. K. (2008). *Narrative methods for the human sciences*. SAGE Publications.

Shulman, L. S. (2004). *Teaching as community property: Essays on higher education*. Jossey-Bass.

Suárez-Orozco, C., Suárez-Orozco, M. M., & Todorova, I. (2008). *Learning a new land: Immigrant students in American society*. Harvard University Press.

Urrieta, J. L., & Calderón, D. (2019). Critical Latinx Indigeneities: Unpacking Indigeneity from within and outside of Latinized entanglements. *Association of Mexican American Educators Journal, 13*(2), 145–174. https://doi.org/10.24974/amae.13.2.432

Wilson, S. (2008). *Research is ceremony: Indigenous research methods*. Fernwood Publishing.

Yosso, T. J. (2005). Whose culture has capital? A critical race theory discussion of community cultural wealth. *Race Ethnicity and Education, 8*, 69–91. https://doi.org/10.1080/1361332052000341006

Yosso, T. J., Smith, W., Ceja, M., & Solórzano, D. (2009). Critical race theory, racial microaggressions, and campus racial climate for Latina/o undergraduates. *Harvard Educational Review, 79*, 659–691. https://doi.org/10.17763/haer.79.4.m6867014157m707l

11

NARRATIVES AS TOOLS FOR AGENCY

Teachers and Students as Activists

Carmen M. Martínez-Roldán

The narratives featured in this book speak to how erasure manifests in the lives of Latina students and their families but, more importantly, how this erasure is resisted. As a collective, there is a sense of urgency in the contributors' narratives that call for change and that advance a transformative activist educational agenda. This agenda involves creating more equitable, humanizing, and decolonizing educational contexts for Latinx students and all students of color through the development of *daring* pedagogies—equity-oriented and caring pedagogical practices and policies. The transformative educational proposal put forward gains more relevance within the current global COVID-19 pandemic, a crisis that made more visible the social and economic inequities in the larger society and especially within communities of color. Echoing the sense of urgency expressed by communities of color, major educational organizations are reflecting on the need to acknowledge the devastating impacts of this moment but also recognize it as a possibility to reimagine what teachers, teacher educators, and educational researchers might do together to create more equitable educational contexts (Suad Nasir & Bang, 2020). The narratives featured in this volume are the authors' contribution to this reimagining.

In the introduction to the book (Chapter 1), I proposed that Latinas in these narrative studies engaged in agentive moves, discourses, and actions that contribute to a transformative activist educational agenda in four ways. First, through their narratives, these Latinas authored themselves as agentic as they mobilized funds of knowledge and orchestrated funds of identity to challenge erasure and to create, express, and develop their identities. Second, the contributors situated their narratives of erasure and agency within larger historical practices of marginalization and advocacy that foregrounded the relationship between Latinx collective histories and individual stories. Third, the authors used writing as activism to develop networks of solidarity. Lastly, the chapters contribute to a transformative activist educational project by explicitly addressing the implications of their narratives for education. This chapter builds and expands on this set of educational implications, organized around 12 tools with the potential to support activism. The discussion of tools includes examples that illustrate some of the different ways in which teachers, students, families, and teacher educators actually participate or could engage in transformative activist efforts in pre-K to higher education. The various implications advance a view of education that moves from adaptation to transformation—transformation that seeks to bring about equity and social justice. Integrated in each of the following sections are also examples of Latinx literature for children and young adolescents that teachers and teacher educators can use to mediate learners' engagements with the particular tool for activism being discussed in each section (see Children's Literature Boxes 11.1–11.8). Examples of titles from culturally specific children's literature from other cultures are also included to promote cross-cultural perspectives that cultivate solidarity.

11.1 A Critical Sociocultural Framework to Learning and Human Development

My reading of the narratives in this volume is informed by a Vygotskian critical sociocultural framework towards learning and development as crystallized in Anna Stetsenko's (2017) Transformative Activist Stance educational proposal. At the heart of this proposal is the question: What can we do in education, in light of Vygotsky's agentive theories for solving educational problems and addressing inequity and social justice issues, debates, and contradictions in our world today, and in our present projects and endeavors? (p. 10). Underlying this question is a theory of the mind, a theory of learning and human development that articulates how we become human: not through competition, but through collaboration and solidarity; not through mere adaptation to circumstances, but by contributing to changing the world for the better, by engaging in transformative activist efforts. In other words, by envisioning future conditions that promote equity and committing to and acting upon them, as imperfect as our efforts might be, we co-create a continuously evolving new reality from which the past and the present can be known and reframed. This ethic is at the center of a theory of change and development grounded in the belief that while engaging in these activist efforts within the structures that constrain or support our efforts, we are simultaneously changed in the process. This theory of development has clear implications for education. The transformative proposal is in line with Freire's (2007) assertion that "'being' in the world means to transform and re-transform the world, not to adapt to it" (p. 3).

The implications of this transformative perspective include, to name just two, a redefinition of students' and teachers' roles, and a redefinition of the goals of teaching and learning. From the transformative perspective proposed by Stetsenko (2017), students and teachers are seen as activists; that is, as contributing to change instead of adapting, assimilating to, or participating in teaching practices that maintain a status quo that dehumanizes marginalized communities and learners, and that sustains inequities. In other words, as Darder (1995) stated more than two decades ago, it is not enough to be a competent teacher; students need competent teachers willing to acknowledge and address the subordination faced by Latinx students in the United States if society is to move towards a democracy that works for all.

The concept of activism at the center of this theory has been articulated in different ways and lived by scholars, teachers, and activists across time in the United States, Latin America, and elsewhere, inside and outside classrooms, and more explicitly by those embracing critical pedagogies, such as equity-oriented, decolonial, and/or anti-racist pedagogies. In my view, these equity-oriented pedagogies share a commitment to daring, as conceptualized by Freire and Stetsenko. Freire uses the concept of daring in its relationship to commitment and solidarity that lead to praxis (action and reflection as a unity) and to becoming a witness (one that offers a "*testimonio*") (1970, p. 228). Daring involves authentic or critical dialogue based on faith in the people and a courage to love, "which far from being accommodation to an unjust world, is rather the transformation of that world in behalf of the increasing liberation of humankind" (1997, p. 157).

In Stetsenko's (2017) proposal, the Transformative Activist Stance is also about "daring to be, to know, and to act" (p. 364); daring to co-create a more equitable world. It is a proposal of hope but acknowledging the role of structural forces in human action. Such transformative efforts and activism can be realized not only through large-scale efforts to change structures and ideologies that perpetuate inequities, an urgent task that is still relevant and critical, but also, in keeping with the main argument of this book, through small actions that become metaphorical fissures, or *resquebraduras*, that open up possibilities and widen the cracks of a transformative and decolonial educational project (Rivera Cusicanqui in Cacopardo, 2018; Walsh, 2017); when it comes to cultivating transformative school environments, everything and everyone matters. Every one of us, including children, possesses "the right to co-authoring the world shared with others through our agentive, authentic, and unique contributions" (Stetsenko, 2017, p. 8). Teachers and students have the right to learn and codevelop tools that will enable their participation in these agentive efforts. This notion of activism is within reach.

11.1.1 Teaching Against the Grain

Developing pedagogies that address issues of equity is easier to say than to do. Given that critical discussions can be uncomfortable, it would be safe to infer that a message of harmony is easier to deliver in classrooms than discussions of difference or inequities, especially for white teachers. Likewise, Latina educators acknowledge that even with a commitment to engage in critical pedagogies, it is difficult to unlearn the many years of Western teaching, with its assimilationist and colonialist pedagogical practices (Saavedra, 2011). Therefore, a strong level of reflexivity is necessary for all involved in education to address our assumptions, ideologies, and positionalities if we want to create schools committed to promoting equity. Sometimes, even if teachers want to engage in these discussions, they may not know enough about their students' cultural backgrounds to be able to enact culturally sustaining and transformative pedagogies and, as Parkhouse, Lu, and Massaro (2019) highlight, these discussions may be emotionally taxing.

Even when teachers have a supportive administration, testing mandates and other state or federal policies can pose insurmountable obstacles to teachers' efforts to engage in these pedagogies and activist efforts. Most of these high-stakes assessments and policies foster competition and an emphasis on adaptation rather than questioning the status quo. Teachers who engage in equity/daring pedagogies find themselves teaching against the grain and need support to sustain those efforts (Cochran-Smith, 1991; Simon, 1992). Notwithstanding these challenges, dedicated and excellent teachers have found many ways to focus on equity and democracy inside and outside their classrooms, as the stories of some committed teachers and the examples included next illustrate (e.g., Darder, 2012; Nieto, 2003).

11.2 Teacher Activism within Classrooms: Co-creating Tools for Agency

The following examples of teachers', teacher educators', and children's contributions to a transformative educational agenda, taken collectively, reflect the principles promoted by various *resource* and *critical pedagogies*. While discussing the overlaps and differences among various critical pedagogies and the *daring pedagogies* promoted in Stetsenko's (2017) Transformative Activist Stance educational proposal is beyond the scope of this chapter, I focus below on their overlap in the way that they redefine students' and teachers' roles/identities and redefine the goals of teaching and learning. Within a critical sociocultural perspective that centers on activism, the goals of teaching and learning shift from an emphasis on knowledge of facts and skills to an emphasis on co-creating tools of agency that support each learner's unique voice (Stetsenko, 2017; Vygotsky, 1978). Important then in daring pedagogies is that while teachers remain key mediators of learning, teachers and students engage *together* in an inquiry process to know themselves and their communities, to create a vision for their communities, and to identify opportunities for activism; the teacher doesn't provide students a voice but rather provides them with opportunities to find or use their own voice, to develop their own interests, motives, goals, and visions for their futures, to co-create tools, and, most critically, to develop their own activist stances (Stetsenko, 2017, p. 340). Efforts to co-create and engage with tools for activism in classrooms require reconceptualizing teacher-student relationships and reconceptualizing students' cultural backgrounds, practices, and communities as assets.

11.2.1 Creating Learning Contexts Based on Critical Caring

As teachers ask what kinds of learning contexts and tools might support their students advocating for themselves, their communities, and others, the responses need to be grounded in a deep respect for students and communities, which may help cultivate relationships of trust. Several chapters in this volume offer examples of how teaching and learning are, fundamentally, about relationships and belonging. Some narrators spoke to the lasting impact of teachers' caring in their educational experiences, and others to the enduring effects of its absence, which speaks to the need to cultivate what some researchers call *cariño conscientizado* as a pedagogy of critically conscious and authentic care as it relates to students' sense of belonging (DeNicolo, Yu, Crowley, & Gabel, 2017).

For Latinx students, strong interpersonal connections that value students' languages, cultures, and ways of knowing are a critical element in supporting them from elementary school through college. Elise in Chapter 7 offers a glimpse of what is lost when white cultural norms remain at the center of the teaching of Latinx students. Teacher-student relationships characterized by critical care reflect pedagogies that actively *sustain* the practices and capabilities of communities of color and other disenfranchised groups (Antrop-González & De Jesús, 2006; Paris & Alim, 2017). To create such critical-caring contexts, some teachers start by getting to know their students and their communities' funds of knowledge, identities, and histories. Such an inquiry process, when aimed at supporting activism and a decolonial stance, decenters white cultural norms and bodies of knowledge.

11.2.1.1 Tool 1: Inquiry into Student Funds of Knowledge and Identities

One crucial way teachers develop trust with their students and their families is by exploring the dynamic and evolving funds of knowledge of their students' households and their students' funds of identity (González, Moll, & Amanti, 2005). *Funds of identity* refers to the resources individuals mobilize and orchestrate to create, express, and develop their identities (Esteban-Guitart & Moll, 2014), including their self-identifying narratives (Sfard & Prusak, 2005), as discussed in Chapter 1. Learning resulting from these inquiries supports teachers' and students' realizations that we cannot assume a unidirectional correspondence between race, ethnicity, language, and cultural ways of being in our classrooms and communities. Hence the call to think about culture not as a noun or a category people belong to, but as a verb, as cultural practices that may or may not be aligned with a certain community or social group relevant to the student (Gutiérrez & Larson, 2007). Inquiry into students' cultures is an invitation for teachers and students to learn about students' ways of living culturally, about the histories of their cultural practices and identities.

Teachers who learn about their students' funds of knowledge, funds of identity, and histories find themselves in a better position to develop a curriculum that supports academic learning while avoiding essentializing students' identities, because they may learn how families' "funds of knowledge, ways of thinking, values, and expectations associated with culturally derived forms of practice are always open to transformation" (Moll, Soto-Santiago, & Schwartz, 2013, p. 181). Such a realization provides students with opportunities to make and remake themselves, their identities, their discursive toolkits, and their relationships. As Diana expressed in Chapter 2, "What it means to be Latina in the expanding diaspora needs to be updated and complicated"; so, what it means to be Latinx, to be a student of color, needs to be complicated.

In exploring students' funds of knowledge, not only would teachers learn about their students, but if we engage students in such exploration, students might also learn about themselves; that is, inquiry into students' funds of knowledge becomes a tool for reconceptualizing students and communities. Such reconceptualizing has activist potential as students mobilize and claim funds of knowledge and funds of identity, and challenge deficit perspectives about their communities. In the equity framework for culturally and historically responsive literacy, Muhammad (2020) invites teachers to ask: "How will my instruction help students to learn something about themselves and/or about others?" (p. 58). Muhammad proposes providing students with opportunities to explore their multilayered identities as the first learning pursuit teachers can use to organize instruction and cultivate the genius within students and within teachers themselves.

CHILDREN'S LITERATURE BOX 11.1

Exploring Multilayered Identities

Marisol McDonald Doesn't Match/Marisol McDonald no combina (Brown, 2011)

Dalia's Wondrous Hair/El cabello maravilloso de Dalia (Lacámara, 2014)

Less than Half, More than Whole (Lacapa & Lacapa, 1994)

Niño Wrestles the World (Morales, 2013)

Cuba 15 (Osa, 2005) (N)*

Gabi, A Girl in Pieces (Quintero, 2014) (N)

Aristotle and Dante Discover the Secrets of the Universe (Sáenz, 2012) (N)

I Am Not your Perfect Mexican Daughter (Sánchez, 2017) (N)

Just ask! Be different, Be Brave, Be You (Sotomayor, 2019)

American Born Chinese (Yang, 2006) (N)

*Note: All young adult novels, chapter books, and poetry collections for adolescents have been identified with an (N) at the end of the title.

For teachers working with elementary students, home visits are a special opportunity to get to know their students better and to develop relationships, which explains why home visits are still a tradition in some schools at the beginning of the school year. Nonetheless, when home visits are not possible, there are other ways that teachers can organize instruction to learn about their students and their communities and for students to learn about themselves. For instance, the use of disposable cameras for students to take photos of their communities has been meaningfully integrated in bilingual contexts to support students' literacies and content-learning experiences, while also helping educators to gain new perspectives regarding their students' communities.

In their work with emergent bilingual learners in two first-grade dual-language classrooms, Martínez-Alvarez and Ghiso (2017) documented the children's engagement in critical inquiry through photographing and writing about their communities. The children were invited to photograph their family and neighborhood experiences, and the images were then used for collaborative storytelling, digital comic-making using iPads, and informational writing. The authors facilitated the lessons in the language of the day, Spanish or English, but encouraged the children to use their full linguistic repertoires in their inquiries. Through their investigations into their own communities, students' dynamic translanguaging practices and their transnational histories became resources that supported not only their literacy learning but their ideas about bilingualism. The authors also learned about these ideas, including the contradiction that more often than not, children reinforce language hierarchies and the dominance of English while still recognizing the value of bilingualism—a contradiction that bilingual education wrestles with, given the linguistic discrimination bilingual groups have historically faced in the United States, as Marisol's narratives in Chapter 6 illustrate.

One example of how educators and researchers have engaged in this inquiry with Latinx adolescents is offered by the Social Justice Education Project (SJEP) and its Critically Compassionate Intellectualism (CCI) model (Romero, Arce, & Cammarota, 2009). In the SJEP, the teachers and researchers developed learning engagements that support the appreciation and validation of students' knowledge, while teachers and students learn about students' local histories. One of the curricular invitations was "My History" writing, an exercise in which students write a five-section narrative piece: "The history of my life," "My family's history," "My history at high school," "My views of my community and the world," and "My future." While each section includes suggested questions, the teacher also follows up with additional questions that might support critical dialogue, such as "Where did that belief come from?" and "Who does that belief benefit?" (Romero et al., 2009, p. 221). Teachers' questions encourage students to reflect critically upon their own and their communities' realities to better capture and appreciate the complexities, challenges, and possibilities of each local community, avoiding essentializing communities' experiences. As students write, engage in critical dialogue, and revise their histories, they are introduced to the notion of counternarratives and counterstorytelling, and the legitimacy of their stories and the stories of their families and communities as "American" stories, "significant and vital component[s] of the fabric that makes America and Americans" (p. 221). While engaged in rigorous academic learning, students also engage in critically questioning the systems and structures that have historically stifled their communities' potential, with the aim of providing students with, and co-creating with them, the tools to engage in agency and activism.

In sum, teaching oriented by a transformative activist stance involves teachers and students getting to know about their communities, about their own histories and their present, and about their role within them. For transformation to occur and to envision more equitable futures, education cannot be ahistorical (Enciso, 2007; Mignolo, 2000). Inquiry into the past and the present will help create a vision for the future. Such inquiry requires an engagement with the histories of domination and colonization of marginalized groups in the United States, as well as with their histories of survival, resilience, and resistance. The book *Arrancando mitos de raíz* [*Uprooting Myths by Their Roots*] by Puerto Rican educators and activists Godreau, Franco Ortiz, Lloréns, Reinat Pumarejo, Canabal Torres et al. (2013) offers teachers and students with resources and counternarratives to engage in anti-racist education.

CHILDREN'S LITERATURE BOX 11.2

Getting to Know Students' Communities

Quinito's Neighborhood/El vecindario de Quinito (Cumpiano, 2009)
Islandborn (Díaz, 2018)
My Colors, My World/Mis colores, mi mundo (González, 2013)
All Around Us (Gonzalez, 2017)
Counting on Community (Nagara, 2015)
An Island Like You: Stories of the Barrio (Ortiz Cofer, 1995) (N)
Grandma's Gift (Velásquez, 2010)
Some Places More Than Others (Watson, 2019) (N)
This is Our House (Yum, 2013)
Pride (Zoboi, 2018) (N)

11.2.1.2 Tool 2: Academic Engagement and Expansive Learning

An essential element of critical caring and transformative pedagogies is the creation of learning contexts that engage students in robust academic content and expansive learning (Engeström, 2001; Gutiérrez, 2008). Developing robust academic curricula without reconceptualizing Latinx learners as capable, though, thwarts the potential for mediating expansive learning. This would require revising deficit views of learners and reconceptualizing notions of students as potential generators of knowledge who can engage with content learning while contributing funds of knowledge from their communities and social group affiliations. Graciela's narratives on her experiences in science and math classes, as discussed by Minosca in Chapter 8, illustrate the consequences of pedagogies that lack high expectations for students. Students would benefit from robust curricular invitations in which they can develop expertise based on engagement with the tools and discourses of the different disciplines; that is, engaging in the cultural practices and the academic identities associated with the various bodies of knowledge that organize schooling. In addition, expansive learning would involve students and teachers in identifying contradictions and problems critical for them and their communities, and in working towards change that advances social justice, equity, and solidarity.

The redefinition of knowledge as inseparable from identity and activism promoted in the transformative activist proposal, as in Freire's (1970) work, is at the center of several critical pedagogies that promote epistemologies grounded in Latinx students' lives, such as the asset-based intelligence framework discussed by Cervantes-Soon and Carrillo (2016) called a Mestizo Theory of Intelligences. These perspectives on intelligence grounded in Latinx and Indigenous epistemologies challenge hegemonic notions of intelligences prevalent in subtractive schooling and bring forth subaltern knowledge and intellectualism (p. 287). Such a perspective on intelligence leads to pedagogies that foster in students "a critical understanding of the world, while achieving academic excellence and being mindful of the role of their roots and 'home' while providing necessary information for holistic notions of success" (pp. 288–289). Cervantes-Soon and Carrillo urge teachers to abandon "savior" practices aimed at "fixing" students. They propose decolonizing border pedagogies, stressing the importance for students to be aware of the world that awaits them, and the expectations and particular cultural capital that is valued in mainstream spaces; however, instead of using this knowledge to assimilate students into dominant ideologies that define success and intelligence in alienating ways for students of color, Cervantes-Soon and Carrillo advocate for supporting students in their ability to enter these mainstream contexts while finding ways in which they can become agents of change in these very spaces.

Two examples of instructional contexts that provided students with tools to engage academically and prepared them for college, while validating students' intellectualism grounded in their communities, come from the Social Justice Educational Project (SJEP) introduced earlier and the UCLA Migrant Student Leadership Institute (henceforth, the Migrant Institute). In the SJEP that supported students' inquiry into their communities, students learned research skills important for future college work but also for developing social consciousness while they were offered opportunities to use their research to critically analyze their social contexts and investigate issues of concern to them (Romero et al.,

2009). The students engaged in inquiry of such issues as the underrepresentation of students of color in advanced placement courses, gifted and talented education, honors courses, and specialty magnet courses. Through their research projects, students advocated for the schooling of Latinx students and for their communities while also writing their own *counterstories*. One learning engagement that supported students' intellectualism was the 'Four Table exercise,' in which students analyzed and interpreted a list of concepts, theories, and keywords that became the theoretical foundation of the course, including such terms as "subtractive schooling, agency, transformation, resistance… power-knowledge" (p. 221). To participate in the Four Table learning engagement, the students were provided with a large piece of paper divided into four fields. Then, they selected a word from the course content and wrote it down, added a word association, wrote a definition, and finally added a picture or image representing their understanding of the concept. The potential of the Four Table activity came from the critical dialogue it generated as students discussed and negotiated their meanings with peers and the teacher while grounding their understanding in their life experiences and the experiences of their communities (see also de los Ríos & Molina, 2020, for an example of an ethnic studies course that highlights immigrant students' community knowledge).

The Migrant Institute was an equity-oriented instructional program that provided migrant students in California with conceptual and material tools to support their academic skills but also, more importantly, to be used as resources that enabled students to become designers of their own social futures (Gutiérrez, 2008). The learning engagements for the students included tutorials, comprehension circles, writing conferences, teatro, mini-lectures, and whole-class discussions. Whether in social science or writing classrooms, the discussions were grounded in the historical and current particulars of students' everyday lives. One genre that merged all these purposes was the writing of their autobiographies, which became testimonios that reflected their particular cognitive, social, and historical realities while learning the traditional conventions of academic writing. Thus, the critical characteristic of the program was that it addressed both the academic and the personal with a critical focus on supporting students' identities as historical actors, or as history-makers. Thinking historically by reading and discussing historically conscious texts was then a central theme and main tool to mediate activism for the students. For instance, students were invited to engage in analysis of historical contradictions, analysis of oppression, and the consequences of poverty, and to use that analysis as a resource for current and future action. The students showed dramatic shifts in their writing, academic literacy, science, knowledge of social theory and its uses, and reading comprehension. Almost all participants applied to a college, including to UCLA, and were admitted to the university in higher numbers than migrant students who did not participate in the program.

In these two examples, the use of what Muhammad (2020) describes as historically responsible texts is conspicuous. These are critical tools because, as supported by Maried's narrative in Chapter 3, engagement with history cannot rely on the official narratives included in history books, in which the history of communities of color is most likely erased or distorted. Teachers committed to daring pedagogies strive for an expansive vision of history that includes divergent histories and absences in relation to the concept of erasure and agency discussed in Chapter 1. Both programs, then, included engagement with historical analysis of the past to reframe the present and reimagine the students' futures. Both centered the production of students' autobiographies and testimonios, alongside the learning of academic genres. In sum, in transformative activism, the roles of teachers are redefined because they are no longer the distributors of knowledge, but rather co-inquirers with students of the tools, knowledge, and histories that can lead to the construction of more equitable educational contexts for all students.

CHILDREN'S LITERATURE BOX 11.3

Cultivating Intellect and Activism

María Calabó: De niña curiosa a mujer líder (Arroyo Pizarro, 2016) (N)
The Tequila Worm (Canales, 2005) (N)
Planting Stories: The Life of Librarian and Storyteller Pura Belpré (Denise, 2019)
Bravo! (Engle, 2017) (N)
The Storyteller's Candle/La velita de los cuentos (González, 2008)
Little Leaders: Bold Women in Black History (Harrison, 2017)
Cinderella Latina/La cenicienta Latina (Salinas, 2003)
A Computer Called Katherine: How Katherine Johnson Helped Put America on the Moon (Slade, 2019)
Turning Pages: My Life Story (Sotomayor, 2018)
Schomburg: The Man Who Built a Library (Weatherford, 2017)

11.2.2 Centering Storytelling and Testimonios: Pedagogies of Daring

In Chapter 1, I discussed the activist nature of testimonios. In her theory of the mind, Stetsenko (2017) proposes that acts of remembering the past serve goal-directed thoughts and action; they serve as commitments to change the present. In other words, remembering is the work of continuously recreating the past and recruiting its resources in the service of one's becoming, a becoming that occurs by changing the world within community practices. Memory, from this activist perspective, is a tool of creating novelty and inventing the future. For Stetsenko, inventing the future involves "reimagining what is possible and who one wants to be within the overall work of identity development and becoming" (p. 305).

The examples presented above and throughout the book suggest that narratives, particularly those identified as counterstories or testimonios, play a critical role in teaching that advances a transformative activist educational project. As a pedagogical tool, testimonios, functioning as the telling of non-majoritarian stories of struggles and agency, would help teachers better understand the lives and experiences of their students of color, and this requires learning how to listen to and hear the messages in counterstories: a deliberate, conscious, and open type of listening (Delgado Bernal, 2002, p. 116). There are powerful examples (some of them mentioned in Chapter 1) of teachers and university partners in the United States and Latin America using testimonios with their Latinx students as part of their pedagogy to support students' learning, identities, and critical consciousness, especially at the high school level.

While there are many examples of the use of testimonios with Latinx adolescents, it is not common to see references to testimonios when talking about children's storytelling. However, because testimonios can include oral or written narratives, digital narratives, and narratives constructed through art and even embroidery, among other forms, there are abundant opportunities for children to engage in testimonios. Their testimonios can be identified when the content of their stories, regardless of the form they take and of the tellers' level of political awareness, connect to larger narratives of injustices that are part of the collective history of Latinx communities, and when their stories reveal counternarratives. Saavedra (2011), a former third-grade teacher, asserts that testimonios are a way for children to act upon the world, a forum in which students feel they have authority of personal experiences, because only they can speak about how they see their world, their experiences as children of color, their transnational experiences, and their negotiations of meaning, language, and relationships. Their testimonios can act as counternarratives to adult hegemony, adult ways of defining childhood, what counts as knowledge and literacies, and what adults determine that children need (p. 266).

11.2.2.1 Tool 3: Storytelling, Testimonios and Children's Literature

One example of texts teachers use to offer an alternative to official narratives is culturally specific literature, or literature that prominently captures the nuances of the daily lived experiences of communities of color—in this case, of Latinx communities—and that reflects language use, attitudes, values, and beliefs of members of the groups portrayed (Bishop, 1992; Clark, Flores, Smith, & González, 2016). Such literature helps teachers and students learn about their students' funds of knowledge, identities, and histories. As teachers carefully select culturally specific literature, this should offer a range of possibilities for students to self-identify and dis-identify. In addition, engaging in a critical content analysis of the books, images, and narratives these promote can help teachers and students evaluate literature, because books and literature can reproduce colonialist perspectives or support anti-colonial and equity stances (Johnson, Mathis, & Short, 2017, 2019).

CHILDREN'S LITERATURE BOX 11.4

Identity Texts

My Name is María Isabel (Ada, 1995) (N)
They Call Me Güero: A Border Kid's Poems (Bowles, 2018) (N)
The Name Jar (Choi, 2003)
René Has Two Last Names/René tiene dos apellidos (Colato Laínez, 2009)
Gaawin Gindaaswin Ndaawsii /I Am Not a Number (Dupuis & Kacer, 2019)
Call Me Tree/Llámame árbol (González, 2014)
Alma and How She Got Her Name (Martínez-Neal, 2018)
My Name is Jorge: On Both Sides of the River: Poems in English and Spanish (Medina, 1999)
The Proudest Blue: A Story of Hijab and Family (Muhammad with S. K. Ali, 2019)
My Name is Sangoel (Williams & Mohammed, 2009)

Advocating for culturally specific literature does not mean that this is the only literature that students could benefit from; however, Latinx literature, in particular that which is described as *literatura fronteriza* (border literature) or critical fictions, has the potential to mediate Latinx students' negotiation of identities as border-crossers. Literatura fronteriza deals with border-crossing experiences and physical, cultural, linguistic, and identity crossings (Benito & Manzanas, 2002; Medina, 2006). Culturally specific literature also provides opportunities for students to critique, rewrite, and co-author those stories through their own narratives. That is, possibilities are created for the students to position themselves as children and youth with agency, reinventing themselves through narratives in response to the literature (Martínez-Roldán, 2003).

Literature discussions that prioritize both students' negotiation of meanings and criticality can create the conditions for children's production of testimonios. In a bilingual second-grade classroom, the children were discussing the picture book *Friends from the Other Side/Amigos del otro lado* (Anzaldúa, 1997) when seven-year-old Rosita shared her family's experience with immigration (López-Robertson, 2011). Like in the picturebook, the border patrol came in search of immigrants who might be undocumented. Unlike in the picturebook, the border patrol actually deported Rosita's parents, in the girl's words: "*tumbaron la puerta y luego entraron y se los llevaron a todos"* [they (Border Patrol) knocked the door down, and then they went in and took them all away] (p. 55). When the kids returned from school, there was no one at home. Rosita and her brother had been advised that if someday there was no one at home, they were to stay with their nana.

This short but painful story takes on the form of testimonio as Rosita's story is not only hers, but that of many immigrants, youth and adults, facing the effects of inhumane policies that separate families at the border. This experience had occurred two years later when she was in kindergarten. While the family was reunited after five months, the story was still present in this young child's memory. In her transaction with the text, Rosita recruited her own family's experience to make sense of the text and of the difficult personal experiences she shared. Her teacher validated the children's experiences and ways of knowing, creating a learning context to which they could bring their testimonios while supporting their language and literacy learning. These (re)membering processes have implications for healing, humanizing, and ultimately transforming teaching and learning (Dillard, 2016, p. 406).

Likewise, the immigrant children participating in the discussion of *The Arrival* (Tan, 2006) as part of an international project imagined new possibilities for themselves and created a new narrative for their communities (Arizpe, Colomer, & Martínez-Roldán, 2014). A common response across contexts for the children in Barcelona, Arizona, and Glasgow involved affirming that immigrants in the text and in their own communities go to another country to work. In the words of one of the students from Barcelona: *"Porque nosotros venimos a trabajar"* [Because we come to work] (p. 104–106). In their responses, the children challenged deficit narratives circulating about immigrants in their communities, offered a counterstory, and asserted their agency. That is, the context of the literature discussions provided a space for these transnational students to co-create new identities for themselves and new visions for their communities.

11.2.2.2 Tool 4: Testimonios and Popular Culture

Literature for children and young adolescents is but one of the literacy tools with the potential to support students' academic, cultural, and activist identities. Less official literacy practices and texts that are part of students' literacy repertoires could be leveraged in school to support students' levels of engagement and identity work. Among those literacy practices, researchers have documented the use of music (using their lyrics in writing or creating lyrics), whether Mexican *corridos*, Spanish rap, or superhero stories.

An example of how texts from students' culture can support learning and activism in elementary classrooms is described in Torres and Tayne's (2017) study on the use of superhero comics—a popular culture genre—in third- to fifth-grade classrooms. The curricular invitations contained an activist orientation that sought to integrate students' interests, funds of knowledge, and agency as they engaged in a 12-week superhero unit. It took place within the context of the 2016 presidential campaign, in which Latinxs faced heightened xenophobic and racist discourses that the students knew all too well and brought into their study and creation of superheroes. Torres and Tayne indicate that while the genre of superheroes is still dominated by primarily white, male heroes, the students were able to create superhero narratives set in their communities. The students identified problems within their communities that could be addressed by the superheroes in their collaborative stories, and also developed a villain or an archnemesis for their superheroes. Once they identified a problem for the storyline, the students were introduced to the trope of superheroes traditionally serving as protectors of their communities and to the ways in which superheroes typically defeat their villains in a nonviolent manner (p. 377). The authors of various stories developed an alternative world or a counterstory that pushed back against the xenophobic discourses and misrepresentations of their communities. As with the other engagements and curricular invitations discussed in this chapter, it was not the use of the superhero genre per se that supported students' creation of counterstories. The instructions and activities designed around those engagements "were grounded in practices of equity and rooted in the lived realities of the students as they read and created their own superhero stories" (p. 382).

The second example comes from de los Ríos (2018), in which she focuses on how reading, writing, and performing corridos are among the myriad transnational and translingual literacy practices that bilingual students engage in daily and bring to schools (p. 456). De los Ríos documents the academic and critical affordances of corridos—balladry in Spanish that often emphasizes injustice and border strife—in the lives of bilingual transnational young people. For one Mexican-American student, Joaquín, corridos were a source to learn about his communities and the struggle of their ancestors. Because this history is practically invisible in the official curriculum, Joaquín asserted that corridos reminded the members of his community of who they really are. While corridos and other popular culture literacy texts and practices tend to be disregarded in academic settings, Joaquín's engagement with corridos involved intellectual and critical work. He analyzed the lyrics and assessed some as really good, such as El Cachorro's song, *El Rancho*, which, through the allegory of *Los pollitos desaparecidos* [The missing chicks], is referring to the 43 student teachers who disappeared from the Ayotzinapa Normal School in Iguala, Mexico, or those by Los Tigres del Norte, which challenge the dominant narrative of immigrants as "a drain to the economy." His everyday language and literacy practices with corridos and his analysis of them showed his highly evolved literary understanding of the use of allegory in this genre, reconciling his everyday knowledge with the demands of subject-matter literacy learning. Through corridos, youth living on the border can thus be recognized as the authors and storytellers of their transnational lives. When youth engage critically with corridos and other popular genres, they have the potential to become tools for anti-colonial resistance.

In these two examples, popular culture was embraced as a legitimate source for literacy learning, in both cases with criticality, in the way Hall (1998) approached it. That is, both examples focused on the activist potential of corridos or superhero stories as they challenged hegemonic perspectives and invited engagement with civic and social imagination.

11.2.2.3 Tool 5: Testimonios, Arts, and Imagination

A pedagogy that sees knowledge, identity, and activism as inseparable recognizes teachers' and students' roles as contributing to a more just world rather than merely participating in existing practices (Stetsenko, 2017). In this new role, teachers and students co-create visions for the future from which the past and the present can be known and transformed, using and transforming the tools available to them and even creating new ones. Such transformative work is possible, as Maxine Greene (1995) proposed, when individuals tap into their social imagination. Cultivating a social imagination in education is an invitation to break "with what is supposedly fixed and finished … [to] become freed to glimpse what might be, to form notions of what should be and what is not yet" (p. 19). It is a call to reflect on what is not working in society, and in schools, and to reach for something new, to envision a better world, and work towards that; it is a call for action. This orientation towards something that is not yet there is one of the factors that renders so relevant the role of arts as special contexts that support imagining new possibilities for individuals' improvement and the improvement of society; new possibilities for empathy, for solidarity, and for activism.

Improvisational arts have been particularly promising in supporting students' imagination, agency, and activism. Pretend play and improvisational drama come together in the curricular engagement of the *playshop* (Wohlwend & Medina, 2014). The playshop is a curricular invitation that recruits young students' engagement with various forms of art while bringing students' voices and imagination to the forefront. It is an engagement that can extend the writing workshop by going beyond the focus on honing an author's craft or producing individual child-made books. While this focus is still important, the authors claim a more central and critical role for play and drama as core literacies in which children participate in the collective cultural production of texts. For example, the dramatization of telenovelas written by the students in one Puerto Rican classroom and the play and writing developed among children who had transnational connections in a classroom in Iowa provided the students with ways of improvising scripts, negotiating, and performing identities that have rich potential for reclaiming writing. Through playshops, the children accessed familiar cultural spaces encountered at home, at school, on television, in the mall, on the internet, on the phone, or across international communities. These multiple spaces made diverse literacy resources available (e.g., popular drama, music, art genres, and scripts; multilingual writing forms) that the children combined to reimagine cultural contexts in ways that stretched classroom practices. The playshops' agentive perspective becomes a context in which bilingual/bicultural and transnational Latinx students can potentially negotiate identities, engage in critical literacies, and imagine new worlds.

The second example shows high school students from Latin America engaged in art-based testimonios. Errázuriz Besa's (2020) work in Chile focused on the discourses and practices of female high school students who self-identified as feminists. Errázuriz Besa was interested in understanding the relationship of youth activism and testimonios to citizenship engagement and civic education. Through their testimonios, sometimes represented in embroidery, the students explored their gendered biographies and shared their historical narratives and collective memories while challenging the "normality" of gender violence and school policing of gender. Given the sometimes extremely painful experiences, art testimonios became an important activist tool the adolescents used to make meaning and denounce the general and specific gender discrimination many women, young and adult, experience. The young women asserted how the curriculum they were exposed to at school contributed to the erasure of women in history, because women were absent from their history and social studies classes—especially women that had been politically active in nontraditional ways. Such invisibility of women's contributions in schools' academic offerings can also be found in schools in the United States, especially if the women are descendants of Indigenous or Black ancestors (Godreau et al., 2013).

11.2.3 Supporting Young Learners' Engagement in Action

Supporting students as actors of social transformation involves providing them with access to, and opportunities to co-create, the tools that afford such agency. This transformative activist pedagogy is possible, as mentioned earlier, when educators see children and families, no matter what their socioeconomic or cultural background, as contributors of knowledge, ideas, and change. Nevertheless, adults' notions of children and childhood often underestimate children's abilities to engage in discussions of critical issues, leading to limited expectations about their abilities to participate in and contribute to change efforts (Soto & Swadener, 2002). These limited expectations are often compounded with low expectations for children from minoritized communities. As the previous examples show, teachers who believe in children's ability to contribute and engage in agentive efforts find many ways to organize curricula around this belief.

11.2.3.1 Tool 6: Inquiry as Knowledge to Foreground Action

The concept of *foregrounding* children's action is used to acknowledge that some children are already engaged in critical readings of their worlds, and that what they need are spaces in the classroom to bring their voices and experiential and political funds of knowledge (Batista-Morales, Slamerón, & DeJulio, 2019).

208 Carmen M. Martínez-Roldán

However, some structures for student participation have more potential than others for supporting and foregrounding children's transformative actions, such as curriculum that engages children in authentic inquiry processes. Maestra Nydia, one third-grade teacher in Puerto Rico, supported children's action through an inquiry project designed to address their concerns as well as their academic needs after the hurricanes hit Puerto Rico in September of 2017 (Martínez-Roldán, 2019). The teachers and the principal expressed that their primary concern after the hurricanes was the children's well-being; however, while the aftermath of the hurricanes represented a devastating experience for many families, once the school restarted, the teachers did not receive the children with a sense of pity. On the contrary, caring for the students involved listening to their concerns and providing learning experiences that could help them academically, as they had lost so much time due to the school's two-month closure.

When their elementary school reopened, the children found out they had lost the school library where, in addition to books, teachers secured all art materials and musical instruments. Some of the children were used to visiting the library during recess time, while others ran around the schoolyard; however, after the hurricanes, the patio was not in its best condition for the children to run around. In a meeting with their teacher, the children expressed their concerns about the lack of recreational activities they could enjoy during recess: "pero es que aquí no hay nada, y ahora hay menos maestra, no hay biblioteca" ["but there is nothing here, and now there is less, teacher, there is no library"]. The children raised concerns about a vital activity, which had been seriously impacted by the hurricanes and its aftermath. Maestra Nydia listened to this concern and took it seriously. She asked the children what things they would like to have, creating a conceptual web as they brainstormed. Elevating their discussion via analysis, the teacher did not treat play and academics as separate activities. From the students' concern regarding free time, the teacher decided to involve the class in an inquiry on the topic of leisure, its definition and benefits, making connections to various content area subjects and different types of texts. The group's concern expanded to include other students in the school community, and as part of their inquiry, they wanted to know whether they also felt the same, so the children surveyed their fellow students about what they would want to see happening during recess. They collected that information and, with the teacher, tabulated the data, made graphs, and analyzed the data in order to propose solutions and make decisions.

This example of third-grade curriculum with Puerto Rican children reflects a transformative activist pedagogy in which both teacher and students engaged in agentive moves that foregrounded children's action. The academic approach to play led to solutions, so knowledge was tied to action from the start. Driven by the problem the students posed, the students and teacher engaged in research, and the children learned new concepts and vocabulary, but more importantly, they collectively proposed solutions, such as the adaptation of certain areas of the school with blackboard paint where they and students from other classrooms could play, draw, and write. The students developed a sense of agency that cultivated solidarity during a time of crisis while engaging in robust learning. Maestra Nydia trusted that the children could contribute ideas and solutions to a problem that impacted the whole school, incorporating knowledge from texts but also from their lives, while having high expectations for their learning. The students and the teacher imagined together a new future for their local school community that led to the physical—and perhaps emotional—transformation of their environment.

11.2.3.2 Tool 7: Inquiry as Meaningful Action for Social Justice

In a four-year school-based inquiry, Short (2016) and the teachers of an elementary school designed learning invitations to engage children in authentic and meaningful social justice action. There was a clear commitment to enact a critical pedagogy, as the adults engaged in efforts to support children's intercultural understanding and their becoming global citizens. Engagements around global literature, in which sometimes the children characters appear taking action, played a major role as the children engaged in a school-wide inquiry on human rights and hunger as global issues. The engagements included read-alouds, independent reading, literature discussions, writing workshops, and inquiry studies in the classrooms. Children explored, for example, the concept of 'power' as connected to 'hunger,' the difference between 'needs' and 'wants' in tight times, and others. After examining root causes for the problem of hunger, the children identified various ways they wanted to take action; some engaged in research action, direct and indirect action, and advocacy for action.

From these efforts, Short and the teachers identified a set of principles to consider in creating a learning environment with the potential to engage children in authentic action. They found that authentic action develops out of children's inquiry and experiences, no longer completely dependent on adult knowledge. The action project meets a genuine need recognized by children. It builds collaborative relationships; that is, it is not the result of just one leader or student in a protagonist role but occurs with other community members. The action results in mutual exchanges among everyone involved in that action so that it is not a one-way process that could reduce the project to an act of charity between savior and receiver; instead, it is a process in which all participants contribute ideas, skills, information, and knowledge. The project involves not just action but also reflection on what occurs, accepting responsibility for consequences, and acting again. The action invites student voice and choice; no one voice should silence another, and in particular, no adult should silence students in the pursuit of engaging in real dialogue and reflection. Lastly, the action involves civic/global responsibility for social justice, and questions about power, oppression, and social conditions within local and global communities (Short, 2016). It is clear from these principles that, when engaging students in social action projects or projects that afford them possibilities to engage in activism, it is not the teacher who should select the problem or impose her perspectives on learners. It all starts with listening to students' concerns. From a transformative activist perspective, through the different actions the children took, they were contributing and daring to create a more just society; they were taking a stand with transformative activist potential.

Transformative pedagogies such as the ones reflected on these two inquiry projects were not adds-on to the curriculum but, as Vasquez (2004) asserts regarding critical literacy, they are a critical frame through which to participate in the world; they constitute a perspective that guides the selection and organization of instruction and policymaking in public schools.

CHILDREN'S LITERATURE BOX 11.5

Children and Youth Agency and Activism

Friends from the Other Side/Amigos del otro lado (Anzaldúa, 1997)
This Promise of Change: One Girl's Story in the Fight for School Equality (Boyce & Levy, 2019) (N)
The Epic Fail of Arturo Zamora (Cartaya, 2018) (N)
Let the Children March (Clark-Robinson, 2018)
A Good Kind of Trouble (Moore Ramee, 2019) (N)
A is for Activist (Nagara, 2013)
Between Us and Abuela: A Family Story from the Border (Perkins, 2019)
By Sit-in: How four friends Stood up by Sitting Down (Pinkney, 2010)
Van a tumbar el húcar (Rivera Izcoa, 2004)
That's not fair! Emma Tenayuca's struggle for justice/¡No es justo! La lucha de Emma Tenayuca por la justicia (Tafolla & Teneyuca, 2008)

11.2.4 Teachers as Professionals and Activists Beyond the Classroom

For a long time, teachers' professionalism has been undermined by standardization and testing efforts and by the increasing number of teacher preparation programs designed around technical training; yet, teachers have been actively resisting de-professionalization forces (Edelsky, 2006). Teachers' activism beyond the classroom is manifested through their efforts to resist district, state, or federal policies that negatively impact students of color. One example of this activism is bilingual teachers' advocacy efforts with colleagues, families, community groups, and legislators as dual-language (DL) programs are increasingly being reclaimed as a powerful way to ensure educational equity for Latinx students (see how to combat inequalities within two-way language immersion programs that do not live up to this ideal by Cervantes-Soon, Dorner, Palmer, Heiman, Schwerdtfeger, et al., 2017).

11.2.4.1 Tool 8: Advocacy for Children's Rights

In *Freedom at Work: Language, Professional, and Intellectual Development in Schools,* Torres-Guzmán, a university professor from New York, with Swinney, an elementary school principal at the time, tell the story of how the teachers and administration engaged in professional development, which took the form of advocacy, as an act of freedom for themselves and their students (Torres-Guzmán, 2010). The teachers were committed to bilingual education, to their students, and to social justice. They were acutely aware of the injustices that had historically impacted the lives of the community they served, mostly Latinx students. They named the injustices that manifested, for instance, through efforts to sabotage the language and academic goals of their bilingual program—for example, through the lack of materials in Spanish, the lack of resources, and testing mandates that made it more challenging to make language equity a reality. Thus, advocating for children's rights became a tool to mobilize transformative efforts for their school. Yet, the teachers were able to advance their bilingual agenda because of a school culture and an administration that respected and valued their professionalism and decision-making. With the support of their administration, the teachers also worked at creating a space of intellectual freedom for their students and for criticality. While it is clear that these teachers had a supportive system at the school level, that is not the case everywhere.

For five cohorts of bilingual teachers from various elementary schools in Texas, the support for their activist efforts came through their participation in Proyecto Maestría, a bilingual graduate leadership program that supported the creation of communities of learning (Palmer, 2018). The program offered a strong grounding in theory, policy, and practice of critical bilingual/bicultural education that teachers used to mediate their activist efforts. The courses, taught in English and Spanish as much as possible, mediated discussions on critical perspectives and culturally relevant/sustaining pedagogies in all content areas, with a focus on the particular needs and realities of the teachers' own elementary bilingual classrooms. The teachers' engagement in the project led them to embrace and enact advocacy and transformative pedagogies, and ultimately to take on leadership in a range of forms in their schools and districts. Some of them came to Proyecto Maestría with a strong sense of advocacy, which supported their critical discussions. One of them, with childhood experience as an undocumented student, already saw herself as an advocate. She had spoken at a meeting of the Texas State Board of Education against an initiative they were considering to embrace an English-only program for bilingual learners, and in another instance, organized the community to keep a full-day pre-K program in her district. They were heard.

With the program's support, experienced teachers became mentors of new teachers, and some perceived that their principals were now seeing them in a new light that supported more of a leadership role for them in the school.

Teachers started offering professional development workshops for other teachers at their school and in their districts. Some initiated a teacher-led annual conference as a project that would allow them to "take agency" in their professional lives, to share their experiences and inquiries with others, and to preserve their collaborations, which supported them as they worked at enacting and promoting critical pedagogies. As part of the conference, a program for parents was created, which now has become its sister conference, with parents not only attending but participating in the planning and presentation process. Some teachers engaged with their school parent-teacher associations. Some moved into district curriculum-development leadership roles, and others served in leadership roles in local teachers' unions. Some joined the board of the Austin Area Association of Bilingual Education, which organizes the annual bilingual conference the teachers created. One of the teachers became an assistant principal at a large elementary school with a dual-language program, and another sought credentials to become a principal. That is, as Palmer (2018) states, the teachers became leaders instead of followers. In the words of one of the teachers: "Being quiet is not going to help anything. You have to be part of the process of advocating in different levels" (p. 167).

CHILDREN'S LITERATURE BOX 11.6

Affirming Bilingualism, Biliteracy, Translanguaging

How Tía Lola Came to ~~Visit~~ Stay (Alvarez, 2002b) (N)
Red Hot Salsa: Bilingual Poems on Being Young and Latino in the United States (Carlson, & Hijuelos, 2005) (N)
Under the Mesquite (García McCall, 2011) (N)
The Upside Down boy/El niño de cabeza (Herrera, 2000)
La Mariposa (Jiménez, 1998)
Inside Out & Back Again (Lai, 2011) (N)
Pepita Talks Twice/Pepita habla dos veces (Latchman, 1995)
Los Gatos Black on Halloween (Montes, 2006)
Sing with Me/Canta conmigo (Orozco, 2020)
Call Me María (Ortiz-Cofer, 2004) (N)

That said, even when teachers have strong support at the school level, it is sometimes still insufficient to effect transformative change (e.g., Newcomer & Collier, 2015). Aware of these challenges, Torres-Guzmán (2010) raised a series of questions: "What if you were to wait for the system to allow this to happen, do you think it would happen? …What if you did not wait, like … the teachers [at this school]? How would you know what is possible, and how would a different system be created if we, individually and collectively, do not try?" (p. 183). Torres-Guzmán's questions raise two relevant issues pertaining to this discussion. One, her questions speak to the heart of the tension and argument put forth in this book. Building on Stetsenko's (2017) work, I propose that the narratives in this book reflect a dialectical view of agency that regards individuals' agency as enacted within social forces and structures beyond them. The narrators' testimonios offer a glimpse of the contexts and structures that facilitated or stifled their agentive potential and identity development with real, material consequences. At the same time, their agentive and activist efforts produced new identities for themselves, impacting the people that surrounded them in their families, schools, or the institutions they worked with. For instance, Daniela's narratives (Chapter 10) showed that a person's transformative efforts can impact others; in her chapter, her aunt's transformative efforts supported other parents in an ESL class, while at the same time, the collective of women coming together, supported her aunt's ethnic and activist identities. Therefore, every effort and story of each teacher, student, and parent matters. Two, while there is no insignificant contribution when there is a commitment to produce change, Torres-Guzmán's questions push educators to think of the need for collaboration, as change "is a collaborative project of people changing and co-creating the world together" while being changed through their activist efforts (Stetsenko, 2017, p. 19); that is, the transformative potential of teachers' agentive actions increases when teachers join efforts with others. An indispensable component of the educational community that can support those advocacy efforts for their children and their schools is parents.

11.2.4.2 Tool 9: Advocacy for Family Engagement, Testimonios, and Activism

Several narratives in this volume highlight the need for teachers to learn from and with parents, to acknowledge bilingual, bicultural parents' and communities' resourcefulness, and to organize more culturally responsive family engagement opportunities. As Núñez (2019) reminds educators, investing time in learning with and from parents allows teachers to create more effective academic learning opportunities for all students and to generate meaningful collaborations and respectful relationships with them (p. 15). When schools engage in deliberate efforts to make parents feel welcome and to build relationships, opportunities for parent agency and activism are expanded (see DaSilva Iddings's 2009 work with parents). Teacher activism would involve reconceptualizing parental engagement, shifting from expecting parents to adapt or passively participate in the schooling of their children to recognize a more protagonic role for them; schools and parents must collaborate on transforming the very contexts that often keep parents away from schools.

Parents' activism takes many forms and levels of engagement (Olivos, Jiménez-Castellanos, & Ochoa, 2011). One of these is parental counternarratives that challenge the deficit views of Latinx families that sometimes characterize the discourse around immigrant families in schools. Villenas (2001) shares some Latina mothers' counternarratives, through which they contested deficit views and reclaimed their *educated* identities in a small town in North Carolina. Their narratives challenge what Villena calls *benevolent racism* or well-intentioned peoples' framing of Latinx families as both problems and victims. Such discourses translate into patronizing and *helping* practices that normalize white, middle-class cultural practices while positioning Latinx families as deviant. Through their counterstories, the Latina mothers reclaimed their dignity as good mothers and educators of their children. These mothers positioned themselves as active contributors of Latinx communities in the rural South.

Welcoming parents' testimonios and placing them at the center of family-engagement spaces becomes a necessary tool to reimagine work *with* and *for* families (Flores, 2018; Roxas & Gabriel, 2017). Parents' counterstories can serve as pedagogical tools for all involved in education; not only can teachers learn about their resistance and agency, but so can children, as parents' counterstories sometimes function as consejos to their children, modeling resistance rather than conformity and the possibility of envisioning a better future (Flores, 2018, p. 343).

Parents sometimes exert their agency and activism in more overt actions, such as defending their children's right to bilingual education (e.g., Moje, Ciechanowski, Kramer, Ellis, Carrillo et al., 2004; Pérez, 2004). Other times, parents fight for their children's basic right to education, which happened in Puerto Rico after the hurricanes of 2017. Families in Puerto Rico experienced numerous challenges, whether they remained on the island or sought refuge stateside. One of the major challenges that parents, students, and teachers experienced after the hurricanes was associated with the closure of schools for an average of two months; some schools closed indefinitely. The reopening of schools has been identified as fundamental to the recovery and emotional stability of children that have lived through a disaster (Fothergill & Peek, 2015). Parents across the island denounced the delay on opening the schools, especially when the schools were in good enough condition to receive children.

For example, the parents from the Dr. Antonio S. Pedreira elementary school forced the reopening of their school with a protest (Martínez-Roldán, 2019). They interpreted the delay as negligence of the government and of the Puerto Rico Department of Education. In their narratives, some mothers expressed that governmental priorities did not correspond to community necessities and priorities. Therefore, in the third week of November, two months after Hurricane María, a small group of parents held a demonstration in front of the school gates, an event that received coverage from the media and generated substantial tension. Ms. Fernández, one of the mothers, explained that after some engineers had determined the school was safe, they had expected the school to reopen;

however, the bureaucracy mandated that only schools on a list created by the Department of Education could open. Increasingly desperate for their children's school to be listed, the parents took action and organized in protest:

> Cuando ya oficialmente todo estuvo bien y no se pudo empezar, pues estuvimos aquí con los nenes, con pancartas y con las noticias y todo eso… o sea, una vez nosotros entendíamos que ya se había determinado, o sea se había evaluado y que ya podían iniciar, pues el proceso ese burocrático de esperar una firma, ¿no? ¿un papel?, y hacer que un niño perdiera dos o tres semanas más por eso, pues era como que ilógico.
>
> (p. 79)

> When everything was already officially safe and [classes] could not begin, we were there with the children, with banners and with news and all that…. That is, once we understood that it had already been determined, that is, it had been evaluated and that they could start—because of the bureaucratic process of waiting for a signature, right? A paper? And to make a child lose two or three more weeks for that, well, it was like, how illogical.

The school reopened by the end of the week.

Teachers' activism involves welcoming and supporting bicultural parental involvement that takes the form of activism for equality in education, even if sometimes parents' claims have the potential to disrupt the harmony in teacher-parent relationships.

CHILDREN'S LITERATURE BOX 11.7

Parents' and Communities' Activism

Si un día juntásemos todas las camas del mundo (Albo, 2010)
Before We Were Free (Alvarez, 2002a) (N)
¡Sí, se puede!/Yes, We Can! Janitor Strike in L.A. (Cohn, 2005)
A Sweet Smell of Roses (Johnson, A. 2005)
The Streets Are Free (Kurusa, 1995)
We Are Water Protectors (Lindstrom, 2020)
Vicky and a Summer of Change y ¡un verano de cambio! (Ortiz & Morales, 2021)
Separate Is Never Equal, Sylvia Mendez & Her Family's Fight for Desegregation (Tonatiuh, 2014)
Undocumented: A Workers Fight (Tonatiuh, 2018)
Sélavi, That is Life: A Haitian Story of Hope (Youme, 2004)

11.2.5 Taking Action within Teacher Education

The responsibility of teacher education for the formation of teachers of Latinx students cannot be underestimated. In a study that included more than 68,000 preK-12 instructors from the United States (out of 1.6 million respondents), Starck, Riddle, Sinclair, and Warikoo (2020) found that teachers' racial attitudes largely reflect those held within their broader society, characterized by pro-white/anti-Black explicit and implicit racial biases. While learning to teach is a lifelong journey, teacher education programs for pre-service and in-service teachers have the potential to offer a solid foundation for teachers' journeys as reflective professionals who can develop ideological clarity (Bartolomé & Balderrama, 2001). The challenge is in the level of intention of teacher education programs in integrating in their academic offerings a social justice perspective that includes tools for developing transformative activist pedagogies. In this section, I offer a glimpse at the ways three teacher education programs are engaged in these efforts. The examples offer different ways institutions organize their teaching education transformative efforts through a particular course that could potentially lead to transformation of entire programs. Each of the courses offer specific tools with the potential to engage teacher candidates in transformative activist efforts.

11.2.5.1 Tool 10: Create Engagements on Family's Funds of Knowledge

In a study of K-2 student teachers over a three-year period, a group of teacher educators documented the responses of their teacher candidates to an assignment intended to support the student teachers' learning about families' funds of knowledge at their placements and the development of relationships with families based on trust. The *Family Backpacks* assignment consisted of recruiting families' stories in their student teaching classrooms through the use of four to six backpacks that rotated among families on a weekly basis (Acevedo, Kleker, Pangle, & Short, 2017). The backpacks contained three books (one informational global-concept book and two picture books), a related artifact, and a family story journal that each family kept, adding stories as the backpacks circulated. The teacher educators then created a narrative inquiry space for the teacher candidates to encourage them to engage in storytelling about their experiences in small groups.

Learning about their teacher candidates' stories, particularly about the deficit views of families in the schools, the teacher educators realized the need to transform the teacher education program by introducing programmatic changes aimed at providing more support for the teacher candidates and opportunities for the mentor teachers and the supervisors to understand the two key concepts behind the backpacks. The changes introduced by the teacher educators supported major shifts in the teacher candidates, as expressed in their narratives along four major themes: conceptual understanding of the families' stories and funds of knowledge as related to the backpacks; strategies for classroom implementation; views of families; influence on candidates' own values and beliefs regarding the potential of the backpacks in building relationships.

For the teacher educators, the narrative inquiry on the teacher candidates' stories became a tool that supported the process of disrupting their own dominant narratives as teacher educators and engaging in a process of learning and transformation that led to the transformation of their program. Still, in the third year of the project, despite the space for reflection created in the course, the pressure of the Common Core State Standards that led to a scripted curriculum in classrooms limited the potential of engaging families, and some teachers from various cohorts still appeared to hold deficit views of families' language and family involvement, although these conceptualizations had shifted overall for the majority of the teacher candidates. Given that the majority of teachers teaching Latinx and immigrant students are non-Latinxs, teacher education programs face the challenge of providing abundant opportunities throughout their program of studies for the teacher candidates to learn and develop tools for reflexivity to examine their own assumptions of Latinx students and their communities within the constraints of testing-driven and prescriptive school curricula that often organize the schooling of Latinx students.

11.2.5.2 Tool 11: Create Engagements for Critical Historical Inquiry

The second teacher education example comes from a study in a social studies methods course that is part of a bilingual education program (Salinas, Fránquiz, & Rodríguez, 2016). The course focuses on mediating bilingual Latinx pre-service teachers' understanding of the history of Latinx communities while providing a context to understand their own experiences and testimonios. The tools used to mediate teacher candidates' analysis, reflection, and agency are the *Journey Box* and historical inquiry tools for agency. Aware of the prevalence of deficit views in society, and of historical inaccuracies and omissions, the teacher educator focused on supporting their Latinx elementary teacher candidates in using critical historical inquiry to identify and deconstruct historical inaccuracies and omissions. The Journey Box assignment entailed collecting primary sources and writing a narrative recognizing an alternative perspective to the mainstream narrative of American history. The assignment was a call for students to foreground perspectives that might complicate, nuance, or run contrary to a dominant school curriculum, highlighting experiences of racism, classism, sexism, and other 'isms' encountered by marginalized communities, as well as writing about their agency in response to such acts (p. 420).

Engaging in critical historical inquiry not only exposed the bilingual teacher candidates to the need to address historical omissions and distortions, but also created space for their own experiences of resistance to dominant narratives. That is, critical historical inquiry became a tool for activism. Learning this method supported students to develop counterstories and to expose relationships among power, privilege, and the history curriculum (p. 435). The pre-service and in-service teachers' narratives facilitated insights into the historical systemic contradictions at the root of the organization of an educational system that advances some voices and silences others, so teacher education programs in general need to create spaces for engaging with these contradictions.

This second example highlights that Latinx teachers also need opportunities for engaging in critical reflexivity in order to uncover their own funds of knowledge and testimonios, given that their own experiences as Latinas might have been undervalued as potential rich resources in their teaching of Latinx students. Teacher education programs can support their Latinx teacher candidates by creating opportunities for them to reflect on how their own experiences as Latinx learners, which often involve transnational experiences, have impacted their pedagogy, including both their struggles and resilience within the highly structured environment of educational institutions. There are multiple studies on Latinas within the field of education that document those efforts by focusing on teacher candidates' testimonios (e.g., Brochin-Ceballos, 2012; Sosa-Provencio, Sheahan, Fuentes, Muñiz, & Vivas, 2019; Zúñiga, 2015).

CHILDREN'S LITERATURE BOX 11.8

Inquiry into Communities' Histories

Return to Sender (Alvarez, 2009) (N)
Somos como las nubes/We are like the clouds (Argueta, 2016)
El cuento de Papapedia (Arroyo Pizarro, 2018)
Voice of Freedom: Fannie Lou Hamer, Spirit of the Civil Rights Movement (Boston Weatherford, 2018)
María María: Un cuento de un huracán (Degenhart, 2018) (N)
Silver People: Voices from the Panama Canal (Engle, 2014) (N)
Dreamers (Morales, 2018)
Dear Haiti, Love Alaine (Moulite, 2019) (N)
The Boy and the Wall (Palestinian refugee children in the Aida refugee Camp, 2019)
We Are Grateful/Otsaliheliga (Sorell, 2018)

11.2.5.3 Tool 12: Create Engagements for Transformative Agency

The third teacher education example focuses on a study conducted in a student teaching seminar that is part of a bilingual teacher education program. The program prepares bilingual teacher candidates from various cultural backgrounds, including teaching candidates who did not grow up speaking the minoritized language but that will be using it for instruction, in this case, Spanish, an increasing tendency within bilingual teacher education that poses particular challenges (Chang, Martínez-Roldán, & Torres-Guzmán, 2020). The course is organized around concepts from Cultural Historical Activity Theory and Expansive Learning to engage the teacher candidates in developing new tools for transformative action. The article focuses on two of the tools offered to the teacher candidates to support their identities as bilingual teachers and their agency. The tools, a *Double-Entry Journal* and a *Four-Field Model*, engaged the teacher candidates in an analysis of contradictions and their development of a new model for bilingual education.

The student teaching seminar course was designed to align its sessions with the seven expansive learning actions described in the theory of Expansive Learning (Engeström, 2001), with the goal of engaging all teacher candidates and their instructor in (1) "questioning" and identifying major contradictions within bilingual teaching/learning, manifested through tensions and dilemmas in their placements and in professional readings; (2) "analyzing" the historical roots of the contradiction; (3) "modeling" a new solution, in this case how they individually and collectively envisioned a new model of bilingual education that could address some of the contradictions; (4) "examining" the new model; (5) "implementing" the new model through their own student-teaching lessons, which they video-recorded; (6) "reflecting" on the teaching/learning process individually and with peers; and (7) "consolidating," or generalizing the new practice. The process is presented as nonlinear and recursive, one which never ends and which can be cultivated through mini expansive learning cycles. The "questioning" dimension, for instance, persisted throughout the whole semester, as the pre-service teachers tracked the 'tensions' and 'aha moments' experienced in their student teaching placements in their Double-Entry Journal. Also, the "consolidation" action would require collective efforts throughout their teaching journeys.

The students collectively developed with the course instructor a vision of their new model of bilingual teaching, moving from what they understood were *old ways* of doing bilingual teaching/learning to *new possible ways* of reimagining bilingual teaching/learning. Their model was mediated by and represented as a two-dimensional zone of proximal development that took the form of a Four-Field Model, in which one axis represented beliefs and philosophies, and the other, pedagogies. The Double-Entry Journal (an adaptation of Virkkunen & Newnham's 2013 Disturbance Diary) and the Four-Field Model mediated transformative agency at the individual level within the collective movement of the group towards a bilingual teacher identity formation as they used these tools to reflect on their own weekly teaching in their respective bilingual placements. The individual narratives of the teacher candidates as documented in the different assignments showed that using these two tools crystallized the importance of deepening the bilingual pre-service teachers' analysis of multiple languages

and pedagogy as understood in the new bilingual teaching model. While the
narratives of two of the three focal students highlighted in the study showed
movement and engagement with their own tensions as sources of change, the
narratives of a third student made evident that knowing the language of instruction is insufficient to become a bilingual teacher. Efforts to develop critical consciousness for both Latinx and non-Latinx bilingual students have to contend
with the schooling structures that organize learning in schools, and the teacher
candidates' and teachers' naive assumptions about language, race relations, gender,
and immigration (see McAdam's 2018 work with teachers' storytelling that challenged xenophobic discourses).

Lastly, efforts to develop equity-oriented programs have more potential for
success when they are distributed throughout a whole program and not just one
course, as in the following two teacher education programs: the bilingual teacher
education model *Educar para transformar* (Flores, Sheets, & Clark, 2011), created
as a curricular reform that includes transformation of professors' and pre-service
teachers' ideological positions, knowledge, and skills, and the Bilingual Special
Education Program (BiSPED), which prepares teacher candidates to challenge
deficit views of bilingual students' with dis/abilities by focusing on children's
agentive efforts (Martínez-Alvarez, 2020).

11.3 Daring to Act

This volume is about Latina narratives, activism, and education. These Latinas' stories and testimonios became tools for activism, as the narrators not only asserted
their voices and identities, but also propelled teachers and teacher educators to
reflect on their role in the development of more equitable learning contexts for
students of color, especially Latinx students. This last chapter provided a glimpse
of the myriad ways in which teachers, teacher educators, and parents contribute
to the development of a transformative activist educational agenda for Latinx
students in and beyond their classrooms.

Teachers engage in transformative activist efforts by providing their students
with tools for their own activism. Those tools can be informal conversations with
students in which teachers really listen and learn, but also challenge students to
question taken-for-granted narratives that marginalize their communities. Other
tools for activism involve teachers' critical selection of culturally and historically
responsible texts that support students' identities, academic success, and agency.
Creating space in the curriculum for students to tell their stories and engage in
inquiry about their communities' histories and funds of knowledge has large
implications for students' engagement with learning and activism. Teachers' also
contribute effectively to a transformative educational agenda when they listen
to the families of their students and support the parents' own activist efforts. Yet,
teachers' activism sometimes manifests as they reach people beyond their schools,
at the district or state level.

These different manifestations highlight the importance of unique and diverse contributions to developing equitable learning contexts for Latinx students and all students of color. While some activist efforts seem to have larger visibility and impact, it is critical to demystify what counts as contribution to change and what counts as transformative activism, so that everyone with equity concerns can enter the conversation and have their voices and testimonios heard. Opening up spaces where the narratives and testimonios of students and parents can be shared and taken into consideration to guide decision-making may represent the kernel of the transformation critical educators envision for our youth, for ourselves, for our communities. Within a transformative activist educational stance, efforts to co-create more equitable learning contexts for all students of color are better understood when they lead to collective action, even if collective action seems elusive at times. Recent history has shown that big changes and shifts might be around the corner, even as the status quo still appears firmly established (Stetsenko, 2017). By daring to act, we are already inserted in the struggle for equity of those who preceded us, and we are opening resquebraduras, fissures, that are already creating a new and more just world—a new us.

References

Acevedo, M. V., Kleker, D., Pangle, L., & Short, K. G. (2017). Thinking with teacher candidates: The transformative power of story in teacher education. In A. C. Iddings (Ed.), *Communities as resources in early childhood teacher education (CREATE): An ecological reform design for the education of culturally and linguistically diverse students* (pp. 100–119). Routledge.

Antrop-González, R., & De Jesús, A. (2006). Toward a theory of *critical care* in urban small school reform: Examining structures and pedagogies of caring in two Latino community-based schools. *International Journal of Qualitative Studies in Education, 19*(4), 409–433.

Arizpe, E., Colomer, T., & Martínez-Roldán, C. (2014). *Visual journeys through wordless narratives: An international inquiry with immigrant children and The Arrival.* Bloomsbury.

Bartolomé, L., & Balderrama, M. (2001). The need for educators with political and ideological clarity: Providing our children with "the best". In M. Reyes, J. Halcón, & C. Genishi (Eds.), *The best for our children: Critical perspectives on literacy for Latino students* (pp. 48–64). Teachers College Press.

Batista-Morales, N. S., Slamerón, C., & DeJulio, S. (2019). Their words, their worlds: Critical literacy in bilingual spaces. *Bilingual Research Journal, 42*(4), 471–490.

Benito, B. J., & Manzanas, A. M. (2002). *Literature and ethnicity in the cultural borderlands.* Radopi.

Bishop, R. S. (1992). Multicultural literature for children: Making informed choices. In V. J. Harris (Ed.), *Teaching multicultural literature in grades K-8* (pp. 37–53). Christopher-Gordon.

Brochin Ceballos, C. (2012). Literacies at the border: Transnationalism and the biliteracy practices of teachers across the US-Mexico border. *International Journal of Bilingual Education and Bilingualism, 15*(6), 687–703.

Cacopardo, A. (2018, April 18). Historias debidas VIII. Entrevista a Silvia Rivera Cusicanqui [Video]. Youtube. https://www.youtube.com/watch?v=1q6HfhZUGhc&feature=yo utu.be

Cervantes-Soon, C. G., & Carrillo, J. F. (2016). Toward a pedagogy of border thinking: Building on Latin© students' subaltern knowledge. *The High School Journal, 99*(4), 282–301.

Cervantes-Soon, C. G., Dorner, L., Palmer, D., Heiman, D., Schwerdtfeger, R., & Choi, J. (2017). Combating inequalities in two-way language immersion programs: Toward critical consciousness in bilingual education spaces. *Review of Research in Education, 41*(1), 403–427.

Chang, S., Martínez-Roldán, C., & Torres-Guzmán, M. E. (2020). Struggling to-be or not-to-be a bilingual teacher: Identity formation in a Change Laboratory intervention. *Methodological Innovations, 13*(2), 1–19. https://doi.org/10.1177/2059799120921696

Clark, E. R., Flores, B. B., Smith, H. L., & González, D. A. (2016). *Multicultural literature for Latino bilingual children: Their words, their worlds.* Rowman & Littlefield.

Cochran-Smith, M. (1991). Learning to teach against the grain. *Harvard Educational Review, 61*(3), 279–311.

Darder, A. (1995). *Buscando America:* The contributions of critical Latino educators to the academic development and empowerment of Latino students in the U.S. In C. Sleeter & P. McLaren (Eds.), *Multicultural education, critical pedagogy, and the politics of difference* (pp. 319–347). State University of New York.

Darder, A. (2012). *Culture and power in the classroom: Educational foundations for the schooling of bicultural students.* Routledge.

DaSilva Iddings, A. C. (2009). Bridging home and school literacy practices: Empowering families of recent immigrant children. *Theory Into Practice, 48*(4), 304–311.

Delgado Bernal, D. (2002). Critical race theory, Latino critical theory, and critical raced-gendered epistemologies: Recognizing students of color as holders and creators of knowledge. *Qualitative Inquiry, 8*(1), 105–126.

DeNicolo, C. P., Yu, M., Crowley, C. B., & Gabel, S. L. (2017). Reimagining critical care and problematizing sense of school belonging as a response to inequality for immigrants and children of immigrants. *Review of Research in Education, 41*(1), 500–530.

Dillard, C. B. (2016). Turning the ships around: A case study of (re)membering as transnational endarkened feminist inquiry and praxis for Black teachers. *Educational Studies, 52*(5), 406–423.

Edelsky, C. (2006). *With literacy and justice for all: Rethinking the social in language and education* (3rd ed.). Lawrence Erlbaum.

Enciso, P. (2007). Reframing history in sociocultural theories: Toward and expansive vision. In C. Lewis, P. Enciso, & E. B. Moje (Eds.), *Reframing sociocultural research on literacy: Identity, agency, and power* (pp. 49–74). Lawrence Erlbaum.

Engeström, Y. (2001). Expansive learning at work: Toward an activity theoretical reconceptualization. *Journal of Education and Work, 14*(1), 133–156. https://doi.org/10.1080/13639080020028747.

Errázuriz Besa, V. (2020). *"Hijas de la lucha": Social studies education and gender/political subjectification in the Chilean high school feminist movement.* (Publication No. 27834335). [Doctoral dissertation, Columbia University. ProQuest Dissertations Publishing.

Esteban-Guitart, M., & Moll, L. C. (2014). Funds of Identity: A new concept based on the Funds of Knowledge approach. *Culture & Psychology, 20*(1), 31–48. https://doi-org.tc.idm.oclc.org/10.1177/1354067X13515934

Flores, B. B., Sheets, R. H., & Clark, E. R. (2011). *Teacher preparation for bilingual student populations: Educar para transformar.* Routledge.

Flores, T.T. (2018). *Chicas fuertes:* Counterstories of Latinx parents raising strong girls. *Bilingual Research Journal, 41*(3), 329–348. https://doi.org/10.1080/15235882.2018.1496955

Fothergill, A., & Peek, L. (2015). *Children of Katrina.* University of Texas Press.

Freire, P. (1970). *Pedagogía del oprimido* [Pedagogy of the oppressed]. Siglo XXI.

Freire, P. (1997). *Pedagogy of the oppressed* (M. Bergman Ramos, Trans.) (Rev. 20th anniversary ed.). Continuum. (Original work published 1970)

Freire, P. (2007). *Daring to dream: Toward a pedagogy of the unfinished.* (A. M. Araújo Freire, Ed.) (A. K. Oliveira, Trans.). Paradigm Publishers.

Godreau, I., Franco Ortiz, M., Lloréns, H., Reinat Pumarejo, M., Canabal Torres, I., & Gaspar Concepción, J. A. (2013). *Arrancando mitos de raíz: Guía para una enseñanza antirracista de la herencia africana en Puerto Rico.* [Removing myths by their roots: A guide for the antiracist teaching of African heritage in Puerto Rico]. Instituto de Investigaciones Interdisciplinarias. Universidad de Puerto Rico.

González, N., Moll, L. C., & Amanti, C. (Eds.). (2005). *Funds of knowledge: Theorizing practices in households, communities, and classrooms.* Lawrence Erlbaum.

Greene, M. (1995). *Releasing the imagination: Essays on education, the arts, and social change.* Jossey-Bass Publishers.

Gutiérrez, K. D. (2008). Developing a sociocritical literacy in the third space. *Reading Research Quarterly, 43*(2), 148–164.

Gutiérrez, K. D., & Larson, J. (2007). Discussing expanded spaces for learning. *Language Arts, 85*(1), 69–77.

Hall, S. (1998). Notes on deconstructing "the popular". In J. Storey (Ed.), *Cultural theory and popular culture: A reader* (pp. 508–518). Pearson/Prentice Hall.

Johnson, H., Mathis, J., & Short, K. G. (Eds.). (2017). *Critical content analysis of children's and young adult literature: Reframing perspectives.* Routledge.

Johnson, H., Mathis, J., & Short, K. G. (Eds.). (2019). *Critical content analysis of visual images in books for young people.* Routledge.

López-Robertson, J. (2011). "Yo el otro día vi, um, un mojadito": Young Latino children connecting with friends from the other side. *The NERA Journal, 46*(2), 52–59.

de los Ríos, C. V. (2018). Toward a *corridista* consciousness: Learning from one transnational youth's critical reading, writing, and performance of Mexican corridos. *Reading Research Quarterly, 53*(4), 455–471.

de los Ríos, C. V., & Molina, A. (2020). Literacies of refuge: "Pidiendo posada" as ritual of justice. *Journal of Literacy Research, 52*(1), 32–54.

Martínez-Alvarez, P. (2020). Dis/ability as mediator: Opportunity encounters in hybrid learning spaces for emergent bilinguals with dis/abilities. *Teachers College Record, 122*(5). https://www.tcrecord.org/Content.asp?ContentId=23135

Martínez-Alvarez, P., & Ghiso, M. P. (2017). On languaging and communities: Latino/a emergent bilinguals' expansive learning and critical inquiries into global childhoods. *International Journal of Bilingual Education and Bilingualism, 20*(6), 667–687.

Martínez-Roldán, C. M. (2003). Building worlds and identities: A case study of the role of narratives in bilingual literature discussions. *Research in the Teaching of English, 37*(4), 491–526.

Martínez-Roldán, C. M. (2019). Prácticas pedagógicas después del huracán María: Colaboración de padres y maestros como agentes de cambio en una escuela elemental en Puerto Rico [Pedagogical practices after hurricane María: Collaboration among parents and teachers as agents of change in a Puerto Rican elementary school]. [Special issue: Transforming Pedagogy: Practice, Policy, & Resistance] *Sargasso: A Journal of Caribbean Literature, Language & Culture, I & II,* 71–95.

McAdam, J. (2018). Narratives of change: The role of storytelling, artefacts and children's literature in building communities of inquiry that care. *Cambridge Journal of Education, 49*(3), 293–307. https://doi.org/10.1080/0305764X.2018.1524001

Medina, C. (2006). Interpreting Latino/a children's literature as critical fictions. *ALAN Review, 33*(2), 71–77.

Mignolo, W. D. (2000). *Local histories/global designs: Coloniality, subaltern knowledges, and border thinking.* Princeton University Press.

Moje, E. B., Ciechanowski, K. M., Kramer, K., Ellis, L., Carillo, R., & Collazo, T. (2004). Working toward third space in content area literacy: An examination of everyday funds of knowledge and discourse. *Reading Research Quarterly, 39*(1), 38–70.

Moll, L. C., Soto-Santiago, S., & Schwartz, L. (2013). Funds of knowledge in changing communities. In *International handbook of research on children's literacy, learning, and culture* (pp. 172–183). John Wiley and Sons. https://doi.org/10.1002/9781118323342.ch13.

Muhammad, G. (2020). *Cultivating genius: An equity framework for culturally and historically responsive literacy.* Scholastic.

Newcomer, S. N., & Collier, L. C. (2015). Agency in action: How teachers respond to Arizona's 4-hour Structured English Immersion program. *International Multilingual Research Journal, 9*(3), 159–176. https://doi.org/10.1080/19313152.2015.1048179

Nieto, S. (2003). *What keeps teachers going?* Teachers College Press.

Núñez, I. (2019). "Le hacemos la lucha": Learning from madres mexicanas multimodal approaches to raising bilingual, biliterate children. *Language Arts, 97*(1), 7–16.

Olivos, E. M., Jiménez-Castellanos, O., & Ochoa, A. M. (2011). *Bicultural parent engagement: Advocacy and empowerment.* Teachers College Press.

Palmer, D. (2018) *Teacher leadership for social change in bilingual/bicultural education.* Multilingual Matters.

Paris, D., & Alim, H. S. (2017). *Culturally sustaining pedagogies: Teaching and learning for justice in a changing world.* Teachers College Press.

Parkhouse, H., Lu, C. Y., & Massaro, V. R. (2019). Multicultural education professional development: A Review of the literature. *Review of Educational Research, 89*(3), 416–458. https://doi-org.tc.idm.oclc.org/10.3102/0034654319840359

Pérez, B. (2004). *Becoming literate: A study of two-way bilingual immersion education.* Lawrence Erlbaum.

Romero, A., Arce, S., & Cammarota, J. (2009). A Barrio pedagogy: Identity, intellectualism, activism, and academic achievement through the evolution of critically compassionate intellectualism. *Race, Ethnicity, and Education, 12*(2), 217–233. https://doi.org/10.1080/13613320902995483

Roxas, K., & Gabriel, M. L. (2017). *Que luchen por sus intereses* (To fight for your interests): Unearthing critical counter-narratives of Spanish-speaking immigrant parents. *Journal of Latinos and Education, 16*(3), 243–262. https://doi.org/10.1080/15348431.2016.1229618

Saavedra, C. M. (2011). Language and literacy in the borderlands: Acting upon the world through "testimonios". *Language Arts, 88*(4), 261–269.

Salinas, C. S., Fránquiz, M. E., & Rodríguez, N. N. (2016). Writing Latina/o historical narratives: Narratives at the intersection of critical historical inquiry and LatCrit. *The Urban Review, 48*(2), 264–284. https://doi.org/10.1007/s11256-016-0355-z

Sfard, A., & Prusak, A. (2005). Telling identities: In search of an analytic tool for investigating learning as a culturally shaped activity. *Educational Researcher, 34*(4), 14–22. https://doi.org/10.3102/0013189X034004014

Short, K. (2016). Children taking action on global issues. In Short, K., Day, D. & Schroeder, J. (Eds.). *Teaching globally: Reading the world through literature* (pp. 251–270). Stenhouse.

Simon, R. I. (1992). *Teaching against the grain: Texts for a pedagogy of possibility.* Bergin & Garvey.

Sosa-Provencio, M. A., Sheahan, A. Fuentes, R., Muñiz, S., & Prada Vivas, R. E. (2019). Reclaiming ourselves through testimonio pedagogy: Reflections on a curriculum design lab in teacher education. *Race Ethnicity and Education*, *22*(2), 211–230. https://doi.org/10.1080/13613324.2017.1376637

Soto, L. D., & Swadener, B. B. (2002). Toward liberatory early childhood theory, research and praxis: Decolonizing a field. *Contemporary issues in early childhood*, *2*(1), 38–66.

Starck, J. G., Riddle, T., Sinclair, S., & Warikoo, N. (2020). Teachers are people too: Examining the racial bias of teachers compared to other American adults. *Educational Researcher*, *49*(4), 273–284.

Stetsenko, A. (2017). *The transformative mind: Expanding Vygotsky's approach to development and education*. Cambridge University.

Suad Nasir, N., & Bang, M. (2020, March 20). *An open letter to our community/COVID-19*. Spencer Foundation. https://www.spencer.org/news/an-open-letter-to-the-spencer-community-covid-19

Torres, F. L., & Tayne, K. (2017). Super heroes, villains, and politics: Elementary youth superhero narratives in an afterschool program. *English Teaching: Practice & Critique*, *16*(3), 375–390.

Torres-Guzmán, M. with Swinney, R. (2010). *Freedom at work: Language, professional, and intellectual development in schools*. Paradigm Publishers.

Vasquez, V. (2004). *Negotiating critical literacies with young children*. Lawrence Earlbaum.

Villenas, S. (2001). Latina mothers and small-town racisms: Creating narratives of dignity and moral education in North Carolina. *Anthropology & Education Quarterly*, *32*(1), 3–28.

Virkkunen, J., & Newnham, D. S. (2013). *The Change Laboratory: A tool for collaborative development of work and education*. Sense Publishers.

Vygotsky, L. S. (1978). *Mind in society: The development of higher psychological processes*. (M. Cole, V. John-Steiner, S. Scribner, & E. Souberman, Eds.). Harvard University Press.

Walsh, C. (2017). (Ed.). *Pedagogías decoloniales: Prácticas insurgentes de resistir, (re)existir y (re)vivir. Tomo II*. [Decolonial pedagogies. Insurgent practices of resisting, (re)existing and (re)living. Volume II]. Abya-Yala.

Wohlwend, K., & Medina, C. L. (2014). Producing cultural imaginaries in the playshop. In R. Meyer & K. Whitmore (Eds.), *Reclaiming writing: Composing spaces for identities, relationships, and action* (pp. 198–209). Routledge.

Zúñiga, C. E. (2015). "This is what is happening to my students": Using book talk to mediate teacher discussion on immigration and social justice. *InterActions*, *11*(1). https://escholarship.org/uc/item/8w93f1q7

Children's Literature

Ada, A. F. (1995). *My name is María Isabel* (K. Dyble Thompson, Illus.). Atheneum Books for Young Readers.

Albo, F. (2010). *Si un día juntásemos todas las camas del mundo* (M. Lanzon, Illus.). Palabras del Candil.

Alvarez, J. (2002a). *Before we were free*. Dell Laurel-Leaf.

Alvarez, J. (2002b). *How tía Lola came to visit stay*. Yearling.

Alvarez, J. (2009). *Return to sender*. Alfred A. Knopf.

Anzaldúa, G. (1997). *Friends from the other side/Amigos del otro lado* (C. Méndez, Illus.). Children's Book Press.

Argueta, J. (2016). *Somos como las nubes / We are like the clouds* (A. Ruano, Illus.). Groundwood Books.

Arroyo Pizarro, Y. (2016). *María Calabó: De niña curiosa a mujer líder*. CreateSpace Independent Publishing Platform.

Arroyo Pizarro, Y. (2018). *El cuento de Papapedia*. Editorial EDP University.

Boston Weatherford, C. (2018). *Voice of freedom: Fannie Lou Hamer, spirit of the Civil Rights movement* (E. Holmes, Illus.). Candlewick.

Bowles, D. (2018). *They call me Güero: A border kid's poems*. Cinco Puntos Press.

Boyce, A. A., & Levy, D. (2019). *This promise of change: One girl's story in the fight for school equality*. Bloomsbury Children's Books.

Brown, M. (2011). *Marisol McDonald doesn't match / Marisol McDonald no combina Z* (S. Palacios, Illus.). Children's Book Press.

Canales, V. (2005). *The tequila worm*. Wendy Lamb Books.

Carlson, L. M., & Hijuelos, O. (2005). *Red hot salsa: Bilingual poems on being young and Latino in the United States*. Henry Holt & Company.

Cartaya, P. (2018). *The epic fail of Arturo Zamora*. Puffin Books.

Choi, Y. (2003). *The name Jar*. Dragonfly Book.

Clark-Robinson, M. (2018). *Let the children march* (F. Morrison, Illus.). Houghton Mifflin Harcourt.

Cohn, D. (2005). *¡Sí, se puede! / Yes, we can! Janitor strike in L.A.* (F. Delgado, Illus.). Cinco Puntos Press.

Colato Laínez, R. (2009). *René has two last names / René tiene dos apellidos* (F. Graullera Ramírez, Illus.). Piñata Books.

Cumpiano, I. (2009). *Quinito's neighborhood / El vecindario de Quinito* (J. Ramírez, Illus.). Children's Book Press.

Degenhart, J. (2018). *María María: Un cuento de un huracán*. Puentes.

Denise, A. A. (2019). *Planting stories: The life of librarian and storyteller Pura Belpré* (P. Escobar, Illus.). Harper Collins.

Díaz, J. (2018). *Islandborn* (L. Espinosa, Illus.). Penguin.

Dupuis, J. K., & Kacer, K. (2019). *Gaawin Gindaaswin Ndaawsii / I Am Not a Number* (G. Newland, Illus.). Second Story Press.

Engle, M. (2014). *Silver people: Voices from the Panama Canal*. Houghton Mifflin Harcourt.

Engle, M. (2017). *Bravo!* Holt & Company.

García McCall, G. (2011). *Under the mesquite*. Lee & Low Books.

González, L. (2008). *The storyteller's candle / La velita de los cuentos* (L. Delacre, Illus.). Children's Book Press.

González, M. C. (2013). *My colors, My world / Mis colores, Mi mundo*. Lee & Low Books.

González, M. C. (2014). *Call me tree / Llámame árbol*. Lew & Law Books.

Gonzalez, X. (2017). *All around us* (A. M. García, Illus.). Cinco Puntos Press.

Harrison, V. (2017). *Little leaders. Bold women in Black history*. Little Brown.

Herrera, J. F. (2000). *The upside down boy / El niño de cabeza* (E. Gómez, Illus.). Children's Book Press.

Jiménez, F. (1998). *La mariposa* (S. Silva, Illus.). Houghton Mifflin

Johnson, A. (2005). *A sweet smell of roses* (E. Velásquez, Illus.). Simon & Schuster.

Kurusa. (1995). *The streets are free* (M. Doppert, Illus.). Annick Press Ltd.

Lacámara, L. (2014). *Dalia's wondrous hair / El cabello maravilloso de Dalia*. Piñata Books.

Lacapa, K., & Lacapa, M. (1994). *Less than half, more than whole*. Northland Publishing.

Lai, T. (2011). *Inside out & back again*. HarperCollins.

Latchman, O. D. (1995). *Pepita talks twice / Pepita habla dos veces* (A. P. Delange, Illus.). Arte Público.

Lindstrom, C. (2020). *We are water protectors* (M. Goade, Illus.). Roaring Brook Press.

Martínez-Neal, J. (2018). *Alma and how she got her name*. Candlewick Press.

Medina, J. (1999). *My name is Jorge: On both sides of the river* (F. Vanden Broeck, Illus.). WordSong.

Montes, M. (2006). *Los gatos black on Halloween* (Y. Morales, Illus.). Henry Holt and Company.

Moore Ramee, L. (2019). *A good kind of trouble*. HarperCollins.

Morales, Y. (2013). *Niño wrestles the world*. Roaring Brook Press.

Morales, Y. (2018). *Dreamers*. Neal Porter Books.

Moulite, M. (2019). *Dear Haiti, love Alaine* (M. Moulite, Illus.). Inkyard Press.

Muhammad, I. with Ali, S. K. (2019). *The proudest blue: A story of hijab and family* (H. Ali, Illus.). *Little, Brown Books for Young Readers*.

Nagara, I. (2013). *A is for activist*. Triangle Square.

Nagara, I. (2015). *Counting on community*. Triangle Square.

Orozco, J. L. (2020). *Sing with me / Canta conmigo* (S. Palacios, Illus.). Scholastic.

Ortiz Cofer, J. (1995). *An island like you: Stories of the Barrio*. Puffin Books.

Ortiz-Cofer, J. (2004). *Call me María*. Orchard.

Ortiz, R. M., & Morales, I. (2020). *Vicky and a summer of change y ¡un verano de cambio!* (S. Cintrón, E. Falcón, & E. Miranda-Rodríguez, Illus.). Red Sugarcane Press.

Osa, N. (2005). *Cuba 15*. Ember.

Palestinian refugee children in the Aida refugee Camp. (2019). *The boy and the wall*. New Balanced Literacy Schools. Roosevelt University College of Education.

Perkins, M. (2019). *Between us and abuela: A family story from the border* (S. Palacios, Illus.). Farrar Strauss Giroux.

Pinkney, A. D. (2010). *By Sit-in: How four friends Stood up by sitting down* (B. Pinkney, Illus.).

Quintero, I. (2014). *Gabi, a girl in pieces*. Cinco Puntos Press.

Rivera Izcoa, C. (2004). *Van a tumbar el húcar*. Ediciones Huracán.

Sáenz, B. A. (2012). *Aristotle and Dante discover the secrets of the universe*. Simon & Schuster.

Salinas, B. (2003). *Cinderella Latina / La cenicienta Latina*. Piñata Publications.

Sánchez, E. L. (2017). *I am not your perfect Mexican daughter*. Ember.

Slade, S. (2019). *A computer called Katherine: How Katherine Johnson helped put America on the moon* (V. Miller Jamison, Illus.). Little, Brown Books for Young Readers.

Sorell, T. (2018). *We are grateful / Otsaliheliga* (F. Lessac, Illus.). Charlesbridge.

Sotomayor, S. (2018). *Turning pages: My life story* (L. Delacre, Illus.). Philomel Books.

Sotomayor, S. (2019). *Just ask! Be different, be brave, be you* (R. López, Illus.). Philomel Books.

Tafolla, C., & Teneyuca, S. (2008). *That's not fair! Emma Tenayuca's struggle for justice / ¡No es justo! La lucha de Emma Tenayuca por la justicia* (T. Ybáñez, Illus.). Wings Press.

Tan, S. (2006). *The arrival*. Levine.

Tonatiuh, D. (2014). *Separate is never equal: Silvia Mendez & her family's fight for desegregation*. Abrams Books for Young Readers.

Tonatiuh, D. (2018). *Undocumented: A workers fight*. Harry N. Abrams.

Velásquez, E. (2010). *Grandma's gift*. Walter & Company.

Watson, R. (2019). *Some places more than others*. Bloomsbury.

Weatherford, C. B. (2017). *Schomburg: The man who built a library* (E. Velásquez, Illus.). Candlewick Press.

Williams, K. L., & Mohammed, K. (2009). *My name is Sangoel* (C. Stock, Illus.). Eerdmans Books for Young Readers.

Yang, G. L. (2006). *American born Chinese*. Square Fish.

Youme, L. (2004). *Sélavi, that is life: A Haitian story of hope*. Cinco Puntos.

Yum, H. (2013). *This is our house*. Farrar, Straus and Giroux.

Zoboi, I. (2018). *Pride*. Harper Collins.

AFTERWORD

To Defy Erasure…

Patricia Enciso

Reading through these chapters, I imagined the beautiful scene of a circle of Latina graduate students gathered in the classroom of an elite college of education. Zooming in to a table top, I imagined photographs, sketches, letters, transcripts, and maps, carefully laid out in front of the authors, attesting to their efforts to gather and piece together forgotten and untold stories from across times and places, past and present selves. I imagined their voices, one by one, naming and questioning the litany of authoritative explanations that have excluded, erased, and surveilled Latinx histories, languages, and learning. I imagined their voices describing the principles for educating our new immigrant children, informed by the strongest material we know—our intergenerational knowledge. The stories told by the women in this room defy erasure. Each word contributes to a deepening collective narrative that transforms the meaning of the college classroom and foretells the production of new materials and stories, anticipating the next generation's freedom to learn and thrive, even as they face new forms of deculturalization. I imagine a collective voice echoing through homes and schools and university hallways: *We have educated ourselves, and we will educate our own and others' minoritized children, on our terms, refusing silence or indignity. We will learn from our histories of linguistic, racialized, cultural, and spiritual resilience as we envision more equitable, decolonial futures. We will compose our stories and make our futures, with our brown, black, and white hands, our bold hearts, and the bilingual words that play on our untamed tongues.*

Professor Carmen Martínez-Roldán created this site for change as a dialogic space where the authors could be in conversation with one another—and with themselves—through testimonio storytelling. While reading through their own and one another's stories and by employing theoretical tools developed by Latinx, feminist, poststructural, and critical scholars, the collective identified resonances between their stories and the conceptual insights they found in Latinx scholarship. Together, they lived into multiple intersecting narrative worlds that could both illuminate and undo erasures that had long denied Latina strength and creativity. Drawing on Anna Stetsenko's (2017) revolutionary sociocultural premise that "human development is a collaborative project of people changing and co-creating the world together" (p. 19), Martínez-Roldán recognizes the group's testimonios and analyses as the simultaneous development of the person and the world. I believe Martínez-Roldán's fusion of transformative activist theory with Latinx scholarship represents a new generation of sociocultural and narrative research, oriented toward agentic, feminist, anti-racist self-definition, and educational equity. These chapters represent not only the specificity of Latina experience across generations, but also the labor of making conversational spaces with friends and family, and the subsequent labor of constructing transcripts, rereading, and searching for the compelling patterns of hope and loss, and then shaping a framing narrative—all in a future-oriented effort to replace distorted, historically formed discourses about Latinx children's educations with the clarity of hard-won truths.

In her role as educator and editor, Martínez-Roldán proposes four major themes evident across the authors' narratives and analyses: (a) erasure of being and, in response, (b) the urgency of agency, (c) the value and recovery of testimonios, and the related sense of (d) 'being-knowing-doing' in the moment-to-moment interactions that shape activist identities. These themes suggest a theory of change grounded in critical sociocultural theory (Lewis, Enciso, Moje 2007; Enciso 2007) that asserts histories, identities, and agency as unequally valued and mobilized and, therefore, struggled over in classroom and community contexts. By moving from critical sociocultural theory to a transformative activist stance, also rooted in Vygotskian theories of change, Martínez-Roldán has actively constructed a deliberative space for naming and remaking the stories through which the multiplicity and complexity of Latina agency and identity may be envisioned. Bringing their labor to a book project means that transformative action continues towards more equitable futures among readers who share the authors' commitments to educational equity.

Like many critical narratives describing inequitable relations of power, agency, and identity, these stories begin by recognizing the imposition of colonizing and minoritizing forces across multiple aspects of the authors' everyday lives. These testimonios, however, go further by representing sustained, remarkably intimate inquiry through which new possible futures are formed. As suggested in the opening of this essay, we can sense the embodied gathering, telling, and reflecting on testimonios shared among the authors as they also introduce and experiment with methods of collection and analysis informed by poststructuralist 'tracings' (Chapter 4), Anzaldúan border-crossing through their own inner terrains of minoritization (Chapter 2), and Indigenous (Chapter 10) practices of *comadriando*.

In Chapter 6, for example, Marisol Cantú describes the language loss initiated by her abuela in reaction to the punishment she endured when she spoke Spanish as a child in school:

> She remembers when she was hit on her hand with a ruler by a teacher for speaking Spanish. This was the beginning of my family's language loss. This was a reason she assimilated and learned English and only spoke Spanish to her parents. She did not want her children to go through the same experiences, so she did not teach my father or tíos Spanish. In one generation, my family's language was lost.
> (pp. 112–113)

In response to this story, Cantú set out to regain Spanish for herself:

> From my grandmother's experiences of being punished with a ruler by a teacher for speaking Spanish, to my efforts to recover my heritage language, the findings describe how I reclaimed the ruler through language.
> (p. 104)

Cantú's decision to 'reclaim the ruler' points to the materiality and embodied experience of both defining and defying erasure, while narrating linguistic agency and Latinx identity into existence.

Similarly, in Chapter 5, Victoria Hernandez describes the testimonios she reconstructed across different stages and places in her life as both the material for understanding silence as a form of knowledge and self-preservation and as a method for moving beyond silence to her bicultural-informed navigation and activism in graduate school. She concludes, "Testimonio as a method led me to carefully examine the factors that allowed me to persist and resist the factors that I felt were pushing me out of academia" (p. 98). Through a process of telling stories of being-becoming, in relation with Latinx critical scholarship, Hernandez agentically reflects on a restorative meaning of silence and her transformation from a stance of self-preservation to collaborative critique and activism.

Through the construction of intergenerational narratives, erasures are disrupted by testimonio, agentic dialogue, and discoveries of identities, layered among historically formed identities produced in relations of trust, respect, and what Daniela Conde calls *comadriando* (Chapter 10). Authors realized how ties to a once-detailed narrative of interconnected lives at home can dissipate over time and across life events. In her chapter (Chapter 3) about her mother's life story and migration from la Isla, Puerto Rico, to the mainland, Maried Rivera Nieves wonders how her own identity can be named and claimed in words that were imposed by an indifferent and distant bureaucracy:

> Am I any more a migrant than someone who moves across United States state lines? Puerto Ricans call la Isla un país—is it? Am I an American?

Do I want to be? What is "American"? This is another way in which Puerto Rico's neocolonial status limits my ability to know myself, even if it is through technocratic terms my people did not generate for themselves.

(p. 44)

In a later reflection on her own and her mother's intersecting narratives, Rivera Nieves confides the embodied worry and sense of erasure they both feel. Her double-voiced writing shows how the preservation of a feeling of belonging is intimately tied with presence, identity, and the continuity of stories we tell of ourselves, among others, across generations.

Like I'm watching our family pull away from puertorriqueñidad in real time, that with each familial death and grudge and out-migration and broken promise, our connection to the island fades. Mami feels it, too, I think. She often worries out loud about how once her mother dies, she won't have a reason to go back. Is this how it happens? Will I soon have to grapple with what it's like to be Puerto Rican without a strong familial connection to the island?

(p. 53)

Stories may be the only, and most important, connection that new generations will be able to hold onto as they ask, "Who am I and who might I become?" The authors' testimonios, located in the specificity of their relationships with time, place, people, and institutions, can be read as personal contributions to their own development and as exemplars for enacting this change. At the same time, these chapters represent the labor and artistry that can also contribute to prophetic claims for change that will echo across generations. Mil gracias, mujeres. Mil gracias.

References

Enciso, P. (2007). Reframing history in sociocultural theory: Toward an expansive vision. In C. Lewis, P. Enciso, & E. Moje (Eds.), *Reframing sociocultural research on literacy: Identity, agency, and power* (pp. 49–74). Routledge.

Lewis, C., Enciso, P., & Moje, E. (2007). *Reframing sociocultural research on literacy: Identity, agency, and power*. Routledge.

Stetsenko, A. (2017). *The transformative mind: Expanding Vygotsky's approach to development and education*. Cambridge University.

INDEX

Made in the USA
Middletown, DE
18 September 2023